Brothers of a Vow

Brothers of a Vow

SECRET FRATERNAL ORDERS AND

THE TRANSFORMATION OF

WHITE MALE CULTURE IN

ANTEBELLUM VIRGINIA

Ami Pflugrad-Jackisch

The University of Georgia Press | Athens and London

Paperback edition, 2011
© 2010 by the University of Georgia Press
Athens, Georgia 30602
www.ugapress.org
Set in 10.5/13.5 Adobe Caslon Pro by BookComp, Inc.

Printed digitally in the United States of America

The Library of Congress has cataloged the
hardcover edition of this book as follows:
Pflugrad-Jackisch, Ami, 1972–
    Brothers of a vow : secret fraternal orders and the
transformation of white male culture in Antebellum
Virginia / Ami Pflugrad-Jackisch.
    vii, 181 p. ; 24 cm.
    Includes bibliographical references (p. 153–172) and index.
    ISBN-13: 978-0-8203-3227-7 (hardcover : alk. paper)
    ISBN-10: 0-8203-3227-5 (hardcover : alk. paper)
  1. Fraternal organizations—Virginia—History—19th century.
2. Whites—Race identity—Virginia—History—19th century.
3. Masculinity—Social aspects—Virginia—History—19th century.
4. Group identity—Virginia—History—19th century.
5. Social classes—Virginia—History—19th century.
6. Virginia—Social conditions—19th century.
I. Title.
    HS1507.V8P48 2010
    369.09755'09034—dc22   2009048468

Paperback ISBN-13: 978-0-8203-4047-0
          ISBN-10: 0-8203-4047-2

British Library Cataloging-in-Publication Data available

CONTENTS

Acknowledgments   vii

Introduction   1

ONE
White Male Political Culture in Antebellum Virginia   11

TWO
Secret Fraternal Orders in Antebellum Virginia   26

THREE
Keeping Out the Unworthy   51

FOUR
Securing the Republic   72

FIVE
Civic Brotherhood   99

Conclusion   120

APPENDIX
A Note on Terms and Calculations   125

Notes   127

Bibliography   153

Index   173

ACKNOWLEDGMENTS

This book is the end product of many years of research and writing. I could not have accomplished this goal without the assistance of many people along the way. The help of the librarians and special collections staff at the Virginia Historical Society, Perkins Library at Duke University, the Library of Virginia, the Albert and Shirley Small Library at the University of Virginia, Carrier Library at James Madison University, and Swem Library at the College of William and Mary made my research both easier and more enjoyable. I am also grateful to Odd Fellow Mike Musick and the Grand Lodge of Virginia Freemasons for generously allowing me to use their private records.

This project originally took shape under the guidance of my dissertation advisers at the University at Buffalo, Susan Cahn, Tamara Plakins Thornton, and Erik Seeman. I appreciate all of the time and effort you have each devoted to my scholarly and professional development. Your close attention to my work, constructive criticism, and thought-provoking questions have made me a better scholar. I especially want to thank Susan for her insightful comments, her encouragement, and for giving me the freedom to take my own path. I would also like to thank my colleagues at the University of Michigan-Flint for creating a rigorous academic environment in which scholarship is valued. In addition, the Virginia Historical Society, the University of Michigan-Flint, and the Institute for the Study of Women and Gender at the University of Michigan-Ann Arbor, have provided me with generous financial support for my research.

I am also very thankful for the encouragement I have received from my friends and family. To my lifelong friends Jen, Alison, and Mindy, my grandmother, and my brother, Michael, thank you for your constant emotional support and for putting up with my sporadic phone calls and visits. I have also been blessed with the most wonderful parents anyone could ask for. Thank you for raising me to believe I could be anything I wanted to be. Your unfailing support and encouragement has meant more to me than words can express.

To my husband, Barry, who has read every page of this manuscript—more times than either one of us can remember—your advice, support, and love has been invaluable to me throughout this entire process. Thank you for constantly pushing me beyond my intellectual boundaries. I dedicate this book to you.

Brothers of a Vow

Introduction

On a warm evening in June 1847, Nelson Rodgers, a thirty-seven-year-old butcher from Harrisonburg, Virginia, stood outside the antechamber door of the local Sons of Temperance lodge. He heard three soft raps, and then the door swung open to reveal two rows of men on either side of the doorway dressed in red, white, and blue regalia. As he looked through the lines of men, he saw the lodge's worthy patriarch, twenty-nine-year-old blacksmith William Miller, seated in the distance in a thronelike chair. As the order's conductor led Rodgers through the rows of men toward Miller, the members sang, "Traveler through a world of danger, / Welcome to a refuge here! / Safety to the trusting stranger, / Safety from the tempter's snare."[1]

Once in front of the worthy patriarch, Rodgers swore never to reveal the secret passwords, ceremonies, or other private matters of the fraternity and agreed to only promote harmony among his new lodge brothers. Then, the officers of the lodge formed a triangle around him, and he pledged to abstain from all alcoholic beverages. After these oaths were completed, Miller declared, "Confiding in your integrity, I now invest you with this badge and proclaim you a Son of Temperance!" Rodgers then joined his new brothers in forming a large circle, and the worthy patriarch announced, "In this circle, consecrated to Temperance and Fraternity, we dedicate ourselves anew to Love ... Purity ... Fidelity! Be ye faithful unto death!"[2]

Rodgers's experience was not an unusual one. During the antebellum period, secret fraternal organizations such the Freemasons, the Independent Order of Odd Fellows, and the Sons of Temperance attracted thousands of new members in the state of Virginia. The orders promoted brotherly love and self-improvement and sought to unite white men across class and partisan divisions.

> The whole scope and object of our association is to make its members wiser and better men—by the equality of conditions which it supposes, to break down and soften the arrogance and selfishness of the human heart—to subdue the asperities of sects and parties—to inculcate charity and brotherly love—strengthen and invigorate all relations in which man can be contemplated—towards himself—his family—his neighbor—his country—his God![3]

Antebellum fraternal orders were composed exclusively of white men, and membership was highest in urban areas among men of working- and middle-class status. Although the societies were classified as "secret," the men who made them up proudly displayed their fraternal membership in numerous parades and public ceremonies. What made the orders "secret," however, were the elaborate rituals and guarded passwords known only to members in good standing. The orders' regalia, rituals, passwords, and signs set fraternal organizations apart from other voluntary and men's associations.

This study examines how secret fraternal organizations unified white men across class lines in Virginia during the crucial decades before the Civil War. As fraternity members, white men downplayed class and partisan distinctions. By shelving these differences, the orders were able to foster a shared white patriarchy that focused on common goals such as charity, the protection of widows and orphans, education, and the promotion of white male equality. This fraternal coalition ultimately established a civic brotherhood among white men that marginalized the role of women in the public sphere and bolstered the respectability of every white man regardless of his class status.

Young Virginians who came of age during the antebellum era lived through a time of tremendous economic, cultural, and political upheaval. The spread of a market economy into the cities and towns of the Old Dominion dramatically changed the lives of white men who grew up before the Civil War.[4] New market values promoted a cultural ethos that rewarded individual ambition, altered long-standing social relationships, and aggravated class tensions between working-class men and new middle-class businessmen, merchants, and professionals. As the traditional pathways to social respectability through slave and plantation ownership became more difficult, many men began to seek new ways of acquiring professional recognition, gauging success, and defining white manhood.[5]

Although there is a vast literature on the spread of the market in the North, historians have disagreed about the extent to which the market affected life in the antebellum South. Some argue that it was not until after the Civil War that the South modernized and emerged from its precapitalist existence.[6] Others argue that a "dual economy" emerged in the antebellum South. This group of historians posits that a small group of planter elite engaged in profit-driven commercial agriculture as early as the colonial era. As the market drove industrialization in the Northeast during the 1820s and 1830s, southern planters' desire for profit spurred them to move into the southwestern frontier and establish commercial cotton plantations, giving new life to the institution of slavery. In this "dual economy," only a small number of wealthy planters were involved in the market. White yeomanry remained on the periphery of market activity, and even resisted its changes, throughout the antebellum era.[7]

Studies that downplay the spread of the market in the South, however, primarily examine the cotton South, ignoring the dynamic changes that occurred in places like Virginia during the 1840s and 1850s. As William Freehling has argued, the South comprised several distinctive regions during the first half of the nineteenth century. Papering over the unique complexities of the South and turning the disparate experiences of southerners into one homogenous southern experience drastically oversimplifies the rich and multifaceted histories of the region.[8] More recently, historians have taken a new look at southern industrialization and urbanization before the Civil War. This new scholarship explores the growth of urban areas, manufacturing, class formation, moral reform, and market development in the South and expands our understanding of southern society beyond life on large plantations. It concludes that urban middle-class merchants, clerks, and wage laborers played a significant role in the development of southern urban areas in the late 1840s and 1850s.[9]

Historians' new focus on southern industrialization is not meant to deny that southern urban development and industrialization were relatively limited compared to the rapid economic expansion of northern cities such as New York, Boston, or Philadelphia.[10] Yet the spread of market values in the

South initiated social transformations that were similar to, and in some cases more complex than, those that northern cities underwent during the antebellum era. Furthermore, this new scholarship demonstrates that, although slavery prevented southern cities and industries from expanding on par with those in the northeastern United States, the Old South experienced much more extensive market growth than scholars have previously acknowledged. Thus slavery stifled but did not stamp out market development in the antebellum South.[11]

In fact, some areas of the South experienced a transportation revolution, rapid urban growth, and the formation of distinct working and middle classes by the end of the 1850s. Virginia was one of these places. Virginia has always occupied a unique place in southern history because of its close economic, political, and cultural connections to the northern states it borders. Recent historical studies of the Old Dominion emphasize both Virginia's similarities to and differences from the lower South. In addition, this scholarship claims that despite their use of slave labor, antebellum Virginians became part of an increasingly market-oriented society.[12] For example, by the late antebellum period many young white men, especially in Virginia's urban areas, embraced a new market-oriented culture and did not necessarily see a conflict between market individualism and a southern "way of life." As historian Peter Carmichael notes, the generation of educated white young men born after Nat Turner's revolt "craved bourgeois respectability, hungered for professional success, followed personal ambition, and desired the material trappings of a middle-class lifestyle."[13]

This book is part of a larger wave of new historical scholarship that explores southern urbanization and takes a fresh look at southern masculinity before the Civil War. Only recently have historians of the antebellum South looked beyond the scholarly paradigm that paired white southern manhood with plantation honor and backcountry violence. Indeed this culture of honor and violence did exist, but it was not the only culture of manhood in the South by the time of the Civil War. As Craig Thompson Friend and Lorri Glover point out, past scholarship provided little room for southern urban dwellers, men of color, and men who owned no land or slaves, despite the fact that they collectively composed the majority of men living in the Old South.[14]

In Virginia, although all white men enjoyed special status and privilege because of their race, white manhood was neither monolithic nor harmonious. Conflicts between elite slaveholders and nonelite white men over status became increasingly complex and contentious in the decades before the Civil War. The injection of market individualism and evangelical social humanitarianism in urban areas further complicated what it meant to be a white man in the Old Dominion.

Historian Amy S. Greenberg argues that this crisis in manhood was part of a larger national problem. According to Greenberg, in the 1850s there was no single ideal of masculinity that dominated expectations with respect to the behavior of American men. Instead, two "preeminent and dueling masculinities" emerged in the United States by 1848, restrained manhood and martial manhood.[15] Men in both the North and the South practiced restrained manhood, and these men grounded their identities in their families, in evangelical Protestantism, and in success in business. Restrained men were morally upright, strong proponents of domesticity, and tended to support temperance legislation after 1851. On the other hand, "martial men," Greenberg explains, "rejected the moral standards that guided restrained men; they often drank to excess with pride and they reveled in their physical strength and ability to dominate both men and women."[16]

Although Virginian men did not by and large support temperance legislation (and so this aspect of Greenberg's definition of restrained manhood doesn't apply to them), restrained manhood emerged as an alternative and legitimate masculine ideal in antebellum Virginia as a result of the expansion of the market and urban growth in the state. I argue that secret fraternal organizations, such as the Freemasons, the Independent Order of Odd Fellows, and the Sons of Temperance, provided a medium through which market-oriented men in Virginia could embrace this alternative definition of southern white manhood and respectability that was rooted in self-discipline, moral character, and success at work rather than simply in property ownership. Ultimately, based on these ideals, secret fraternal orders created a civic brotherhood among white men in Virginia that softened class distinctions and carved out a nonpolitical pathway to white male civic authority that was not tied to the ownership of land or slaves.

In addition, although many scholarly studies have been written on antebellum women's groups, historians have only recently begun to examine white men's organizational life. Despite the fact these fraternal orders were enormously popular in the late 1840s and early 1850s, few academic histories of secret fraternal orders from this era exist.[17] The study of these groups provides rich insight into the associational lives of white men before the Civil War and reveals the interconnectedness of men's and women's changing roles in the antebellum era. For example, as this project suggests, fraternal orders played an important role in the decline of women's reform efforts in

Virginia in the 1840s and 1850s by narrowing women's opportunities outside the home and assuming their roles in the public sphere.

Other studies lump secret fraternal orders together with a larger group of organizations such as debating societies, lyceums, historical societies, benevolent associations, and temperance societies that marked the growth and definition of middle-class culture in the antebellum North. According to this scholarship, voluntary associations, including fraternal organizations, shored up middle-class values and identity by instilling sobriety, self-discipline, and industriousness in white men from the rising professional commercial classes and upper strata of the working class.[18]

This was certainly true among Virginia's antebellum secret fraternal orders, but it must be noted that the members of these orders were largely middle-class professionals, shopkeepers, and artisans and mechanics who aspired to become middle class. Defining the middle class in the antebellum era has never been an easy task, but the slave system in the South further complicates this problem.[19] Jonathan Daniel Wells's work on the origins of the antebellum southern middle class highlights the importance of considering both occupation and cultural ideals when defining the middle class in the South. Wells argues that a small group of professional and commercial southern men and their families formed a middle class by the end of the antebellum era. The men and women of this emerging middle class pursued express class interests in educational reform, industrial development, and internal improvements, "coalescing around a set of ideals about the virtue and necessity of economic and cultural modernization." Furthermore, members of this southern middle class envisioned the integration of slave labor into manufacturing as a key part of the southern modernization process.[20]

Many of the men who joined secret fraternal orders were surely trying to carve out the kind of middle-class identity for themselves that Wells describes. However, the artisans and workingmen who also joined these groups fell outside what was traditionally considered to be the middle class, and they would have been turned away from membership in other middle-class institutions such as lyceums, debating clubs, and literary, historical, and philosophical societies. These skilled mechanics and artisans occupied an ambiguous place in this new southern social order. Some artisans intentionally maintained their identity as manual laborers, while others who profited from the boom in construction and growing consumption in luxury goods became business owners. These business owners welcomed emerging ideas about southern industrialization and middle-class notions of self-restraint.[21]

Those skilled artisans who, despite their occupational status, embraced middle-class cultural ideals found secret fraternal orders the most appealing. Secret fraternal orders broadened the opportunity for workingmen to fashion a middle-class identity for themselves. Such a self-identity would have been difficult or even impossible for workingmen to have achieved via other middle-class organizations. Thus, the majority of men who joined secret fraternal orders in antebellum Virginia were either skilled artisans and mechanics who aspired to become part of the new middle class or professional and commercial men who were already solidly middle class.

While antebellum fraternal orders were by no means bastions of white male equality, they did accept a wider range of men from different economic classes than most other male clubs and organizations at the time. Yet it is also important to point out the discrepancies between the orders' class rhetoric and reality. Virginia's antebellum fraternities claimed that their orders personified the words "all men are created free and equal," because all white men of good moral character were eligible for membership in their orders. The first (and most obvious) problem with fraternal rhetoric was that the orders were only open to white men. Second, although fraternity members may have truly believed that they would admit any white man of good moral character into their lodges regardless of economic status, in reality this was not the case. For poor white men in Virginia, the cost of dues, regalia, and perhaps time spent away from work put membership in a secret fraternal order out of their financial reach no matter how self-disciplined and morally upright they may have been.

It is because of this unique set of social relationships and the changing economic environment, then, that Virginia provides an especially good place to examine the growth of secret fraternal orders. In a state increasingly caught between the demands of the growing market and the long-established tradition of unfree labor, secret fraternal orders played a special role in assuaging class tensions between white working- and middle-class men. As the market economy grew and expanded over the course of the antebellum era, many external forces worked to keep these two groups of men apart. Despite these powerful social and economic influences, many of these men chose to join fraternal lodges and instead focus on their common bonds as fraternity brothers.

Researching the history of secret fraternal orders poses special challenges. Printed materials such as speeches, pamphlets, fraternal newspapers, and state grand lodge publications are readily available, but local lodge records are not always as easy to find. Antebellum lodge rosters, in particular, are difficult to locate. Some lodge records for the Odd Fellows and Freemasons are privately held, and because the Sons of Temperance dissolved at the turn of the twentieth century, many of the order's antebellum lodge records have simply disappeared. Researching the Odd Fellows in particular is even more difficult because the current Grand Lodge of Virginia can no longer locate its antebellum records and the Sovereign Grand Lodge of the United States, headquartered in Winston-Salem, North Carolina, lost an unknown number of records when its basement flooded.[22]

Although I was able to find a sufficient number of membership rosters to properly analyze the types of men who joined these orders, complete membership rosters for the lodges of the Sons of Temperance and Odd Fellows in the cities of Richmond and Petersburg were not available. This dearth in rosters makes a systematic examination of how many men were members of more than one secret fraternal order or how many men were members of both a secret fraternal order and a militia group or mechanics' association almost impossible.

In addition, because the majority of the men who joined fraternal orders in antebellum Virginia did not leave collections of personal papers, their thoughts and opinions on a variety of subjects remain unknown. This is particularly evident when it comes to slavery. Although these fraternity members lived and worked in the largest slave state in the Union, surprisingly Virginia's secret fraternal orders left little or no written opinions about slavery. Political discussion inside the lodge room and at lodge functions was explicitly banned because of its controversial and divisive nature. The orders' desire to cultivate harmony among white men from different political perspectives necessarily stifled political debates, including those about slavery.

All of the available written evidence regarding race and slavery that my exhaustive research uncovered is included in this book. It consists mainly of the orders' reaction to nonwhite candidates for membership, policies that allowed only whites to join the orders, and census data on slave ownership. Aside from personal letters that merely document the buying and selling of slaves without further discussion, I have not found any more extensive evidence concerning slavery and fraternal orders. If lodge members did discuss slavery, they did not record those conversations.

As shocking as this may sound to modern historians who understand that race and slavery were interwoven into the very fabric of antebellum southern society, perhaps the absence of discussion on slavery is what is truly significant here. During an era of ubiquitous accusations of abolitionism and raucous, cutthroat, and mean-spirited partisan assaults, these men chose to create relationships and an environment that temporarily suspended the seemingly all-consuming controversies surrounding politics and slavery. Indeed, many fraternity members saw their lodges as a refuge from the political and economic turmoil that went on just outside the lodge-room door.

This book is broken into three sections. The first section provides an overview of white male relationships and the rise of secret fraternal organizations in antebellum Virginia. Chapter 1 describes the environment in which secret fraternal orders became popular. In the decades before the Civil War, the world in which Virginians lived underwent significant transformation as the market economy spread throughout the state and residents experienced the growth of cities and urban culture, battled over the political role of propertyless white men, and adjusted to shifts in Virginia's slave system. During these same years, secret fraternal orders gained enormous popularity in urban areas across the state. Chapter 2 surveys the rise of these orders during this pivotal time in Virginia's history and describes the types of men who joined the fraternities, the orders' membership qualifications, and the fraternities' basic functions.

The book's second section explores the way antebellum fraternal orders helped create a new standard for gauging masculine independence in Virginia. Chapter 3 examines the relationships of fraternity brothers and reveals how their promotion of white male equality cultivated a sense of brotherhood both inside and outside the lodge room. Lodges admitted only "worthy" men, men they claimed had high moral character, exemplified by their adherence to the order's rituals and by their embrace of such values as prudence, temperance, and fidelity. In addition, the orders' network of worthy men fostered external social and business connections that replaced traditional social adhesives, whose dissolution in the wake of the new market economy had left men exposed to swindlers and confidence men, and helped shape a new class of southern professionals.

The final section of the book, chapters 4 and 5, describes how fraternal orders redefined white men's civic responsibilities. Chapter 4 explores how secret fraternal orders carved out a unique role for themselves within Virginia's antebellum political culture as the guardians of republican principles and the manly proponents of civic virtue. Relying on a constructed mythological past that appropriated images of the founding fathers, the orders claimed that women's exclusion from the lodge room was part of an important historical precedent. Moreover, the fraternities claimed that charity, benevolence, education, and partisan harmony were masculine civic responsibilities. Here I argue that there was a direct connection between the decline of women's public autonomy and the success of secret fraternal organizations in antebellum Virginia. Fraternal republicanism did not just redefine the social and political role of nonelite white men in Virginia. It also dramatically affected the status of women by marginalizing their role in the public sphere.

Chapter 5 examines the role of secret fraternal orders in antebellum public ceremonies such as funerals, anniversary celebrations, cornerstone laying ceremonies, and Fourth of July festivities. Fraternal orders' participation in public celebrations physically demonstrated white male equality and fraternal republicanism on the streets of Virginia's cities and played a key role in establishing the community's confidence in these men to guide and protect the state. Public celebrations clearly reinforced fraternity members' public authority and social prestige. In public ceremonies that excluded women and blacks, fraternity members filled the public streets alongside politicians, firefighters, and the militia, reinforcing the validity of a broader white male claim to political power and leaving no doubt in the minds of spectators about the legitimacy of the moral authority of every white man regardless of his class status.

Although this book focuses primarily on the activities of three secret fraternal orders, it is not simply an organizational history. Rather, I have sought to demonstrate the significant role these orders played in the broader transformation of masculine culture in antebellum Virginia. The concept of fraternal brotherhood embraced by the Freemasons, Odd Fellows, and Sons of Temperance was not merely empty rhetoric meant to sustain arcane secret ceremonies. This brotherhood was living evidence of a greater attempt to unify large segments of Virginia's white male population along the lines of race and gender in bonds that it was hoped would extend far beyond the lodge hall. Ultimately, this symbolic fraternal brotherhood came to signify a very real white male unity that had far-reaching implications for other important issues such as slavery, gender relations, and class conflict. The fraternal orders played an important role in a much broader process, a role historians can no longer overlook, whereby the status of working white men was elevated above that of blacks and women, entitling them to all the rights and privileges of citizenship.

ONE

White Male Political Culture
in Antebellum Virginia

Reformers hoping to secure universal white manhood suffrage at Virginia's 1829 state constitutional convention left frustrated and disappointed. Despite weeks of heated debate, the convention chose to maintain freehold suffrage requirements. At the convention, Conservative Philip Nicholas warned that dropping property requirements for voting in Virginia would destroy the state's moral and social order. "Extend the Right of Suffrage to every man dependent and independent, you will immediately open the flood gates of corruption. You will undermine the public and private virtue of your people."[1] Conservatives threatened that if Virginians took literally the phrase from the state constitution's preamble "all men are created free and equal," nothing short of a full-scale collapse in the social order would ensue. Consequently, convention members voted to uphold suffrage requirements, and the state's new constitution left one-third of white men without the right to vote.[2]

By the next state constitutional convention in 1850, however, both convention members and the public overwhelmingly supported not only universal white male suffrage but also the popular election of the governor, local judges, and the Public Works Board, which controlled the state's internal improvements projects. In spite of grumbling from a minority of eastern conservatives, 75 of 108 convention members and 78 percent of eligible voters approved the new constitution.[3]

The changes to Virginia's suffrage requirements were in many ways part of a larger transformation in antebellum Virginia's white male political culture. During the early national period, nonelite white men repeatedly failed to dilute the political power of wealthy eastern planters. As William Shade has eloquently noted, "The Old Dominion lingered as a genteel republic in the age of the common man."[4] Throughout the 1830s and 1840s, proslavery ideology attempted to paper over the social and political inequalities among white men, promulgating the equality of all white men in a slave society. The promise of proslavery rhetoric, however, did not hold. By the end of 1840s, improvements in transportation and economic diversification ushered in a burgeoning market economy in Virginia that changed what it meant to be a white man in the slave South.

The dramatic social and economic changes wrought by urban and commercial expansion disrupted white male solidarity and reignited class tensions that proslavery egalitarianism had supposedly resolved, forcing Virginians to reevaluate their ideas regarding white male independence. It was within this tumultuous environment that secret fraternal orders became popular. The orders claimed that they brought white men together across class lines and bound them together in unique fraternal friendships. By creating a network of white brotherhoods, the fraternities constructed a space outside the political arena where white men could envision an alternative definition of white male independence based on men's moral conduct rather than on the ownership of land or slaves.

In 1829, Virginia state delegates attended a constitutional convention at which reformers attempted to equalize white men's political authority by dropping freehold property requirements for voting and granting universal white male suffrage. The convention's debates reflected the basic tensions among white men in Virginia at the time. Undergirding the opposition to universal white male suffrage was the assumption that propertyless white men were part of a larger group of dependents that collectively consisted of nonfreeholders, women, and slaves. Men without property, they argued, could not be trusted with political authority because their political opinions could be easily coerced by employers, by those who rented them land, or by their social betters.[5]

At the convention, Conservative Benjamin Watkins Leigh went so far as to liken nonfreeholders in the western part of the state to slaves and

European peasants. Men who "labor for their daily bread," he declared, were comparable to slaves in the eastern part of the state because "in [the] political economy [slaves and day laborers] fill exactly the same place," both being subject to the will of others for their own subsistence. Consequently, he claimed that "the peasantry of the west" cannot and should not enter political affairs.[6] In retaliation for the above remarks, men in Harrisonburg burned Leigh in effigy along with a copy of his speech.[7]

Tensions inside and outside of the 1829 convention ran high, as nonfreeholders and their supporters demanded political equality based on their race. In Richmond, for example, nonfreeholders submitted a petition to the constitutional convention complaining that the convention's delegates had "deprived [nonfreeholders] of their rightful equality" and had not treated them with the respect they deserved. They had been "passed by, like aliens or slaves," the men claimed, "as if destitute of interest, or unworthy of a voice."[8] The petition exposed the deep resentment that the city's nonfreeholders felt for eastern conservatives and suggested that there was a growing belief among many men that *all* white men were equal in a slave society.

The implication that nonelite white men were similar to slaves resonated sharply with reformers and further exacerbated their growing hostility toward the political power of elite slaveholders. Reformer Philip Doddridge capitalized on this resentment and flipped the Conservative Party's argument on its head. "Do I misrepresent or exaggerate when I say your doctrine makes me a slave? . . . [S]o long as you hold political dominion over me I am a slave. [Nonfreeholders] are a majority of individual whites in the state, and your equals in intelligence and virtue, moral and political. Yet you say we must obey you. . . . We have felt your weight and suffered under your misrule."[9]

Reformer Charles Morgan pushed the argument even further, claiming that securing an allegiance with propertyless white men was in Virginia slaveholders' best interest. Morgan, a nonslaveholder, warned Conservative Party members that other southern states "deemed it of the utmost importance to make all the free white men as free and independent as Government could make them. . . . [I]t is known that all slaveholding States are fast approaching a crisis truly alarming: a time when freemen will be needed—when everyman must be at his post. . . . Is it not wise now, to call together at least every free white human being and unite them in the same common interest?"[10] These arguments reveal the latent herrenvolk ideology that would become an important part of proslavery ideology in Virginia and that promised to heal class divisions.[11]

In spite of reformers' best efforts, the 1829 convention delegates were reluctant to share political power with all white men in the state, and so the new constitution upheld property requirements for voting and masculine independence remained tied to property ownership. Just one year after Virginians ratified the new constitution, however, Nat Turner's revolt hastened the death throes of old Virginia patriarchy and permanently changed the relationship between elite and nonelite white men in Virginia. Almost as Charles Morgan had predicted, Turner's slave revolt underscored the need for white male unity in this slave society.

On the night of August 23, 1831, Turner and approximately forty other slaves moved quietly through the Southampton countryside and killed more than fifty whites.[12] Turner's rebellion sent waves of fear, shock, and hysteria throughout Virginia, prompting the state legislature to engage in an unprecedented debate over the future of slavery in the Old Dominion. During these 1831–32 legislative sessions, state legislators debated solutions to the "problem" of slavery. Outcry over the rebellion and the closely followed debates in the general assembly publicly exposed the precarious nature of nonslaveholder support for the peculiar institution. Proponents of gradual emancipation argued that the slave system was dangerous to whites' safety and economic prosperity. The peculiar institution, they claimed, had slowed Virginia's economic and industrial progress and forced white laborers to compete with blacks for jobs.[13]

Although the general assembly chose to await "the development of public opinion" on the subject and ultimately did not dismantle Virginia's slave system, Turner's rebellion and the fear it caused among whites ignited a discussion about white male independence. The debates demonstrated to slaveholders with crystal clarity that the loyalty of nonslaveholding whites would be essential to the long-term preservation of the slave system. As a result, proslavery advocates increasingly abandoned older ideas that divided white men based on wealth and property, and they began to assert that slavery made all white men equal. After 1832, the notion that black slavery permitted a greater equality among white men than could be attained in a free society became a critical component of southern proslavery thought.[14]

In the 1830s, this new strain of proslavery ideology touted white male equality and even found favor among Virginians who had been staunch conservatives at the 1829–30 state constitutional convention. Conservative leader Abel Parker Upshur, for example, adopted this new component of proslavery thought in his 1837 essay "Domestic Slavery." The article claimed that in southern slave societies all white men were equal. The "impassable barrier of race," he claimed, elevated white men's social status and self-respect, inspiring even the "humblest white man with a high sense of his own comparative dignity and importance."[15]

This herrenvolk solution, however, was based on the idea that Virginia would remain primarily an agricultural society. The notion that all white men's interests, regardless of occupation, were tied to "the land and negroes" was a crucial part of Upshur's formula for a successful slave society.

> A commercial or manufacturing people will never be slave owners, because they can never profitably employ that kind of labor to any considerable extent. Wherever African slavery exists in a large class of the population, agriculture must of necessity be the chief occupation and the predominant interest.[16]

At the time Upshur wrote his essay, the goal of making agriculture Virginia's primary occupation seemed easily accomplished. Approximately 80 percent of adult white men were engaged in agricultural occupations, and only a small handful of white wage laborers complicated the Jeffersonian vision of white yeoman independence that Upshur and other proslavery advocates endorsed.[17]

Yet over the course of the next decade the hopes of men like Upshur faded.

If Virginia had remained a primarily agrarian society throughout the antebellum era, perhaps the herrenvolk democracy that proslavery advocates envisioned would have fostered harmony among white men. During the 1840s, however, the state underwent a series of important social, economic, and political transformations that altered the nature of its society, hastened its transition to a market economy, and engendered the growth of towns and cities. These changes not only put Virginia on the road to industrialization but also reawakened old tensions in white male relationships.

The expansion of Virginia's transportation networks was one of the most important developments during these years. By the 1850s, the state's cities and towns were linked to coastal, foreign, northern, and internal urban markets. Transportation improvements in Virginia began in the 1830s, most notably with the development of the James River and Kanawha Canal from Richmond to Lynchburg. Many hoped this waterway would become the Erie Canal of Virginia.[18] During the 1840s, the state's Board of Public Works and private corporations constructed bridges, dredged rivers, and laid thousands of miles in plank roads, turnpikes, canals, and railroad lines. By the eve of the Civil War, state and local governments had invested approximately $55 million in internal improvements, and railroads connected smaller urban centers like Staunton, Lynchburg, Danville, Abingdon, Fredericksburg, and Charlottesville not only with Richmond, Petersburg, and Norfolk but also to markets in Baltimore, Philadelphia, and Washington, D.C.[19]

This new transportation network expanded opportunities for merchants and led to an increase in commercial activity. Faster and cheaper shipping gave businessmen access to larger markets for their goods and enabled Virginia's merchants to make frequent buying trips to Baltimore, Philadelphia, and New York. Newspapers across the state advertised the availability of a wide assortment of goods that had "just arrived" from northern cities. As a result, farmers increasingly bypassed local mills and merchants, opting to market crops and buy finished goods in larger urban centers instead. This loss of protected local markets affected artisans the most, and many saw their business decline.[20]

Some artisans and mechanics, however, were able to transform themselves into middle-class shopkeepers or factory owners. Artisans in the luxury crafts who faced new competition from northern industry adapted to these changing economic conditions by becoming merchants and retailers of the goods they had previously produced themselves. Also, men in the construction trades, such as carpentry, flourished in urban areas during these years as demand for new housing and commercial buildings grew. As historian L. Diane Barnes explains, many prosperous artisans and mechanics turned entrepreneurs wanted to protect their new status. They embraced the emerging middle-class culture, supported the industrial development of the South, and celebrated the importance of manual labor to the modernization process. Those outside of the luxury crafts and construction trades found the new economic environment more difficult. The rise of a market economy resulted in uneven opportunities that allowed some artisans and mechanics to prosper more than others. The majority of white men were not able to start their own businesses, and mechanics and artisans moved to urban areas in large numbers in order to fill new occupations on the lower social stratum as skilled and unskilled workers.[21]

At the same time that improved transportation networks created new opportunities for work outside of agriculture, intensive soil exhaustion coupled with the economic depression of the late 1830s encouraged Virginia's farmers to diversify their crops. The unpredictable nature of the tobacco market pushed many farmers away from cultivation of the "stinking weed," and in the 1840s many farmers began growing wheat or corn or raising livestock instead.[22] Virginians also placed a greater emphasis on using the raw materials they produced, such as wheat and coal, to create finished products that could be sold nationwide. Richmond, Petersburg, Lynchburg, Staunton, and Danville all became important national manufacturing and marketing centers for flour and industrial iron. In addition, smaller regional industries expanded, such as the textile industry in Augusta County, which earned it the nickname "the Lowell of the South."[23]

The tobacco market eventually rebounded in the late 1840s, and prices rose significantly with the new popularity of bright leaf tobacco. As with other crops, Virginians went beyond cultivation and began processing and manufacturing flavored tobacco, tobacco chews, plugs, and other products. In the decade before the Civil War, Richmond alone had fifty-nine tobacco factories, and the Old Dominion emerged as the world's leading producer of tobacco products. This successful diversification of Virginia's economy fueled commercial growth, and over the course of the 1850s the value of the state's manufacturing output grew from $30 million to $50 million.[24]

As local markets withered, the traditional route to becoming a freeholder through slave ownership and farming became increasingly difficult. Young men from the countryside flooded into Virginia's urban centers to seek out new business opportunities and find work. In just ten years, for example, the number of white carpenters and clerks in Danville tripled.[25] Noting the rapid influx of artisans into Richmond in 1845, one saddler remarked to his cousin that within six weeks four new saddle- and harness-making shops had opened and that saddlers were "as thick as forty cats in a bag."[26]

Between 1830 and 1850, urban centers across the state expanded, and the free white population of Richmond and Petersburg doubled as young white male cabinetmakers, carriage makers, blacksmiths, hatters, and other artisans moved to cities in order to fulfill the growing needs of middle-class consumers. Work for skilled tradesmen abounded in urban areas as new warehouses, marketplaces, and other physical structures had to be constructed to keep pace with the new market economy in Virginia. Skilled white laborers also found work in small factories, flour mills, and iron foundries and as overseers in tobacco factories, while a new class of merchants, shopkeepers, agents, clerks, and other businessmen grew up around the state's expanding commercial sector.[27]

According to the federal census, by 1850 less than half (48 percent) of the white male population in Virginia considered themselves to be farmers or planters. Approximately 50 percent or more of the white men in the state worked in nonagricultural occupations. This relatively high percentage of nonagricultural occupations among white men made Virginia different not only from every other slave state but also from some northern states, including Ohio.[28]

At the same time, southern urban boosters and businessmen strove to reconcile slavery with the burgeoning market culture in Virginia. They did not always succeed.[29] The rising number of white men who worked outside of agriculture in the slave society of Virginia complicated white male class relationships. Not only had new market relations in Virginia decreased the possibility of upward mobility for poor rural white men, but white work-ingmen—skilled and unskilled—also began to compete with free blacks and slaves for jobs in the state's urban centers.[30] These changes exacerbated old tensions among nonelite white men and the growing class of wealthy professionals and industrialists, further casting doubt on proslavery ideals that tied white male equality to land and slaves.[31]

One issue that sorely divided middle-class white men and working white men was the use of free blacks and "hired out" slaves in skilled and un-skilled manufacturing jobs. In the late 1840s and 1850s, slave hiring became an increasingly popular and cost-effective way to fulfill the sudden demand for labor, first during the period of intense internal improvement projects and then during the boom in tobacco manufacturing. Rural slaves were frequently hired out in Virginia's urban areas to factories, to residences for domestic service, and to prosperous artisans' shops.[32] Slave hiring was very profitable for both slave owners and the companies that hired them. In southwestern Virginia, for example, railroad companies that used hired slaves to build new lines cut labor costs by approximately 50 percent.[33]

In addition, the cotton boom in the lower South created a lucrative do-mestic slave trade that made selling Virginia's surplus slave labor very prof-itable. The so-called slave drain from Virginia to states like Alabama and Mississippi fostered the growth of slave hiring. This was a very profitable trade for Virginia's slaveholders, who no longer needed to rely on local mar-kets to sell their slaves.[34] The high demand for slaves as both laborers in the cotton South and as unskilled factory workers in Virginia, however, drove up the price of slaves in the 1840s and 1850s. Ironically, then, the system of slave hiring, which seemed to reinvigorate the profitability of slavery in Virginia, made it more difficult for lower and middling white men to buy slaves of their own.

Nevertheless, poorer white men could experience a "divided mastery" of sorts by renting slaves. Historian Jonathan Martin argues that the practice of slave hiring allowed for a shared mastery of slaves, giving white men who could not afford to purchase their own slaves a taste of slave owner-ship. Despite the potential elevation in status this seemed to promise, it became a significant source of conflict between slave renters and owners. Urban slave hirers and overseers often butted heads with slave owners over the extent to which slaves could be disciplined. Slave owners by and large resented someone else severely disciplining their property and feared that if a slave was overworked while rented out, he or she would be of no use to them at home.[35]

Slave hiring also gave slaves the opportunity to play their two masters against one another, affording them leverage in situations they might not otherwise have had. Other consequences of slave hiring, such as "living out," where slaves received additional money from employers to find their own room and board, "self-hiring," where slaves negotiated their own con-tracts, and "overwork," where slaves received cash incentives for increased or extra work, collectively gave whites the impression that the hiring out of slaves encouraged blacks to step out of "their place."[36]

Further conflict developed as antebellum employers in urban areas began to see the financial benefits of using slave labor in skilled labor positions, particularly in the railroad, tobacco, and iron industries. White skilled la-borers vehemently protested against this new practice and eventually began refusing to do what had become "nigger work" in their eyes. Artisans and mechanics from Portsmouth, Petersburg, and Richmond petitioned the state legislature in the 1850s, requesting that slaves be banned from skilled trades and that the "mechanical arts" be made the exclusive privilege of white men.[37]

In the well-publicized case of the Tredegar ironworkers' strike, white workers quickly learned that their race did not always take precedence where business was concerned. Beginning in the early 1840s, Tredegar Iron Works hired and trained slaves for skilled positions as puddlers, rollers, and heaters because they argued it would save them almost $12,000 per year in labor costs. This outraged white mechanics and artisans, who had traditionally held these jobs, and workers called for a strike to ban the use of black labor in skilled positions at the foundry. Tredegar's owner, Joseph Reid Anderson, responded to the striking workers by defending his right to use slave labor in his factory as he saw fit. The white workers at Tredegar were then unpleasantly surprised when Anderson publicly fired them.[38]

As historian Jonathan Daniel Wells explains, the use of slave labor in southern factories generated significant class tensions among white men. "The business owners and middle-class managers of mills and factories had a keen interest in reducing labor costs by utilizing slave artisans, thus driving a wedge between middle-class and working-class whites in the urban South. White labor responded in the only way it could by demanding that slaves be kept on the plantation and off the factory floor."[39] The Tredegar strike received national attention, and white workers across Virginia vehemently protested Anderson's decision to fire the men. Thus, the strike further deteriorated the relationship among white men of different classes.[40]

The changes in Virginia's economy only highlighted the lingering political inequality that existed among white men. Growing resentment against the state's political system fueled a rancorous debate over universal white male suffrage and the basis of representation in the general assembly. Representation in the Virginia legislature was determined on a "mixed basis," which gave extra political weight and influence to regions that paid more taxes on property. Although easterners were a numerical minority, the value placed on their land and slaves gave them a majority of delegates in both the house of delegates and the senate.

As a result, easterners were able to pass or defeat legislation according to what was in the best interest of large plantation owners. Eastern slaveholders bitterly clashed with small slaveholders and nonslaveholders in western Virginia and the Shenandoah Valley over state funding for internal improvements projects as the market economy spread westward. Tidewater interests defeated projects that promised to connect valley counties and the western part of the state to the Ohio River valley and eastern markets. Many traditional eastern conservatives believed that state funding for internal improvements was unconstitutional and, moreover, felt that their constituents would not benefit from state money spent on the extension of the railroad in the Valley of Virginia.

By the 1840s, pro-internal improvements men from the valley and western counties declared that they would no longer tolerate the state's failure to provide them with a safe and convenient means of marketing their products, and they openly discussed dividing the state into two parts. At an internal improvements meeting in Staunton, market-oriented men adopted a resolution warning their "eastern brethren" that the continued stifling of valley internal improvement projects threatened to destroy the bonds that held Virginians together in a "common brotherhood."[41]

In 1847, the same year as the strike at Tredegar Iron Works, men in the valley reached their boiling point after the general assembly initially voted down another bill that proposed to fund an extension of the James and

Kanawha Canal from Lynchburg to the town of Buchanan. Their frustrations were reflected in Henry Ruffner's controversial 1847 pamphlet. Ruffner, the president of Washington University in Rockbridge County, had been a reformer at the 1829 convention and was a staunch advocate of internal improvements in the Valley of Virginia. His pamphlet, which emerged from a series of weekly discussions at the Franklin Society and Library Company in Lexington, argued that slavery had limited manufacturing in the South, retarded the state's economic development, and degraded the value of white labor in Virginia. To resolve these problems, Ruffner suggested that either the state be divided in half or that the slaves in western Virginia be gradually emancipated and colonized in West Africa.[42]

Not surprisingly, at a time when Virginians were forcefully condemning the Wilmot Proviso in national politics, easterners declared the Ruffner plan an abolitionist plot. Although the pamphlet received support in the western part of the state and in some parts of the valley, many questioned the timing of the statement, while others felt the emancipation plan was too radical. Still, the pamphlet highlighted not only existing discontent over the lack of universal white manhood suffrage and mixed basis representation in the general assembly, but it also demonstrated how far some Virginians were willing to go to rectify the situation. Thus, it contributed to a growing movement for a new constitutional convention.

Agitation for a new state constitution had begun in the early 1840s, and by 1846 reformers had submitted a bill calling for a new convention to the Virginia House of Delegates, but it was defeated. By the late 1840s, however, both Whigs and the Democrats in Virginia began to publicly support the push for a new convention and nonfreeholder suffrage. The Democratic *Richmond Enquirer* openly courted the workingman's vote, and the state's Whigs asserted that a new constitutional convention would undermine eastern elite planters' capacity to quash internal improvements. By 1849, the calls for a new state constitution had become deafening, and a convention bill passed through the state legislature in February 1850.[43]

The convention began in the fall of 1850 and continued through the summer of 1851. Two of the key debates concerned universal white male suffrage and the basis for representation in the legislature. Creating harmony among white men in Virginia was an important goal underlying these debates. At the convention, Henry A. Wise from Accomack County became a strong and vocal advocate for white male equality and universal white male suffrage. He argued that class tensions were at the bottom of the sectional debates over power in the legislature, and he played an important role in brokering a compromise that both protected the interests of slaveholders and politically empowered nonelite white men.[44]

The convention first took up the so-called basis debate over representation. "Mixed-basis" supporters favored awarding the seats in the state legislature based on both the slave and free white populations. "White-basis" advocates argued that representation should be based solely on the white population. Urban white workingmen and nonslaveholding westerners were drawn to the white-basis argument, while large slaveholders in the eastern part of the state generally supported the mixed-basis argument.[45]

In the end, the convention struck a temporary compromise that awarded a majority of the seats in the house of delegates to western representatives and a majority of seats in the state senate to eastern representatives. This arrangement was contingent on the calling of another convention in 1865 to reconsider the issue.[46] The basis issue underscored the division between slave interests and nonslave interests in Virginia and, more importantly, suggested the formidable political force that a combination of urban workingmen and western nonslaveholders had the potential to become in the future.

The convention then took up the question of universal white male suffrage. As historian Craig Simpson points out, the convention occurred at a pivotal time, when the national debate over the Compromise of 1850 was raging. As the convention sat down for its first meeting, Virginia's newspapers repeatedly called for southern unity on the slavery issue, making white male solidarity more important than ever.[47] Delegate Charles J. Faulkner of Berkeley County summed up the issue at stake: whether slaveholders could have confidence in nonelite white men to protect "the interests of society."

> When you have ascertained who shall exercise the right of suffrage, you have given us the measure of your confidence in the people. . . . If you have confidence in the justice, the virtue, and the intelligence of the people . . . you will enlarge the right of suffrage to its greatest practical limits . . . [and will] have given to us your own solemn conviction as statesmen as to the persons in whose hands the safety and control of all the dearest interests of the state may be safely deposited.[48]

Although a handful of staunchly conservative delegates continued to oppose dropping property qualifications for voting, universal white male suffrage was adopted by a vote of eighty-three to twenty-six with minimal debate. The new constitution declared that "every white male citizen of the

Commonwealth of the age of twenty-one years ... —and no other person—shall be qualified to vote."[49]

The people of Virginia ratified the new constitution in October 1851, and the men who had gained the right to vote were quick to exercise their new power. In local, state, and national elections in the early 1850s, candidates fervently courted the workingman's vote, and participation in elections greatly increased. In Richmond, for example, voter participation increased 197 percent in the elections that followed the ratification of the new constitution. As a result of these changes the *Richmond Enquirer* predicted that the new, more democratic constitution would "unite all classes of our citizens together like a band of brothers."[50] In 1855, the hotly contested gubernatorial election between Henry Wise and Thomas Flournoy garnered a record 156,488 votes, the largest in any Virginia state election before the Civil War.[51]

In many ways the 1850–51 constitutional convention was the high point of a crisis in white manhood that had been building throughout the 1840s. At the heart of this crisis was the changing definition of white male independence and the realization that in Virginia a true herrenvolk democracy could not be based on proslavery ideals alone. The spread of new market individualism, the large number of men who worked in nonagricultural occupations, the Tredegar ironworkers' strike, the Ruffner pamphlet, and the demand for universal white manhood suffrage underscored the fractured state of white male relationships in the Old Dominion.

It was within this contentious environment that secret fraternal orders became popular in Virginia. Secret fraternal orders created a new social space in which bridges between white men from different classes and political opinions could be built. Between 1840 and 1860, white men from a variety of professional, business, mechanical, and artisanal occupations clamored to join one of Virginia's secret fraternal orders. The majority of men who made up these organizations worked in nonagricultural occupations near or in urban centers, and they were primarily small slaveholders or nonslaveholders.

Pre–Civil War membership in the Sons of Temperance, Freemasons, and Odd Fellows peaked in the early 1850s, at which point the three orders collectively had approximately twenty-eight thousand members from across the commonwealth.[52] Although the orders were popular in most parts of the state, membership was particularly concentrated in urban areas. For example, by 1850, 44 percent of the adult free white male population in Richmond were Sons, Odd Fellows, or Masons.[53] Furthermore, these numbers

TABLE I. Percent of Adult White Male Population in Freemasons, Odd Fellows, and Sons of Temperance, 1850.

City/town	White male population age twenty-one and older*	Combined membership of the Freemasons, Odd Fellows, and Sons of Temperance**	Percent of white male population in a secret fraternal order
Lynchburg	1204	656	54
Fredericksburg	576	271	47
Richmond	4044	1780	44
Petersburg	1580	505	32
Portsmouth	1842	564	31
Norfolk	2056	609	30

* Population numbers taken from the 1850 federal census documents and presented in "A Statement Shewing the Number of White Males and White Females, over Twenty-one Years of Age, in the Several Counties, Towns, and Grand Divisions of the State of Virginia," in *Documents Containing Statistics of Virginia Ordered to Be Printed by the State Convention Sitting in the City of Richmond, 1850–1851* (Richmond: William Culley, 1851), n.p.

** Membership numbers for each group were calculated from lodge rosters or membership statistics found in each fraternal order's official proceedings. The 1851 proceedings of the Odd Fellows and the Freemasons reflect the membership numbers collected in 1850. Because only the Freemasons printed full lodge rosters in their proceedings, membership numbers from the Sons of Temperance and the Odd Fellows are based on the raw number printed for each lodge by the orders. Therefore, it is impossible to tell how many men belonged to more than one order. See *OF Proceedings*, 1851, *FM Proceedings*, 1851, and *ST Proceedings*, July 1850.

represent only the three most popular fraternal organizations that are the subject of this study. References to other secret fraternal orders (Improved Order of Red Men, United Order of American Mechanics, the Druids, and Brotherhood of the Union) can be found in antebellum Virginia newspapers, but unfortunately the records for these groups no longer exist or are unavailable for scholarly use.[54]

One of the reasons secret fraternal orders were so wildly popular in Virginia's urban areas was that, in addition to softening class distinctions among white men, they reinforced a new standard of masculine independence that was based not on property or economic status but on character, proper conduct, adherence to fraternal rituals, and success at work. Ultimately, these groups not only united men across class lines but also created a shared investment in white patriarchy that eroded the idea that white male independence must be tied to land and slaves.

Thus, in this period of tumultuous change and growing class tensions, these fraternities worked behind the political scenes to cultivate harmony and foster white male unity. The orders brought together both middle-class and workingmen and united slaveholders and nonslaveholders under the banners of brotherly love and white male equality. In light of the political, economic, and social conditions that tore these men apart, this was no small feat. The men who joined these orders made a conscious choice to overlook their cultural, political, and economic differences and create a united white male public front. In this sense, the Virginia case offers insights into the importance of secret fraternal orders to the development of white male solidarity in the two decades before the Civil War, a time of profound change and upheaval.

TWO

Secret Fraternal Orders in Antebellum Virginia

After over a decade of steep decline, membership in Virginia's secret fraternal orders rebounded in the 1840s. The orders' rhetoric of brotherly love and white male equality appealed to antebellum men who navigated the new economic and social challenges wrought by the market revolution. A broad survey of the white male social landscape in antebellum Virginia reveals that most other men's associations were traditionally distinguished from each other by the class, occupation, or political persuasion of their members. These organizations differed from secret fraternal orders in important ways. First, with the possible exception of Greek-letter college fraternities, none of these other male groups practiced elaborate secret rituals, nor did they stress the importance of white male brotherhood to the same extent that fraternal orders did.

Second, most white all-male organizations were composed of men from similar social, economic, or political backgrounds. College fraternities, debating clubs, societies, and other university associations were naturally composed only of the sons of wealthy merchants and planters who could afford to attend college.[1] Mechanics' organizations, such as the Petersburg Benevolent Mechanic Association, for example, formed to promote the interests of exclusively white mechanics and artisans.[2] In addition, the handful of white male organizations that primarily focused on charity during the antebellum era, such as the Richmond Male Orphan Society and the Gentlemen's Benevolent Society, were established in conjunction with pre-existing women's organizations and drew their membership from Virginia's social elite.[3]

Political affiliation also shaped the membership of other men's organizations in the antebellum era. During the 1840s, partisan organizations, such as "Clay," "Old Hickory," and "Rough and Ready" clubs, were popular during election seasons but functioned mainly as arms of a larger state political machine whose main goal was to secure votes for the Whig or Democratic Party. In addition, although all white men and sometimes women were welcome at partisan rallies, these groups attracted mostly men who were wealthy enough to meet the property requirements for voting.[4]

Civic groups such as voluntary firemen and militia groups had a more socially diverse group of members and were more similar to secret fraternal orders in terms of class composition. Volunteer fire companies and state militia organizations, such as the Lynchburg Hose Company, the Richmond Light Infantry Blues, and the Petersburg Grays, drew members from both working and middle classes. These groups stressed manly behavior and may have been a way for artisans and petty shopkeepers to attract business and acquire the social prestige that came with civic service. In theory, any adult white male could join a militia group or a fire company, but in most cases members had to pay yearly dues and buy their uniforms (and sometimes their equipment as well). This made militia groups in particular too expensive for many workingmen in Virginia.[5]

In goals and values, however, fire associations and militia groups were very different from secret fraternal orders. Beyond protecting the community, firemen and the militia did not subscribe to any broader philosophical ideals; they did not, for example, promote self-restraint, temperance, moral discipline, or interclass fellowship. In fact, Virginia's militia groups were known for drinking and conviviality that occasionally got out of hand. At one point the Richmond Blues attempted to ban drinking at militia events, but the ban only lasted for six months. Voluntary fire companies also sanctioned excessive drinking and fighting, and some reformers even thought of firemen as "corrupters of youth."[6]

Thus, the Freemasons, Odd Fellows, and Sons of Temperance were different from other exclusively male organizations in Virginia during the antebellum era. No other groups combined fraternal rituals, moral improvement, and sick and death benefits, nor did they attract members from both the working and middle classes. The orders' widespread popularity did not come easily, however. The Morgan affair and the subsequent anti-Masonic movement of the 1830s threatened to stamp out American secret fraternal organizations once and for all. Beginning in the 1840s, however, secret fraternal orders resurrected their fraternities and remade their public image, becoming even more popular than they had been during the early national period. In the decades leading up to the Civil War, white men established more than a dozen new secret fraternal orders modeled on the Masons and Odd Fellows.[7]

History of Secret Fraternal Orders in Early America

The history of secret fraternal orders in America dates back to the colonial era and begins with the Freemasons. Originally a European stonemasons' guild, the fraternity became a private society of merchants and gentlemen in the early eighteenth century. Within only a few decades of the order's founding, British settlers brought Freemasonry to the American colonies. By the late 1730s, colonists had opened lodges in New England, New York, Pennsylvania, Georgia, and South Carolina. The first Virginia lodge opened in Norfolk in 1741.[8]

In the decades surrounding the American Revolution, Freemasonry played an important role in transforming the British colonies into an independent republic. The fraternity helped transmit Enlightenment cosmopolitanism and republican values to the new nation's up-and-coming urban professionals and politicians. During the Revolutionary era, Masonic membership significantly increased, and the order became part of the new nation's republican landscape, both literally and figuratively. President George Washington, representing the Grand Lodge of Virginia Freemasons, laid the cornerstone of the U.S. Capitol building in 1793, and Masons dedicated new statehouses, bridges, and monuments all across the country.[9]

The Freemasons of the early republic continued to represent the upper echelons of American society, despite the fact that the fraternity's membership had broadened beyond the aristocratic colonial elite who joined the order before the Revolution. The bulk of post-Revolutionary Masons were young ambitious men seeking to attain social prominence, political influence, or commercial reputations as independent professionals.[10] In addition, the Masons were known not only as political power brokers in early America but also as imbibers and merrymakers. Drinking— occasionally to excess—was a normal part of lodge activities. According to historian Marc

Carnes, the promise of status and convivial entertainment were some of the order's chief attractions during the early national period.[11]

A second secret fraternal order also emerged in the United States in the 1820s. London-born Thomas Wildey formed the first American Odd Fellows' lodge in Baltimore in 1819. The Independent Order of Odd Fellows (IOOF), a British fraternal order, spread to cities in Massachusetts, Pennsylvania, and New York and then southward into Washington D.C., Cincinnati, and New Orleans.[12]

The popularity of fraternalism in the early national period, however, came to a screeching halt in 1826 after Masons from western New York allegedly abducted and murdered wayward lodge brother William Morgan for threatening to reveal the order's secret rituals. While awaiting the publication of his book, *Illustrations of Masonry*, Morgan was arrested by six men (five of whom were Masons) for failing to pay a two-dollar debt. Contemporary accounts claim that a stranger arrived at the jail, paid Morgan's bail, and forced him into a carriage as he screamed, "Murder, murder!" Morgan's fate was never officially determined. Some accounts of the story suggest that, after killing him, the Masons pitched Morgan's body over Niagara Falls to dispose of evidence against them. Others claim that the Masons held Morgan at Fort Niagara and then released him into Canada.[13]

Accounts of Morgan's abduction spread across the country, and its effect was to paint Freemasonry as the antithesis of republicanism. As investigators further unraveled the story, they discovered that a large number of the police and local magistrates involved in the case were also Freemasons. When the alleged abductors received only minimal punishment, the members of the community who were not Masons began to argue that a Masonic conspiracy existed within their local government. The most strident opponents of Freemasonry charged that the order had betrayed republican values by pooling power in the hands of a secret few and that it had corrupted the teachings of Christianity. Some even contended that the order sought to overthrow the government.[14]

These concerns and accusations culminated in a political crusade against Freemasonry. The Antimasonic Party, the nation's first third party, ran candidates for the presidency in 1832 and 1836 and persisted in small pockets into the 1840s. The party enjoyed only minimal success, but it effectively destroyed Masonry for at least a decade in much of the Northeast, and it severely damaged the order's reputation in the South. In Virginia, early membership peaked in 1825 but then dipped to its lowest point in 1835, after the Morgan affair. Unlike in the Northeast, the fraternity continued to operate in Virginia, although on a very minimal basis throughout the 1830s.[15]

The revival of secret fraternal organizations in the antebellum era marked an important new phase of American fraternalism. After a ten-year lull, American Freemasonry and Odd Fellowship experienced a dramatic resurgence in popularity in the 1840s. In addition, dozens of new secret fraternal orders, such as the Sons of Temperance, the Improved Order of Red Men, the Order of United American Mechanics, the Independent Order of Rechabites, the Brotherhood of the Union, and the United Ancient Order of Druids, formed and spread rapidly throughout the country.[16]

The new and modified secret fraternal orders that emerged in the antebellum era were different from early national fraternities in several important ways. First, antebellum secret fraternal orders stressed the new market values of temperance and self-restraint. This new group of Freemasons and Odd Fellows made drinking in the lodge illegal in the 1840s and deemed intoxication to be grounds for suspension or expulsion. This, of course, was also the policy of the Sons of Temperance from the very beginning of that order. Thus, in the antebellum era Freemasons and Odd Fellows sought to distance themselves from their orders' old reputation. They gathered not to drink, gamble, or escape from their wives, they argued, but to accomplish something much more important. Antebellum Masons and Odd Fellows claimed that the purpose of their orders was to promote white male equality and self-improvement and to better the communities around them.[17]

Antebellum fraternities also added elaborate new rituals. The orders put much emphasis on these rituals in the hope that they would foster a special bond among members, a bond different from that which characterized regular male friendships and that would create a fictive kinship among other members of their lodge. Increasingly, they also conceived of the space within their lodges as sacred, demarcating the boundary between public and private much more strongly. During the antebellum era, members considered their lodge space a sacred refuge from rancorous partisan, commercial, and sectional strife.[18]

Sick and death benefits were another new feature of antebellum fraternalism. In the post-Revolutionary era, the Freemasons had provided special money to help brothers in need, raised funds to educate Masonic orphans, and buried deceased brothers. However, it was during the antebellum period that the Masons created a more centralized system for the collection and distribution of charitable funds.[19] The Odd Fellows were the first to combine a centralized mutual benefit system with secret fraternal rituals in the late 1830s, and other newly created antebellum orders quickly followed suit.[20] Members paid monthly or weekly dues and in return became eligible for weekly payments in times of sickness. The orders also helped make provision for members' burials and the burial of their spouses.

Moreover, the governments of antebellum fraternities were also much more centralized and hierarchical than they had been before the Morgan affair. In addition to local lodge government, the fraternities established governing bodies at the state level (the "grand" lodge) and the national level (the "supreme," "sovereign," etc., grand lodge of the United States).[21] Each of these governing bodies had its own constitution and representative body, which met annually to vote and to discuss fraternity rules, regulations, and constitutional issues.

The Freemasons were the only antebellum order that did not have a formal national governing body. In the 1820s, several state grand lodges suggested forming a grand lodge at the national level, but there was never enough agreement among the state lodges to make it a reality.[22] In the early 1840s, however, representatives from the Masonic state grand lodges agreed to gather annually and took important steps to centralize the government of the fraternity and standardize the order's rituals nationwide. Virginia Mason John Dove authored the *Masonic Textbook* under the auspices of the Grand Lodge of Virginia, which provided state grand lodges across the country with a handbook for the order.[23]

Membership in secret fraternal orders grew dramatically around the country during this new phase of antebellum fraternalism. In Virginia, Masonic membership had climbed above pre–Morgan affair numbers by the late 1840s, and by 1851, the order had almost thirty-one hundred members and 118 subordinate lodges across the state.[24] Odd Fellowship was not established in Virginia until after the Morgan affair. The first Virginia Odd Fellows' lodge opened in Harper's Ferry in 1833. The order spread quickly to Norfolk and Wheeling, and by 1837 five more lodges had opened in Richmond, Winchester, Portsmouth, and Petersburg, and the Grand Lodge of Virginia had been established. Between 1840 and 1850, the Odd Fellows enjoyed tremendous growth. In 1840, the fraternity had 1,404 members and twenty subordinate lodges. By 1850, 5,429 men had joined the Odd Fellows, and the order had opened eighty-nine subordinate lodges.[25]

The most successful of the new antebellum orders was the Sons of Temperance. Formed in New York City in the early 1840s, the Sons applied the concept of fraternalism to the temperance movement. The order modeled itself after Masonry and Odd Fellowship but tailored its rituals, passwords, benefits, and hierarchies to the temperance cause. The Sons led the temperance movement during the 1840s and 1850s and, in contrast to earlier temperance societies, advocated total abstinence from all alcohol and pushed to legally ban the sale and public consumption of alcoholic beverages.[26]

The Sons distanced themselves from the evangelical arm of the campaign against alcohol. Temperance reform in the 1820s and 1830s had been largely a product of the Second Great Awakening. Men and women, both elite and middle class, had led this phase of the movement, characterized by the moral suasion approach of the American Temperance Union that allowed for the occasional drinking of wine.[27] One of the most striking new trends in late antebellum temperance reform was the large numbers of workingmen who were drawn to the movement. The male-run Washingtonian Society, a precursor to the Sons of Temperance, was the first temperance organization to harness the reform efforts of workingmen. All-male temperance organizations reshaped and refocused much of the debate over alcohol. They deemphasized the role of women and the church and instead highlighted masculine self-restraint and the importance of male friendship in securing a temperate lifestyle. The Washingtonians, however, enjoyed only brief success and faded out of existence within a few years. Historian Ronald Walters notes that the group grew rapidly but without direction or structure.[28]

The Sons of Temperance replaced the Washingtonians in 1842. The Sons not only attracted a large number of workingmen to their new order but also made fraternal ritual an important part of the organization. The order grew quickly and ultimately became the largest and most successful temperance organization of the antebellum era. As a systematized and highly structured secret fraternal order, the Sons of Temperance remedied the institutional and organizational problems of the Washingtonians, and the order spread rapidly throughout the country. Like the Washingtonians, the Sons also had a policy of total abstinence from the use of alcohol.[29]

The Sons of Temperance was the most popular of the three fraternities in antebellum Virginia. In 1852, at the peak of antebellum state membership, the Sons had over twice as many members as the Odd Fellows and the Freemasons combined. Like the rest of the country, Virginians began their first organized efforts at temperance reform in the 1820s in conjunction with the church. Temperance societies connected to Baptist, Presbyterian, and Methodist churches and composed of both men and women led the state's early temperance movement. By the 1830s middle-class and elite white women were actively participating in the state's temperance movement, and in some areas women were voting members of their associations. However, as temperance reform became increasingly associated with abolition in the North, Virginia's organizations began to distance themselves from national temperance groups such as the American Temperance Union.[30]

Beginning in the 1840s, a second, male-run phase of temperance reform reconnected Virginia's temperance advocates to the national antiliquor movement through the Sons of Temperance. The Sons founded their first Virginia lodge in Norfolk in 1843. The following year the order established the Grand Division of Virginia, and the fraternity quickly spread through the Shenandoah Valley and across the state.[31] By 1850, the order had over three hundred subordinate lodges, and state membership climbed to 15,375. Moreover, the Grand Division of the Virginia Sons of Temperance was the sixth-strongest state division in the country.[32]

The members of the Virginia Sons of Temperance gave several reasons for the popularity of their order. In particular, they claimed that earlier temperance societies, including the Washingtonian Society, were unsuccessful because they were not well organized. Thomas J. Evans, the grand secretary of the Virginia Sons of Temperance, remarked that, although the Washingtonian Society actively supported and was enthusiastic about the temperance cause, its lack of unity and a national system of organization made it weak.[33] Similarly, Virginia Son of Temperance Alexander Martin explained that the Sons had given the temperance cause stability, which produced uniform success. "Our operations are conducted with uninterrupted regularity and system," Martin boasted. "We illustrate the might of compact[,] associated effort. Everyone knows his duty:—everyone has his post. We present an undivided front."[34]

Brotherhood was another reason fraternity members claimed the order was more successful than past temperance societies. Members insisted that the Sons' fraternal rituals and exclusivity created a unique bond among its members. Their fraternal ties helped them to maintain their temperance pledge because their brothers encouraged, supported, and chided them when necessary. According to lodge brother Pike Powers, brotherhood furthered the fraternity's twin goals of temperance and self-improvement.[35]

The Freemasons attracted fewer members during in the 1840s and early 1850s than the Sons of Temperance and the Odd Fellows. It was not until just before the Civil War that Masonic membership surpassed that of the other two fraternities. This was likely due to a combination of factors. First, the effects of the Morgan affair lingered into the early 1840s. Also, the government of Freemasonry was more decentralized than the Odd Fellows and the Sons. This allowed the Masons to better withstand the increasing sectional tensions that bred divisiveness in most national organizations in the late 1850s. Thus, the Freemasons continued to steadily gain members in the late 1850s, while membership in the Sons and Odd Fellows declined precipitously in Virginia after 1855.

Financial concerns may have been another reason why the Freemasons initially drew fewer members than the Odd Fellows and the Sons. Masonry was the most expensive of the three fraternities. Masonic dues were double those of the other orders, and the initiation fee for the Freemasons was $15, compared to $5 for the Odd Fellows and between $2 and $4 for the Sons.[36] As a result, the Masons also tended to have more socially prominent men as members than the other two fraternities.

Joining the Lodge

Men interested in joining an antebellum fraternity submitted a written petition stating their name, age, residence, and occupation. Only adult white men were eligible for membership in the Sons, Masons, and Odd Fellows during the antebellum era. Moral character, the ability to support oneself, and belief in a supreme being were the most important factors in determining whether or not a man was accepted into a lodge.[37] To become a member of the Sons of Temperance, a man was also required to take the following pledge: "No Brother shall make, buy, sell or use, as a beverage, any spirituous or malt liquors, wine or cider."[38]

After a man requested admission to a fraternity, the lodge chose between three and five men to form a committee of investigation. The committee was charged with looking into the character and reputation of the applicant. This could involve simply speaking with other lodge members who already knew the man or speaking with family members or business associates to ensure that the applicant was "of good moral character." For example, Freemason Phillip Barziza of Williamsburg Lodge, no. 6, wrote to fellow lodge member Charles Montague concerning the membership application of one of Montague's neighbors, inquiring as to "the fitness of the applicant to become a Mason."

I will as one of the committee of investigation & deem it my duty to address you, who being as it were a neighbor of his will be able to give me back information concerning Mr. T as, is proper for the lodge to know. You may know if he has contracted habits which [are] not objectionable to a gentleman of the [world], yet would unfit him to be made a member of our fraternity.[39]

Investigators and those who vouched for the character of applicants were asked to consider whether or not they would feel comfortable lending the applicant large sums of money, if they could trust him to protect and "intermingle" with their families in times of crisis (particularly their wives and daughters), and if, upon their death, they would trust the applicant to visit their bedside or oversee their funeral arrangements.[40]

The committee of investigation informed the lodge of its findings and made its recommendation. The lodge then voted whether or not to accept the candidate for membership. If the candidate received three black balls (voting was anonymous), he was rejected and could not apply to the order again for six months. Once accepted into a fraternity, candidates were expected to read the constitution of their new lodge, pay the lodge's initiation fee, and undergo the order's initiation rituals.[41]

When explaining the membership requirements to the public, the fraternities stressed the importance of a man's integrity rather than his economic status. As Mason John Bowie Strange noted, his order abolished "all distinctions founded on wealth" and "all hereditary honors," judging a man only "by his *internal* and not by his external qualifications."[42] Moreover, the orders claimed to function as the embodiment of liberal meritocracy, promising equal opportunity for white men of good character.

The orders also insisted that they united men from different social classes who might not otherwise have associated with one another. Odd Fellow James D. McCabe explained to a public crowd that one of the benefits of his fraternity was that it brought "men together of the most discordant opinions, and unite[d] them in bonds of brotherly love."[43] Fraternity members argued that they "esteem[ed] each other as children of the same parent."[44] This "perfect and lasting friendship" could only truly exist, the orders asserted, among men who believed they were equal in status.[45]

The literature of Virginia's Freemasons, Odd Fellows, and Sons of Temperance loudly proclaimed the orders' advocacy of white male equality based on character. The groups fervently asserted that their orders welcomed men of any status into their lodges, provided they were of good moral character. Robert G. Scott Jr., a Richmond lawyer and past master of Randolph Lodge, no. 19, celebrated the insignificance of class distinctions in the Masonic brotherhood at the 1845 annual meeting of the Grand Lodge of Virginia. He explained to the crowd that

> [Freemasonry] knows no distinction of caste, or of sect. Its comprehensive love embraces in its fold alike the tenants of the palace or the cottage[.] . . . [T]he humble daily laborer, we should be proud to call brother, as he who rolls in luxury and wealth, and they meet together with us on the same common level of equality. Equality did I say? Yes, equality in its best, its broadest, its most fascinating forms.[46]

Similarly, the Sons of Temperance noted the members of their order met as a "band of brothers" dedicated to the dual causes of brotherhood and temperance. After all, remarked Robert Taylor of Lexington Division, no. 45, rich and poor men alike were susceptible to the vice of intemperance.[47]

One Odd Fellow directly linked the principles of his order to natural rights ideology. "We carry out, in fact, in our little polity," he boasted, "what others hold in theory, 'that all men are created free and equal.'"[48] Furthermore, he claimed that men from all different occupations found common ground in the principles of Odd Fellowship.

> Enlisted under the banners of "Friendship, Love and Truth" the hardy mechanic and artisan, the sturdy yeoman and the learned divine are seen shoulder to shoulder and hand to hand, upholding this glorious fabric reared upon the imperishable principles of Odd-Fellowship.[49]

Thus, these new and reformed secret fraternal orders in antebellum America both promoted the ideal of white male equality, an equality that many men in Virginia craved, and emphasized the importance of the new market values found in Virginia's urban centers, such as self-restraint, upright moral character, and temperance. White men who worked in nonagricultural occupations and valued the standards of white male independence that lauded success at work and good moral character found this rhetoric especially appealing.

Membership

In the antebellum era, the men who joined fraternal orders represented a much broader cross section of the white male population than those who joined the fraternities of the early republic. Although only a handful of scholarly studies have analyzed the membership of these antebellum fraternities, several conclusions may be drawn from the existing scholarship. In all parts of the country, the majority of men who joined secret fraternal orders were artisans and skilled laborers (blacksmiths, carpenters, tailors, cabinetmakers), commercially oriented men (merchants, shopkeepers, clerks, salesmen), and professionals (lawyers, doctors, dentists, editors, clergy, teachers). In other words, the bulk of fraternity members, in all regions of the nation, worked in nonagricultural occupations. Existing studies further demonstrate that the men who joined fraternal orders also were more likely to embrace the market economy and evolving values of self-restraint, industriousness, and temperance associated with middle-class propriety. The orders created a code of conduct that guided members through the evolving labyrinth of middle-class etiquette and promised upward social mobility based on character, not economic status.[50]

Thus, changes in American fraternalism during the antebellum period, such as the increasing significance of ritual, the fictive kinship of the lodge, and the introduction of a system of benefits, brought middle-class men and skilled workingmen together and helped them to cope with the dramatic social and economic upheavals wrought by new market relations. Furthermore, the new rituals, benefits, and cross-class bonds, combined with the exclusion of free blacks and women, resulted in a promise of respectability for all white men.

This promise of respectability extended to the members of Virginia's antebellum secret fraternal orders as well. The majority of Virginians who joined the fraternities were skilled artisans or professional and commercial men who sought to improve themselves and their community. The men who joined the Masons in Richmond were overwhelmingly (approximately 70 percent) professionals or men who were connected in some way with business. Skilled craftsmen made up the second-largest group of men who joined one of the five Masonic lodges in Richmond. Approximately 22 percent of members worked as artisans or as skilled laborers, and based on available information for 165 men, there were no unskilled laborers who joined the order, and only one farmer.[51] In smaller towns such as Harrisonburg and in more rural areas such as Appomattox County, less than half of the men who joined the Masons were professionals or connected with business. Still, even in these areas the majority of Masons held nonagricultural occupations, as many men who joined were artisans or skilled craftsmen.

Information about members of the Odd Fellows in antebellum Virginia is more difficult to locate than information about the members of other fraternities because Odd Fellow lodge rosters from this era are extremely scarce. The records for Chesapeake Lodge, no. 89, in Mathews County and Marshall Lodge, no. 44, in Gloucester County contain some of the few remaining (and accessible) antebellum lodge rosters. The names of the Odd

TABLE 2. Occupational Distribution for the Freemasons in Antebellum Virginia: Percent of Members in Each Occupational Group.

	Richmond city lodges, nos. 10, 19, 36, 51, and 53 (1851)	Harrisonburg, Rockingham County, Rockingham Union Lodge, no. 27 (1851)	Fredericksburg lodges, nos. 4 and 63 (1851)	Williamsburg Lodge, no. 6 (1851)	Appomattox County Lodge (Clover Hill), no. 107 (1851)	Staunton, Augusta County, Staunton Lodge, no. 13 (1851)
Artisan/craftsman	21.2	28.1	13.2	5	11.1	30.4
Commercial/professional	69.7	37.5	48.5	58	38.9	52.1
Laborer	0	0	0	0	5.6	2.1
Farmer/planter	.6	25	7.4	16	26.5	4.3
Government/miscellaneous	9.6	9.4	7.4	21	4.4	8.7

Fellows' officers and representatives to the Grand Lodge of Virginia, however, can be gleaned from newspaper ads and the published proceedings of the grand lodge. Based on this information, it can be determined that the majority of Virginia Odd Fellows were also skilled artisans, professionals, and businessmen.[52]

Like the Masons and the Odd Fellows, the majority of the men who joined the Sons of Temperance had jobs unrelated to agriculture. Occupational information for members of lodges in Rockingham, Spotsylvania, and Augusta counties and for the officers of lodges in Richmond demonstrates that between 54 and 82 percent of members were skilled craftsmen, artisans, businessmen, and professionals or involved in commercial activity in some way. In four of the lodges only a handful of members listed themselves as "laborers" on the 1850 census. In Mount Crawford and Charles City County, for reasons unknown, approximately one-quarter of the lodge members were listed as laborers on the census. However, this appears to be an aberration from the typical makeup of Sons of Temperance lodges.[53]

A large number of Virginia's white fraternity members were also slaveholders. Between 50 and 75 percent of Virginia Freemasons and Odd Fellows owned slaves. Among the Sons of Temperance, approximately 49 percent of the officers and grand representatives in Richmond owned slaves, and in Rockingham County between 11 and 16 percent of all Sons were slaveholders.[54] Like the Sons of Temperance in other slave states, the order's members in Virginia were overwhelmingly small slaveholders, owning fewer than five slaves.

Overall, however, compared to places like Georgia, Alabama, and South Carolina, where between 57 and 67 percent of the Sons of Temperance were slaveholders, a smaller percentage of Virginia's Sons owned slaves.[55] As several recent studies have demonstrated, slavery was not incompatible with temperance or other types of moral reform in the South.[56] By 1850, men from slave states represented 44.3 percent of the total American membership in the Sons of Temperance.

In fact, southern temperance advocates believed that reform aimed at restricting black access to alcohol would boost the productivity of their slaves and reduce disorderly conduct among urban slaves and free blacks. Southern temperance reformers also equated drunkenness with a dependence on "slavery" to alcohol. The concept of total abstinence as "independence" from alcohol certainly would have appealed to middling white men attempting to prove their independent status.[57]

TABLE 3. Occupational Distribution for the Odd Fellows in Antebellum Virginia: Percent of Members in Each Occupational Group.

	Officers and representatives to the Grand Lodge of Virginia from Richmond (1849–53)*	Harrisonburg, Rockingham County, Valley Lodge, no. 40 (1857)	Fredericksburg, Myrtle Lodge, no. 50 (1857)	Gloucester Court House, Gloucester County, Marshall Lodge, no. 44 (1848–54)	Mathews County, Chesapeake Lodge, no. 89 (1851–52)
Artisan/craftsman	53.8	35.1	36.4	23	11.1
Commercial/professional	34.6	23.5	48.5	35.9	44
Laborer	0	11.8	0	0	3.7
Farmer/planter	3.85	17.6	0	15.4	29.6
Government/miscellaneous	3.85	11.8	9.1	12.8	7.4

* Because lodge rosters were not available for the Richmond Odd Fellows from the early 1850s, officer/member names were compiled from those listed in ads in the *Richmond Daily Dispatch* and from the names of representatives to the state bodies as listed in the fraternities' official proceedings. See: *Richmond Daily Dispatch*, January 15, 1852, March 26, 1852, April 1 and 2, 1852, and *OF Proceedings*, 1849 and 1853.

TABLE 4. Occupational Distribution for the Sons of Temperance in Antebellum Virginia: Percent of Members in Each Occupational Group.

	Officers and representatives to the Grand Division of Virginia from Richmond (1848–52)*	Harrisonburg, Rockingham County, Marshall Division, no. 3 (1844–48)	Fredericksburg and Spotsylvania County divisions, nos. 67, 109, and 348 (1851–52)**	Charles City County, Monguy Division, no. 226 (1852–54)	Staunton, Augusta County, Charity Division, no. 6 (1849)	Mount Crawford, Rockingham County, Mount Crawford Division, no. 19 (1848–54)
Artisan/craftsman	31.3	49.7	28.2	17.6	71.4	44.3
Commercial/professional	50.7	31.5	33.3	5.9	12.2	14
Laborer	2.9	3.5	2.6	23.5	0	23.6
Farmer/planter	5.9	8.4	33.3	35.3	4.1	16
Government/miscellaneous	8.9	7	0	0	2	1.8

* Because lodge rosters were not available for the Richmond Sons of Temperance from the early 1850s, officer/member names were compiled from those listed in ads in the *Richmond Daily Dispatch* and from the names of representatives to the state bodies as listed in the fraternities' official proceedings. See *Richmond Daily Dispatch*, February 21, 1852, February 26, 1852, April 4, 1852, June 3–5, 1852, and *ST Proceedings*, July 1848, October 1849, October 1850, January 1852.

** Sons of Temperance names taken from the roster of Mount Hermon Division, no. 348, and a partial list of members from a broadside published by Mercer Division, no. 67, and Spottswood Division, no. 109.

TABLE 5. Slave Ownership Among Virginia's Secret Fraternal Orders.

Virginia Freemasons	Percentage of members who owned slaves	Virginia Odd Fellows	Percentage of members who owned slaves	Virginia Sons of Temperance	Percentage of members who owned slaves
Richmond City Lodges, nos. 10, 19, 36, 51, 53 (1851)	52.7	Officers and Representatives to the Grand Lodge of Virginia from Richmond (1849–53)*	50	Officers and Representatives to the Grand Division of Virginia from Richmond (1848–52)*	49.3
Harrisonburg, Rockingham County, Rockingham Union Lodge, no. 27 (1851)	65.6	Harrisonburg, Rockingham County, Valley Lodge, no. 40 (1857)	35.3	Harrisonburg, Rockingham County, Marshall Division, no. 3 (1844–48)	15.4
Fredericksburg Lodges, nos. 4 and 63 (1851)	44	Fredericksburg, Myrtle Lodge, no. 50 (1857)	42.4	Fredericksburg and Spotsylvania County Divisions, 67, 109, and 348 (1851–52)**	56.4

Lodge	%	Lodge	%	Division	%
Williamsburg Lodge, no. 6 (1851)	68	Gloucester C.H., Gloucester County, Marshall Lodge, no. 44 (1848–54)	71.8	Charles City County, Monguy Division, no. 226 (1852–54)	29.4
Staunton, Augusta County, Staunton Lodge, no. 13 (1851)	43.4	Staunton Odd Fellows Lodge, Staunton Lodge, no. 45	No data available	Staunton, Augusta County, Charity Division, no. 6 (1849)	20.4
Appomattox County Lodge (Clover Hill), no. 107 (1851)	50	Mathews County, Chesapeake Lodge, no. 89 (1851–52)	70	Mt. Crawford, Rockingham County, Mt. Crawford Division, no. 19 (1848–54)	11.3

Figures based on percentage of slaveholding members who could be found on 1850 census. Dates in parentheses indicate year(s) of lodge roster.

*Because lodge rosters were not available for the Richmond Odd Fellows or the Sons of Temperance from the early 1850s, I compiled officer/member names from the Richmond *Daily Dispatch* and from the names of representatives to the state bodies as listed in the fraternities' official proceedings. For the Odd Fellows see: *Daily Dispatch*, January 15, 1852, March 26, 1852, April 1 and 2, 1852, *OF Proceedings*, 1849 and 1853. For The Sons of Temperance see: *Daily Dispatch*, February 21, 1852, February 26, 1852, April 4, 1852, June 3–5, 1852, and *ST Proceedings*, July 1848, October 1849, October 1850, January 1852

**Sons of Temperance names taken from the roster of Mt. Hermon Division, no 348, and a partial list of members from a broadside published by Mercer Division, no. 67, and Spottswood Division, no. 109.

In general, only a handful of men who owned more than twenty slaves joined the orders, and the large majority of Virginia's Freemasons, Odd Fellows, and Sons owned fewer than ten slaves. Among men from the upper-middling and working classes, then, the orders brought together small slaveholders and nonslaveholders. These men joined together largely in the state's urban centers under the banners of white male equality, moral propriety, temperance, and brotherly love. This was quite an astounding display of public unity among men who, living in an era of white male class turmoil, oftentimes had competing political and economic interests outside of the lodge. The glue that held them together was a new faith in the importance of moral character in judging a man's respectability.

Policies on Race

Although the orders' requirement that members maintain good moral character provided for the inclusion of white men from different economic classes, the same requirement was used as a way of excluding African Americans from the fraternities. The purportedly degraded morality of slaves and free blacks warranted their automatic exclusion from the Masons, Odd Fellows, and Sons in Virginia.

African Americans were not just excluded from the southern lodges of these orders. The national governing bodies of all three organizations limited membership across the country to white men. Virginia's fraternal orders fully supported the exclusion of African Americans and fought to maintain this national policy when other state lodges challenged it later in the antebellum period. The slave state that had witnessed Nat Turner's rebellion forbade African American Freemasonry and Odd Fellowship. Historians have found evidence of black mutual aid and burial societies in antebellum Virginia, and a few claim that secret fraternal orders met without whites' knowledge in places like Norfolk and Richmond in the late 1850s.[58] Unfortunately, it is impossible to know for certain whether such lodges existed.

Virginia did, however, become a hub for black secret fraternal orders after the Civil War. In the decades following the war, black fraternal orders such as the Independent Order of St. Luke, the Prince Hall Masons, the Grand United Order of Odd Fellows, the United Order of Galilean Fisherman, and the Grand United Order of True Reformers established important state and national headquarters in Virginia.[59] The prevalence of black secret fraternal orders in postbellum Virginia gives credence to the claims that black orders met secretly before the Civil War. In addition, it reinforces the notion that men, both black and white, viewed secret fraternal orders as a way to advance themselves socially and economically.

In northern states, black secret fraternal orders met openly, but blacks and whites maintained separate secret fraternal orders throughout the antebellum era and into the twentieth century. The Prince Hall Masons, named after the founder of African American Freemasonry, received their initial charter from a British soldier during the American Revolution. After the war, Prince Hall and fourteen other black men applied to the Grand Lodge of Massachusetts for permission to open a lodge of their own. The Massachusetts Masons rejected their request "on account of color." The men then applied for and were granted a charter from British Masons and opened African Lodge, no. 459.[60]

Throughout the early republic, Prince Hall Masonry continued to attract educated and politically conscious free blacks. It was rumored that David Walker was a Prince Hall Mason, and copies of Walker's famous *Appeal to the Coloured Citizens of the World* were discovered in both Richmond and Norfolk just before Turner's rebellion. After the revolt, rumors circulated through Virginia that Turner was also a black Mason.[61] Slave uprisings fueled white speculation regarding the potential threat that black fraternal orders might pose to the slave system and white supremacy in general. In Norfolk, one citizen suggested that black secret fraternal orders had been illegally meeting in the city and had gathered weapons and money for potentially nefarious purposes.[62]

Although black fraternal orders were illegal in antebellum Virginia, present-day Virginia Prince Hall Masons maintain that their first lodge, Universal Lodge, no. 1, was founded in Alexandria in 1845.[63] Current Prince Hall Masons also suggest the existence of at least three other lodges in the Norfolk-Portsmouth areas. An article appearing in a Norfolk paper supports their claim.

> A gentleman of this city, was applied to a few days since for advice by a negro, who declared himself a member of the colored Lodge of Masons in this city, which according to his account, was organized some months since.... We understand that there are other secret societies in existence here among the negroes.... [W]e think in these times of impudence and insubordination among this class of our population, that these societies should be ferreted out and broken up.[64]

Although there may have been orders that met in secret, no formally organized black lodges existed in Virginia during the antebellum period. After the Civil War, black Masons met openly in Virginia for the first time in Norfolk, and by 1869 twelve lodges had joined together to form the state's Union Grand Lodge.[65]

In 1846, the Grand Lodge of Ohio forced white Freemasons nationwide to confront the issue of race in their fraternity by proposing that free blacks be allowed to join the order. Although Masonic constitutions did not specify that members must be white, from the very beginning of American Freemasonry, the order had required that members be "freeborn."[66] After some debate among the leaders from several state grand lodges, the decision to admit free blacks was left up to the Grand Lodge of Ohio in the interest of preserving the sovereignty of each grand lodge's jurisdiction. The Ohio Masons, however, ultimately voted against admitting the "descendants of Africans." They asserted that it "would be inexpedient and tend to mar the present harmony of the fraternity to admit any of the persons of colour (so called) into the fraternity of Free and Accepted Masons."[67]

In reaction to the Grand Lodge of Ohio's decision, the Grand Lodge of Virginia's Committee of Foreign Correspondence issued a report that appeared in the 1846 annual proceedings. Committee members Robert G. Scott, John Dove, James Evans, Sidney S. Baxter, and Samuel H. Myers reassured members that the proposal had been defeated and the race issue would not become a serious topic of Masonic debate in the near future.

> It is enough for the present to say, that the unhappy and demoralized condition of this portion of our population is such, that we cannot expect any serious attempt to unite them, in the bonds of Masonry, from the benefits of which all whose moral standard is so low must be forever excluded. It can only be for purposes of evil, and not to strengthen and build up Masonry, that such an inquiry can be seriously and recklessly urged.[68]

The order's assertion that the degraded state of black character permanently excluded blacks from the Masons would work to prevent white Masonic lodges from recognizing the legitimacy of Prince Hall Masonry or admitting black members until the twentieth century.

Like the Prince Hall Masons, African Americans in northern states also established Odd Fellows lodges under British jurisdiction. In 1843, several free black men in New York applied to the British Odd Fellows, the Grand United Order of Odd Fellows (GUOOF), for permission to open a lodge after American Odd Fellows rejected their request. The men had applied twice to the American Odd Fellows (the IOOF) for a charter but were rejected "with contempt" both times because of their race. Then, a British black man named Peter Ogden persuaded them to apply for a charter from the GUOOF in England. Their request was accepted without hesitation. The GUOOF expanded rapidly throughout northern cities, first in New York, Albany, and Poughkeepsie and eventually in cities in Pennsylvania, Connecticut, Massachusetts, and New Jersey.[69]

The GUOOF attempted to establish a lodge in Alexandria, Virginia, in 1847, but the lodge encountered strong opposition from white Odd Fellows. A letter to the grand scribe of the GUOOF reported that the members of the Alexandria lodge made every effort to keep the lodge open, but white fraternity members had "opposed them tooth and toenail."[70] The GUOOF did not attempt to open any other lodges in the South, and there are no records that indicate the existence of any official GUOOF lodges in Virginia before the Civil War.

Early on in the antebellum era, the national constitution of the IOOF stipulated that all members must be "free white males" of good moral character.[71] In other words, no free blacks would be accepted into the order. Upon the application of a Polynesian man to the order in 1857, the Grand Lodge of the United States, IOOF, reviewed its guidelines on racial purity. The national body repeated that only "pure Caucasian or white" men would be accepted into the order. The Grand Lodge of the United States also explicitly excluded Chinese, Polynesian, and Native American men from the fraternity. "Every protection should be afforded," they warned, "to prevent the amalgamation of the races."[72] Representatives from the Grand Lodge of Virginia fully supported the decision of the Grand Lodge of the United States to ban free blacks from the order and reported to members in Virginia that "we cannot, without endangering the Order itself, introduce races into its bosom whose characteristics are falsehood, sensuality, and social and moral degradation."[73]

The Sons of Temperance on both sides of the Mason-Dixon Line excluded blacks from membership as well. Although the tradition of black temperance reform in the North extended back to the early national era, there is no evidence to suggest that African Americans formed their own Sons of Temperance lodges in northern states before the Civil War.[74] The question of admitting blacks to the Sons of Temperance was formally raised as a national issue at a national division meeting in Boston. In 1850, the national division declared it "illegal and improper" to admit blacks into the order, and the following year, the body mandated that the word "white" be included in the membership requirements section of subordinate lodge constitutions.[75] This decision sparked controversy within some northern state divisions, and in Wisconsin one local division even disbanded in protest.[76]

Virginia's grand worthy patriarch, William R. Drinkard, who attended the meeting, made the following report to Virginia's grand division:

> The solemn declaration of the National Division, by a vote of 74 to 6, that
> the admission of negroes, or colored persons, into our Order was "*illegal and
> improper*," relieved the oppressive fears of many of our best friends, both
> North and South, and, in a satisfactory and just manner, effectually disposed
> of a subject pregnant with ruin and dismay, to the dearest interests of our
> united and great fraternity. . . . Thanks to the wisdom, the prudence and
> the firmness of the National Division, by which this imminent peril was
> removed, to the satisfaction and joy of all, save a few whose "zeal lacketh
> understanding."[77]

Virginia's subordinate divisions expressed their relief over and satisfaction with the National Division's ruling. However, they wanted to ensure that question could not be raised again in Virginia. Thus, the Grand Division of Virginia resolved to include the word "white" in their qualifications for membership.[78]

The Sons of Temperance not only enhanced the social status of white men by excluding blacks from membership. They also made restricting black access to alcohol an important goal of their fraternity, and they sought to punish white shop owners who sold liquor to slaves and free blacks. Early on in the Sons' history in Virginia, the fraternity tied controlling black behavior to temperance reform. In 1846, the Barboursville Division in Orange County presented the very first antiliquor resolution to the grand division, which proposed banning the sale of alcohol to slaves.[79]

Despite the fact that it had been illegal to sell liquor to slaves without their master's consent since early in the nineteenth century, prior to 1831 Virginians had more or less ignored these laws. After Turner's rebellion, however, authorities made new attempts to rigidly enforce this law and passed a series of additional acts that further restricted slaves' and free blacks' ability to purchase alcoholic beverages. As Virginia's commercial centers grew, reformers argued that black access to alcohol needed to be more tightly controlled in order to preserve public order and to protect whites.[80]

Ellen Eslinger's study of the antebellum temperance reform movement in the town of Lexington also ties temperance reform to race relations and urban growth in Virginia. She argues that commercial growth in the state's midsized urban centers, and subsequently racial tensions, created a need among whites to further regulate black drinking. Consequently, Lexington's Sons of Temperance organized public temperance meetings to discuss the revision of state liquor laws and how to punish liquor retailers who sold alcohol to minors, known drunkards, and blacks.[81]

According to the Sons' leaders, the duty to protect one's community from the evils of intemperance acquired an even greater significance in a slave society. Speakers at an 1852 state temperance convention in Staunton argued fervently that Virginians, as southerners, had a special interest in the passage of more restrictive liquor laws.

> In Virginia and other slave States, we must not lose sight of another element in ascertaining our loss by this [liquor] traffic. We allude to its effect upon our slaves ... Our interest as well as our duty, requires us to use our utmost efforts to save [slaves] from this destructive vice of intoxication. They have not the same motives that their masters have to restrain them. They have no intellectual pleasure to lose—their intemperance will not deprive them of a home, nor make their wives and children hungry or naked, nor cast them upon cold charity of the world.... We have, therefore, additional motives, which have no force in the northern states, to put down a traffic which so seriously injures our slaves and their masters.[82]

Thus, the Sons of Temperance, composed of slaveholders and nonslaveholders alike, adroitly employed temperance reform to place themselves in the position of paternal protectors. They argued that they must protect social order and save slaves from themselves. Consequently, the Sons' active involvement in restricting black access to alcohol further elevated the status of all white men in their group.

Virginia's secret fraternal organizations thus elevated the status of its nonelite members both by excluding African Americans as well as by bolstering the politics of white supremacy within their communities. Antebellum fraternities used their orders to uphold white social order across class lines in both the North and the South. The rejection of free blacks from these orders made clear that preserving harmony among the white men who made up their lodges was more important than bridging racial divides.

It also drew important distinctions between black and white morality that could be used to deny free blacks respectability and social status.

Thus, this new wave of antebellum fraternalism in Virginia extended the promise of respectability to all white men based on character. These fraternities attracted urban white artisans, shopkeepers, and middle-class professionals and both small slaveholders and nonslaveholders to their orders. Membership was based on whiteness and adherence to a specific code of conduct that advanced the market-oriented ideals of self-restraint, industriousness, and temperance. The orders' emphasis on brotherly love also worked to ease the stress placed on the relationship between white middle-class and workingmen by the spreading market economy. In effect, the orders constructed an alternative standard of southern white manhood, based explicitly on the exclusion of women and black men, that disentangled white male independence from the ownership of slaves and property by emphasizing moral character. This new understanding of southern manhood not only reinforced white supremacy outside the realm of plantation slavery but also supplemented proslavery ideology in the places where it had fallen short.

THREE

Keeping Out the Unworthy

On March 25, 1841, in downtown Richmond, Virginia, colorful banners with the words "Friendship, Love, and Truth" waved in the air, and a large crowd watched as members of the Independent Order of Odd Fellows dressed in full regalia laid the cornerstone of their new grand lodge building. In his commemoration speech, Brother Raleigh T. Daniel extolled his fraternity's virtues. The Odd Fellows, he claimed, strove not merely to improve the character of the men who joined the secret fraternal organization but also to benefit society as a whole by making its members better sons, husbands, fathers, and citizens.[1] At public meetings, in speeches, and in print, each of Virginia's fraternal orders worked to define its organization as a band of brothers that united men from all ranks of society and to portray its members as exemplary and morally upright citizens.

Beginning in the mid-1840s, Virginia underwent fast-paced and significant economic change as the Old Dominion increasingly became a market-oriented society. Rapid population shifts and the forces of urbanization broke down traditional pathways to respectability and drove a wedge between white middle-class men and workingmen in Virginia's cities. This new culture of business placed a high premium on good moral character and encouraged skilled craftsmen turned shopkeepers, new merchants, and the owners of small manufactories to promote harmonious cross-class relations as they sought to establish a good reputation with lenders, employers, clients, and consumers.

The Sons of Temperance, Odd Fellows, and Masons recreated face-to-face societies within their lodges and carried out the work of reforming men's characters. To accomplish these goals, the orders developed and refined secret fraternal signs and symbols that allowed members to distinguish between men of good character (other members) and urban swindlers in their own neighborhoods and those they might meet on their travels. The orders used these rituals and ideals to reinforce new standards of masculine conduct that gauged white male respectability and independent status in relation to moral character and a man's ability to support himself and his family. Fraternal orders played a key role in Virginians' acceptance of restrained masculinity as a new way of judging a man's character—a new way that they claimed would mitigate the harsh competitiveness of business and politics and improve society as whole.

Safety in a World of Strangers

New mobility, demographic change, and the increasingly impersonal institutions Virginians encountered as a result of the market disrupted their small familiar networks of kinship and community. One Richmond resident commented to a friend, "I meet every day hundred[s] of new faces."[2] In this new world of strangers, one could not easily determine a person's moral character. Traditional norms governing face-to-face relationships at the end of the Revolutionary era allowed men and women to become acquainted with each other gradually and within the well-defined context of family and neighborhood. Long-term knowledge of a person's family history and conduct had revealed which men were of good character and which were not. The social and economic changes of the early nineteenth century, however, had dislodged these older norms and left a void in prescriptive guidance on how to safely judge a man's character.[3]

In order to protect fraternity members and their communities from disingenuous swindlers and confidence men, fraternal orders developed complex secret rituals, passwords, and signals. Odd Fellow William Rooker explained that his fraternity was both a "benevolent institution" and, by necessity, a secret society.[4] Secret signs and rituals set fraternal orders apart from other charitable organizations and established an "impassible barrier" across which neither the "idle and immoral" nor "the intemperate and the profane" could set "their polluting feet."

We value not our signs, pass-words, or tokens, any farther than they enable us to recognise the Brotherhood, and test the legality and justice of every claim to our confidence, regard or benevolence. By these, the unworthy or the pretender can always be detected.[5]

Without this threshold, members argued, men lacking proper moral values might corrupt or, even worse, fleece their fraternities. Consequently, Rooker stated that members must "guard well the doors of admission" to the lodge. Otherwise, he warned, a "host of shameless imposters would soon empty our treasury, and deprive us of the ability of relieving the wants and necessities of those who are specially entitled to the assistance, compassion and sympathies of Odd Fellows."[6]

Standards of conduct, regalia, and fraternal rituals created a protective barrier that the confidence man theoretically could not cross. To admit an applicant to a fraternal order, the lodge had to deem him "worthy" of their trust and brotherhood. Freemason Robert Enoch Withers cautioned fraternity members that a candidate's moral character had to be carefully scrutinized to determine whether he was "worthy" or "unworthy" of admission.

Ask yourself if he is [of] such a character as you would entrust your money with—your secrets—your wife or daughter with—your character with. . . . If you have sons old enough to become Masons, would you be willing to point *him* out to them as a standard and exemplar of Masonry? . . . These may seem a formidable array of questions to apply to anyone, and yet, if these cannot be answered satisfactorily, I tell you brethren, the applicant, if admitted, will bring *dis*-honor instead of honor on our Craft. . . . Guard well, then, the *outer* door of the sanctuary, and you will have peace and prosperity within.[7]

Once a fraternal order accepted a man into their organization, he had proven his trustworthiness and good character. This made him worthy of becoming a trusted friend or business associate.

For the residents of Virginia's rapidly growing cities and towns, the ability to judge a man's character when lending money, extending credit, or hiring employees could mean the difference between being swindled and securing a livelihood. The orders claimed that membership in a fraternity not only helped a man to establish a good reputation for himself but also helped the orders by giving them access to network of "worthy" skilled artisans, clerks, mechanics, professionals, and businessmen.

Frank Byrne's recent study on southern merchant culture conveys just how crucial a man's reputation was to obtaining credit in the antebellum business world. A good reputation was necessary to secure credit and establish relationships with business colleagues, customers, and employees. In addition, storekeepers scrutinized clients for signs of economic difficulties or moral lapses when extending them credit. Because local farmers and families often bought between 60 and 70 percent of their purchases on credit, a merchant's economic survival depended on guaranteed payment for goods sold.[8]

Antebellum businessmen often took part in a complex and stressful web of lending and borrowing practices to keep their businesses afloat. Merchant and Son of Temperance Adam Plecker of Rockingham County anxiously wrote to lodge brother and business associate Peter S. Roller that he had used all the money he had to pay a creditor, and now two men had inquired about money Plecker owed them. Presumably hoping to borrow from Roller, who was in Baltimore, Plecker wrote, "I know not what to do. For these considerations I hope you will at least get home on Friday morning or I can't keep these fellows off me [a]nd Skelton wants to borrow one hundred dollars next saturday night if he can get it."[9] Dealings such as these occurred with great frequency.

In addition, because travel could be difficult or take them away from their homes and businesses for extended periods, men commonly asked their neighbors and acquaintances to buy or sell goods (including slaves) for them at a distant marketplace, arranging to pay them back or collect their money later. Fraternal orders facilitated these types of transactions by creating a network of trustworthy businessmen. For example, John H. Blakemore, a Son of Temperance in Augusta County, asked merchant Peter Roller to order him a clarinet from Roller's wholesaler in Philadelphia. Blakemore asked Roller to advance him the money and assured Roller that he would pay him back right away.

> You will please advance the money for me and I will pay you the first time I come to [Mount] Crawford. . . . I will pay you the amt. whether I get the instrument or not. Yours in the triple bond of Love, Purity and Fidelity, [John] H. Blakemore.[10]

Although these two men may have had a long-standing friendship that would have eased Roller's mind in advancing the money, Blakemore's insertion of their fraternal motto, "Love, Purity, and Fidelity," reminded Roller that he was dealing with a brother.

Lodge brothers often conducted business with one another as well. The lodges bought goods from companies owned by fraternity brothers and hired members to do work in the lodge. For example, the Freemasons of Randolph Lodge, no. 19, in Richmond paid John Regnault, a fraternity brother who owned an upholstery and wallpaper shop, $154.08 for carpets, oilcloth, and other materials for the lodge. The lodge also hired another brother, Isaac Shriver, a house painter, to paint the lodge's closets and glaze the windows.[11] Madison Division of the Sons of Temperance hired one of their brothers, John W. Lamon, a carpenter, to build the tables, chairs, benches, and shelves for their new temperance hall.[12] These relationships not only created business for lodge members but also had the potential to advance members' reputations in their craft or profession.

Since lodge members also did business with men who were not fraternity members, it is difficult to assess the extent to which fraternal bonds influenced a man's business decisions. It seems likely however, that since the orders performed a background check of sorts upon entrance to the order and expelled members who exhibited poor moral judgment or did not pay their dues, fraternity brothers would make good business associates. As early as 1841, *the Independent Odd Fellow*, Virginia's Odd Fellows magazine, announced it would publish a directory of Odd Fellow–owned businesses.

> It is desirable that members of the Odd Fellows visiting our towns should know who of the business men are Odd Fellows. . . . The advantage resulting to our brethren from this thing will be great. All of our subscribers will thus be enabled to know with whom they deal.[13]

By the outbreak of the Civil War, Philadelphia Freemason Leon Hyneman had published a national directory of Masonic businesses, *The Universal Masonic Record and Directory*, which claimed to list the name, profession, and town of residence of members in good standing.[14]

In the same way that being a member of a fraternal order could help men establish a good reputation in the business world, fraternity members who failed to pay their dues on time, were caught drinking, or expelled for poor moral conduct risked damaging their standing in the community. The Sons, Odd Fellows, and the Freemasons each had a system in place through which the name and infraction of wayward lodge brothers could be disseminated to every subordinate lodge in the state. The Sons listed each man's occupation as well, harming his social and economic reputation. Subordinate lodges regularly sent a list of expelled men to the orders' state headquarters, and these governing bodies printed the names in the annual communications or on broadsides that were distributed across the state several times a year.[15] For example, the name of "Wm. Griffis, confectioner," from Samson Division, no. 4, of Richmond was listed in the quarterly minutes of the Grand Division of Virginia Sons of Temperance for being expelled for violating article 2 of the order's constitution prohibiting drinking.[16] Some lodges also kept a "black book" of expelled, suspended, and rejected members from across the state as a way of keeping unscrupulous men from unknowingly being accepted into a different lodge. The books listed men's names, the charges against them, and sometimes their occupation.[17]

Having his name placed on an order's expulsion list or in a black book marked a man as a risk to creditors, employers, and clients, especially if he had been charged with nonpayment of dues, drunkenness, lying, or "immorality." When transferring his membership to a new lodge, Son of Temperance John Pascoe learned that because of a paperwork error, his name, to his "great mortification," had been "placed on the Black Book."[18] Most men who wished to voluntarily terminate their membership in a fraternal order were careful to pay the dues they owed and apply for an official withdrawal card from the order. This ensured that they would be considered "in good standing" when their connection with the fraternity ended and made certain they would not appear on the expulsion list for nonpayment of dues.

In addition to keeping lists or black books of expelled members, secret fraternal orders publicized names and descriptions of unscrupulous men who had been rejected or expelled from their orders, claiming that by so doing, they were protecting their communities from the urban confidence man. The orders placed warnings in local newspapers, fraternity magazines, postings, and correspondence to other lodges. For example, a notice in the September 1841 issue of the *Independent Odd-Fellow* warned readers to "guard the public against" recently expelled Odd Fellow James T. Bennett.[19] A resident of New York City, Bennett, who worked in the willow basket business, was apparently in Richmond for only one year. The Odd Fellows' notice claimed that Bennett had passed counterfeit notes and then quickly fled Richmond "in a clandestine manner, leaving many debts unpaid."[20] As these and other announcements indicated, lodge members and the public generally advised against doing business with this well-dressed, well-spoken, and seemingly respectable urban confidence man.

Another essential part of business life in the antebellum South was making buying trips to northern cities like Philadelphia, Baltimore, and New York. Antebellum travel, however, could be precarious.[21] Men who became ill or who fell on misfortune could find themselves in a dangerous situation while far from home. According to Freemason David Caldwell, one of the benefits of fraternal membership was peace of mind while traveling. Freemasons did not have to fear strange or unfamiliar places, he claimed, because they had "*a sort of universal language.* Wherever we wander, . . . we can every where make ourselves known as Masons and secure all the privileges of Masons."[22] Theoretically, anywhere in the country, a Mason, Son, or Odd Fellow who was ill or in trouble merely had to flash his order's secret sign of recognition or find the nearest lodge, and brothers would come to his aid. This was particularly comforting to geographically mobile Virginians, and it quickly became one of the major selling points of fraternal membership.

> Reclining on yonder couch, is a sick and pain worn man. A stranger in a
> strange land, he is dying far away from his home, and from those who have
> sympathy for his fate. . . . [B]ehold, entering the door of his death chamber,
> a few who bear the token of Odd-fellowship. A mutual recognition takes
> place. They discover him a brother. And what but *friendship* is it which leads
> them to visit him day by day. What but *love* that urges them to watch by his
> bedside night by night.[23]

The confidence man, then, posed no threat to brothers who were new to an area or who were traveling. Members of a secret fraternal order could be assured that only men of good character would assist them in these situations.

Fraternal literature was replete with examples of men who had became sick or been involved in an accident while traveling and needed assistance. The *Abingdon Virginian*, for example, reprinted a story from the Odd Fellows' national periodical that told the tale of a young Odd Fellow traveling from Boston to Alabama. While on a steamer on the Ohio River, the young man became acquainted with a very ill man who was also an Odd Fellow. The young man found an Odd Fellows' lodge in Cincinnati, the Ohio Odd Fellows offered the sick man comfort, located a good doctor, and stayed with him until he was well enough to travel.[24] The story illustrated the national network of brothers ready and willing to assist Odd Fellows in times of distress.

That men would take care of sick brothers whether they were at home or on the road was touted as evidence of the genuine existence of love, fidelity, and friendship among fraternity members. D. J. Mandell explained to a crowd of Odd Fellows in Fredericksburg that their taking care of sick brothers not only made Odd Fellows a blessing to the community but also

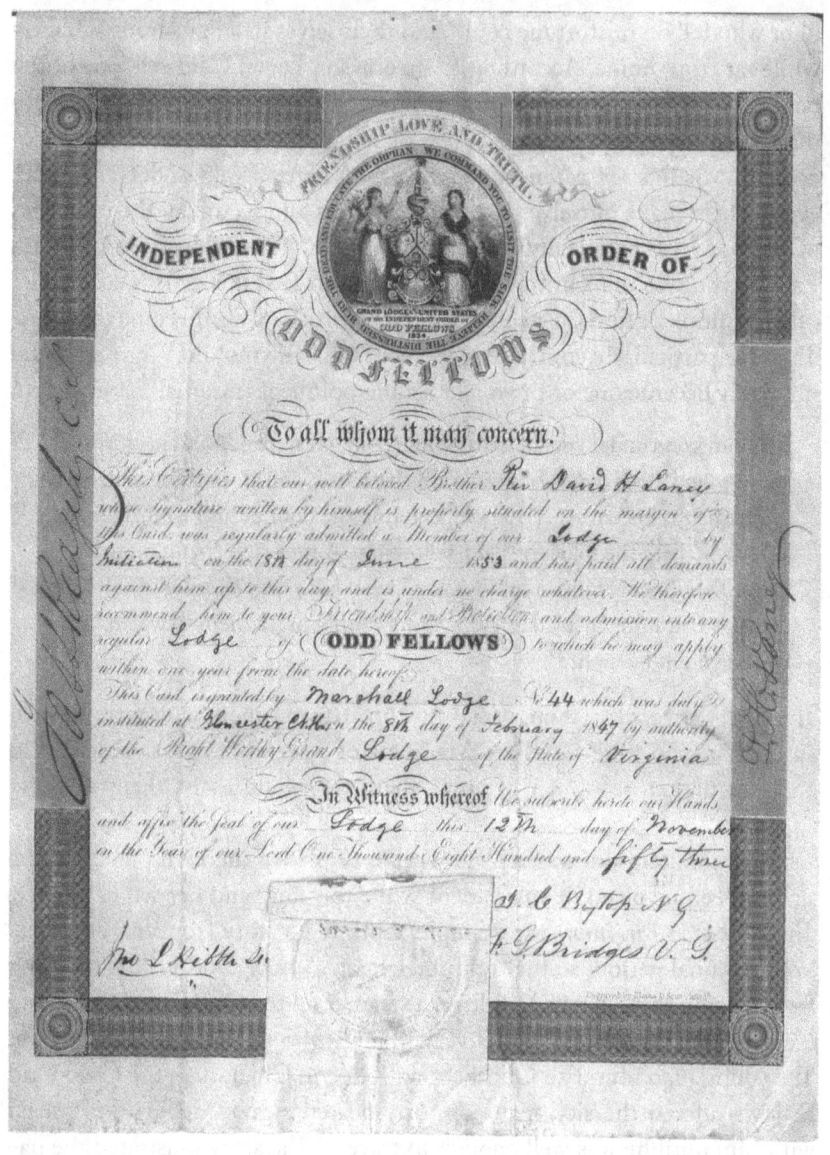

Figure 1. Odd Fellows traveling certificate, 1853. Michael P. Musick, private collector, Harpers Ferry, West Virginia.

made them emblems of the true meaning of friendship.[25] Each order made provisions for "watchers," men assigned to sit up during the night with sick brothers. These men served as nurses for their sick brethren and would "gladly minister to his weakness and wants" by "wiping the clammy sweat from his pale brow . . . and holding the cooling draught to his parched and burning lips."[26]

Fraternal membership also benefited men when they moved to a new town. Membership in a fraternal order created an instant network of "brothers" and business associates. In the early 1840s, Albert D. Clarke moved to Smithfield, Virginia, from Massachusetts, where he joined the local Odd Fellows lodge, Smithfield Lodge, no. 20. After a nasty bout with pleurisy, which he believed had cost him "between fifty and one-hundred dollars and thirty pounds of flesh," Clarke wrote to his (biological) brother back home to tell him how lodge members had nursed him through his illness.

> I was attended through every night by two gentlemen belonging to a large Lodge of Odd Fellows in this country who perform this duty in rotation as [our] obligations require in sickness—I have [been] for more than a year an officer in [this] Lodge and found this assistance [so] beneficial during the dreary nights of painful illness.[27]

Clarke, then, almost instantly created a niche for himself by joining the Odd Fellows. Having access to a network of at least sixty people, he was no longer a "stranger in a strange land" but a member of a large extended family. Membership in a secret fraternal order eased Clarke's settlement in his new community and assured Smithfield's residents that he was not a confidence man but a man of good character. Thus in the emerging world of impersonal business transactions and urban strangers, secret fraternal orders created a system for gauging white men's character and establishing personal contacts. The orders established a network of "worthy" men with whom members could do business or become friends, and that promised safe passage for members when traveling.

The Refuge of the Lodge

Antebellum fraternal orders also claimed to provide refuge from the competitive and unfriendly public world by reconstituting a face-to-face society within the lodge. The lodge became a safe haven where members did not have to fear the unworthy urban stranger—he would be turned away at the door. As brothers of a "common parent," fraternal orders also claimed to create a fictive kinship, one that compelled brothers to take care of one another when sick, comfort each other upon the death of their wives, gently and fairly resolve problems among one another when they arose, and generally provide men with a place to escape from the aggressive world of business and politics.

Freemason James Lawson Kemper, a future governor of the state, described time spent with fraternal brothers as a reprieve from divisive partisan politics.

> We have turned aside from the cares of business; we have deserted the feverish paths of ordinary excitement and toil. We have met to mingle together in a spirit of the broadest fraternal kindness. We are here to indulge in a festival of good feelings; to partake of a cup which is mingled with none of the rancor of political conflicts,—which is unembittered by any of the venom of party strife or personal malignity.[28]

Asked to speak at the dedication of a new Masonic hall in Northampton County in 1848, educator John Bowie Strange likewise described the lodge as a place where "all the good and true" could meet as brethren, regardless of political or religious affiliation.

> The angry elements which too often lash the sea of life into mighty billows of discord and strife, are here lulled to rest and harmonized by the influence of brotherly love and affection. . . . [D]ifferences of opinion are never suffered to intrude into this sacred retreat of friendship and virtue.[29]

It was not uncommon for Masons, Odd Fellows, and Sons to refer to the lodge as a kind of sacred space, a "snug harbor," a "sanctum sanctorum," and a "second home."[30] Historian Steven Bullock notes that it was in the nineteenth century that the Masonic lodge became more than just a meeting place. Many Masons began to refer to their lodges as Masonic "temples" to indicate that they were places where sacred rituals were performed.[31]

Ideally, it was within this refuge that brothers would get to know one another and cultivate brotherly bonds. The atmosphere of the lodge did not stress individual accomplishments but instead encouraged members to make sacrifices for one another in the spirit of friendship and brotherly love.

Fraternal rituals further strengthened the quasi-familial bonds forged at lodge meetings and in taking care of sick brothers. In the nineteenth century, Virginia's antebellum fraternal orders ritualized almost every aspect of their procedures. The Odd Fellows, Masons, and Sons had elaborate and meaningful rituals for initiation, the completion of each degree, funerals, the consecration of new lodges, and the installation of officers. These important ceremonies reinforced the idea that a man's behavior, not his economic status, determined his worthiness. A man's attention to his conduct and to the regalia and rituals of his order was part of a larger performance that indicated the quality of his character and reinforced the "familial" bonds of the lodge.[32]

Members were expected to pay close attention to their brothers' behavior from the moment they came through the lodge door until the ceremonies that officially ended the evening were over to ensure that the unworthy would not gain admittance into their sacred space.[33] "Guard with a jealous eye the door of entrance to the Lodge," warned Mason David Caldwell. "Look to it that none but the virtuous cross its threshold."[34] Accordingly, Virginia's secret fraternal organizations also employed a guard whose job it was to literally guard the outer door of the building. The Masonic order had a "tyler" who guarded the outer doors of its lodges. The Odd Fellows and Sons employed, in addition to outside guards (the outside sentinel and outside guardian), a second set of inside guards to restrict access into and out of the lodge room where ceremonies were conducted (the inside sentinel and the inside guardian).

When a member arrived at the outer door of the lodge, the guard first inspected his appearance. The Sons, Masons, and Odd Fellows each had an elaborate scheme of regalia involving a hierarchy of colorful collars, ribbons, aprons, and jewels. It was essential that brothers keep their regalia clean and wear them according to lodge specifications. If they did not, they ran the risk of being rejected by the outer guard or being assessed a fine once they entered the lodge. Furthermore, the inside and outside guards could be fined or suspended for admitting a brother into the lodge who was not properly dressed.[35]

The purpose of the regalia when worn outside of the lodge was to distinguish brothers from the "multitudes," just as a military uniform sets the solider apart from the civilian.[36] Inside the lodge, regalia served two different objectives. First, it was used to show the hierarchy of members within an order. Brothers were considered of equal status upon entering each order, but, once a member, a brother had the opportunity to move up in the ranks of the organization by either becoming an officer or completing various degrees of self-improvement. This internal hierarchy further promoted the idea that status and respectability were based on one's behavior. Each officer could be identified visually by the regalia he wore. Upon completing each

Figure 2. Son of Temperance, Currier and Ives, 1848. Library of Congress, Prints and Photographs Division, LC-USZC2-3019.

degree and taking a step up on the organizational ladder, members received special pieces of regalia to signify their success. Second, regalia served to remind the wearer of the order's principles. Each piece of regalia had a specific symbolic meaning. For example, a member of the Sons of Temperance wore a white collar, white tassels, and a red, white, and blue rosette corresponding to the order's motto, "Love, Purity and Fidelity."[37]

After passing the physical inspection, members were required to give the outside guard the quarterly password. The secret passwords, signals, forms, and ceremonies were necessary, members argued, to prevent the intrusion of the unworthy.[38] At specific times during the year, the Grand Lodge of Virginia transmitted an encoded password to the presiding officer of each subordinate lodge. The key to the code was a combination of numbers that could be translated into letters of the alphabet. The presiding officer of the lodge then transmitted the password to the keepers of the door and then to members, provided their dues were not in arrears.[39]

The members then went through a series of intricate steps that were extremely important to fraternity members. It was in one's strict adherence to each ritual's minutiae that a man's true worthiness was revealed. Once inside the building an additional set of passwords and secret signs was required. In the Sons, for example, members were required to give a second inner guard the proper salutation (right hand on left breast) and the "explanation" of the password. The inside guard would then ask a series of scripted questions that had specific answers known only to the worthy, such as "Who knocks?" "Why cometh the stranger?" and "Is he worthy?" (for "Our Gates . . . are only closed to the unworthy").[40]

Members also asserted that their order's secrets and rituals promoted social harmony and further cultivated brotherly bonds among members. Moreover, they claimed that secrets taught men to be loyal not only to other lodge members but also to their family and their country.

> The man who divulge[s] the secrets, whether of his friend, his fraternity
> or country, placed in his keeping under the pledge of confidence expressed,
> or implied, is a traitor in the heart; and an institution which, like this, in-
> culcates this lesson upon mankind, and promotes the indulgence of mutual
> confidence, enlarges the bounds of virtue and adds another tie to that great
> bond of Human Nature.[41]

A member who betrayed his brother's confidence could not be trusted in any situation, inside or outside of the lodge. Strengthening the bonds

Figure 3. Unidentified antebellum Freemason. Library of Congress, Prints and Photographs Division, LC-USZ62-110183.

Figure 4. Freemason contemplating Masonic principles. John Dove, *Masonic Textbook* (1847), Virginia Historical Society, Richmond.

of brotherhood was another important function of the lodge. Members claimed that "familial" ties created within the lodge were not merely superficial or for show. They argued that members truly came "to esteem each other as children of the same common parent."[42] William Rooker explained that the Odd Fellows' "bond of union is not a mere nominal thing." Rather, "in regarding our order as a family, where one member suffers, then all the members suffer with him."[43]

Disagreements between brothers were to be quelled immediately. Members believed that nothing was more important than maintaining harmony and unity among brothers. Factions and personal animosity had no place within the sacred refuge of the lodge.

[The Freemason] is particularly to banish from his heart all personal resentments, all angry feelings against a brother; to forgive him if he has offended, and to extend to him the hand of fellowship and love—Should he still offend—should he accumulate wrong upon wrong, and add injustice to injustice, still he is to be considered as a *brother*.[44]

Clearly, members held their lodge relationships in high regard. The importance of reestablishing harmony among brothers within the lodge necessarily carried over into their lives outside of the lodge, helping to ameliorate the class and political tensions—the "angry elements" of life.

Thus, the increased importance of ritual in antebellum fraternities functioned as a line of defense to prevent the entrance of unworthy men or outsiders into the lodge and protect men from swindlers. The rituals, taking care of sick brothers, and the refuge of the lodge also established a fictive kinship that bound men together as "brothers." Furthermore, the new attention to the men's observance of rituals and physical appearance demonstrated, members claimed, the depth of a man's internal character and integrity.

In addition to serving as a second home, the lodge room also provided a virtuous environment in which to meet and taught men the proper standards of conduct. Members argued that the very nature of each group's meetings, always among other men of good character, safeguarded the morality of its members and the community. Time spent at fraternity meetings was time *not* spent in the tavern, the gaming house, or involved in other immoral activities. Meetings took place within either a building owned by the organization or in a hall that they rented, often from another fraternal organization. Members claimed that the environment of the lodge fostered the moral behavior in its members and created a space for social intercourse "free from the contaminating influence of vice."[45]

Robert J. Taylor of the Sons of Temperance explained in his speech to Lexington Division, no. 45, that the order would not tolerate any illegal or immoral behavior.

> The guardianship, which this organization assumes over the conduct of its members, requires of them sobriety, order and uprightness. If anyone be found guilty of felony, fraud or disgraceful crime, or any wicked or notorious practices, or using unlawful means to procure a livelihood he is expelled by constitutional decree from the Division.[46]

Proper conduct was expected from fraternity members while inside the lodge. Drinking, profane or disrespectful language, and fighting were expressly forbidden in the lodge room, as was spitting on the floor.[47] The Sons in Mossy Creek Division in Augusta County passed a resolution stating that brothers must bring their own spit boxes for their tobacco because spitting on the floor was not acceptable behavior. Officers fined Brother R. H. Robertson twelve and a half shillings for disregarding this resolution only three weeks after it was passed.[48]

Tightly controlled behavior in the lodge was necessary not merely to maintain a vice-free environment. The regulations also tempered human passion and excess, qualities that threatened nonelite men's independent status. Strictly scripted rituals and rigid codes of conduct also allowed men to demonstrate their self-discipline. Men who could not control their passions were unworthy of the role of public protector. Men were expected to subdue their passions and to be "prudent" and reasonable in their actions. Intoxication and violence were the reckless results of excess and a lack of self-discipline. "Who can claim to be *Prudent*, whose every action is regulated, not by the dictates of reason, but by the impulse of passion?" asked Robert Enoch Withers.[49]

The Freemasons, the Odd Fellows, and the Sons of Temperance all required total abstinence from alcohol. Drunkenness, members argued, made men slaves to vice, and no man who was "addicted to the slavish vices of intemperance and excess" could be considered a worthy member of any fraternal order.[50] F. L. B. Shaver clearly stated the Odd Fellows' policy regarding alcohol in his 1848 address to Lebanon Lodge, no. 66:

> Odd Fellowship regards drunkenness as the vilest and most pernicious of all vices; and teaches that the drunkard, deprived of the reason given him by

God, lowers himself to the condition of brutes; contracts ruinous engage-
ments; neglects his business; squanders his property; abuses his health; fills
his house with troubles; and if not cut off by a premature death, is doomed
to an old age comfortless and diseased.[51]

Because fraternal orders considered intoxication such a serious offense,
they often encouraged members to keep an eye on their brothers to make
sure they refrained from drinking. In April 1851, Adam Miller, a joiner from
Worth River, was expelled after Brother James Coursey spotted him drinking French brandy at a local dry goods store.[52] Intoxication was the second
most common reason for suspension or expulsion (nonpayment of dues was
the most common).

Virginia's fraternal organizations were very proud of their policing of
members' behavior. It was one of the many ways they felt they were keeping
moral decay at bay in their communities, and such watchfulness guaranteed
the worthiness of all its members.[53]

> It is not only the privilege, but it is made the imperative duty of every
> Mason, to advise, admonish, and reprove any member of the fraternity
> whose conduct may require it. And this we consider one of the most
> admirable features of the institution, since it must make its members walk
> uprightly; they know their actions are closely watched, and that should
> they prove unworthy and resist all the kind influences which will be thrown
> around them in order to cause a reformation, they will be *branded* as unwor-
> thy, and as such their names sent on lightning's wings throughout the length
> and breadth of the land. . . . This, we say, must tend to make its members
> good, and in this way society must be greatly benefitted.[54]

Thus, policing the morals of their fraternity brothers was another way that
the members of Virginia's secret fraternal organizations protected both
their orders' reputation and their communities from confidence men.

Members took the idea of being their brother's keeper very seriously,
and in addition to reporting brothers who drank they also took note of
other moral peccadilloes. In December 1851, Brother Eakin, for the "good
of the order," called the attention of Covington Division "to the fact that
some of the members were in the habit of indulging in Card playing—and
pointed to a certain By-Law of [the] Division bearing upon the morals
of its members."[55] Other punishable offenses included adultery, theft, "immoral conduct," contempt, and "conduct unbecoming" of an Odd Fellow,
Mason, or Son.[56]

"Conduct unbecoming" could involve a variety of bad behavior, including disturbing the harmony of the fraternity and creating tension between members. In April 1848, Brother James Pfifer of Mount Crawford Division of the Sons of Temperance charged Brother John M. Smith, a laborer from the Mount Crawford area, with "Conduct Unbecoming of the Sons of Temperance." According to Pfifer, Smith had repeatedly mocked and insulted him in public.[57]

He has repeatedly and dose [sic] every time he meets me in company maks fun of me and insults me which I as a Son of Temperance feel myself bound to submit to in order to sustain the reputation of the order and I would request you to appoint a committy to investtigate the matter and acertain whither the brother is at liberty to [sport?] with an other's feelings in that manner.[58]

A bizarre incident then pushed Pfifer to his breaking point. Apparently, in order to insult Pfifer, Smith had publicly offered him "Corn bread and a dead Muskrat." When offered "said cornbread and dead Muskrat," Pfifer threatened to kill Smith.[59] The report of the committee of investigation sheds little light on the disagreement between the two men. It stated that the order had found it impossible to bring about a reconciliation between the two brothers and that it had officially charged Smith with conduct unbecoming of a Son of Temperance. The committee felt that Pfifer had made a reasonable effort to mend his relationship with Smith. Smith, however, had refused to cooperate, claiming that the only solution to their problem was "to go into the street and knock it out, or to drop the matter and let it rest as it is."[60]

The committee further instructed that the men were required to meet in friendship and treat one another with "due respect for their feelings." Failure to comply with this demand would result in a severe reprimand from the worthy patriarch, possible suspension or expulsion, and damage to the men's reputations. Following the dead muskrat episode, Pfifer did not bring further charges against Smith. For almost two years following this incident, Pfifer and Smith remained members of the lodge without visible disagreement, until Smith was expelled in March 1850 for nonpayment of dues.[61]

This incident reveals how important it was to members who took pride in their order and who sought to protect their lodge's reputation and principles to stifle outside personal disagreements with one another. Fraternal orders privately moderated disagreements among members while giving the appearance of a united public front. The incident also elucidates how the orders reined in inappropriate behavior. Despite Smith's suggestion that the two men fight, after the incident was over Pfifer and Smith voluntarily complied with their fraternity's rules of conduct, until Smith apparently quit paying his dues to withdraw from the order.

In another incident in 1846, several Odd Fellows from Maffitt Lodge, no. 21, accused members from Gratitude Lodge, no. 24, both in Berkeley County, with threatening physical assault outside of the lodge at a local civil trial. In this case, because the conflict was between members from two different lodges, the Grand Lodge of Virginia formed a committee of investigation to determine the validity of the charges.

The committee, composed of three of the most high-ranking Odd Fellows in the state, Jacob H. Robinson, S. J. Poisal, and H. Swisher, found the charges to be "grossly false." Moreover, the committee wrote a scathing censure of the members of Maffitt Lodge, stating that they had "carelessly and indiscreetly" proffered charges against their brothers, creating discord among lodge brothers.[62] In conclusion, the committee reminded Virginia's Odd Fellows that

> we are all brothers emphatically—brothers, bound by connections stronger than those of blood. We are, indeed, BROTHERS OF A VOW! It is the recollection of the faithful spirit which should ever prevail in our grand family of harmony.[63]

In this kinship without blood, worthy white men were oathbound to treat one another as members of the same family. In addition, as the muskrat incident also demonstrated, disagreements were to be resolved internally. Members who publicly besmirched the reputation of their orders were subject to penalties.

Clearly, cultivating lasting brotherly affection among members was an important goal of fraternal orders. The refuge of the lodge offered those free white men who abided by fraternal standards of conduct and dress comfort when sick and a fictive kinship among members. Moreover, as new market forces transformed social order in antebellum Virginia, secret fraternal organizations reconstituted a new face-to-face society among white men, and encouraged harmony among men.

It is not surprising that white men in nonagricultural occupations would be drawn to secret fraternal orders. In the new uncertain economic climate of Virginia's antebellum towns and cities, the orders portrayed fraternity members as morally upright, temperate, and honest men. They also connected members to a network of "worthy" businessmen, creditors, employers, and customers. Moreover, each order's careful screening of new members, their attention to regalia and ritual, their tempering of human passions, and their policing of brothers' moral conduct reinforced the ideals of restrained manhood that promised equality, respect, and financial success to white men with good moral character and self-discipline. This combination of strong brotherly bonds and a new standard of masculine conduct softened class lines among white men in antebellum Virginia and mitigated the festering tensions between middle- and working-class men. This shared patriarchy of "worthy" men within the lodge helped justify white men's claim to public authority outside of it and laid the groundwork for a redefinition of white men's civic responsibilities in the 1840s and 1850s.

FOUR

Securing the Republic

For many antebellum Americans, commercial and industrial development in urban centers posed fundamental questions about the survival of
republicanism. The framers' classical republican notions of political disin-
terestedness, economic independence, and sacrifice for the common good
clashed with emerging values touting competition, individualism, and the
importance of commercial success. Would, many Americans began to won-
der, their generation protect and carry forward the republican ideals of
the American Revolution? Or would rapid economic growth give rise to a
generation of self-interested men who would disregard the cornerstone of
American republicanism, moral virtue?[1]

Virginia Odd Fellow James D. McCabe expressed similar concerns for
the nation at a cornerstone-laying ceremony on July 4, 1849. Fearing that
his generation had drifted away from the ideals and goals of the founding
fathers, he warned the audience that an "abyss of licentiousness" threatened
the very survival of the country. However, McCabe reassured his listeners
that Odd Fellowship would restore, preserve, and transmit the "blessings of
our fathers" to future generations. The order's emphasis on upright moral
conduct, brotherly love, education, and judicious charity, he asserted, would
"widely disseminat[e] that moral virtue which is the true cement of our
civil institutions."[2]

Antebellum secret fraternal orders argued that they cultivated the civic virtue and white male equality crucial to preserving American republicanism. The orders claimed to foster moral character in men and to make them better husbands, fathers, and citizens. In addition, secret fraternal orders believed the job of strengthening the moral conduct and civic virtue of white men was uniquely theirs. The orders maintained that their bonds of brotherhood, and especially their ability to act as a coordinated group, made them better suited for public benevolence than other voluntary associations, which included women's benevolent reform organizations. In the name of safeguarding republicanism and moral order, the fraternities implemented a system of sick benefits, created charities for the widows and orphans of members, launched projects for new schools, and sought to bring white men together across class and partisan lines. These activities marginalized women's activities in the public sphere and made benevolence, charity, education, and the quelling of partisan conflict masculine civic responsibilities.

Male Friendships and the Benefits of Brotherhood

As the Old Dominion's growing cities and towns experienced an increase in crime and poverty and underwent the fast-paced demographic and social changes that accompanied commercial expansion, Virginians became increasingly worried that their society's moral standards were in rapid decline. In Richmond, for example, the number of white men and women charged with both violent and property crimes in Richmond's hustings court in the antebellum era increased by 600 percent.[3] The new penny presses heightened the public's awareness of crime, reporting that bands of "young ruffians" roamed the streets robbing respectable citizens. In lurid detail, they chronicled incidents of drunken disorderliness, assault, gambling, burglary, rape, and murder.[4] One Virginian from Danville remarked, "The papers are rife with accounts of rebellions, insurrections, mobs, highway robberies, thefts, murders, forgeries, swindling—and all manner of crimes and villainies, until 'the ear is pained, and the soul is sick.'"[5] As news of crime made its way through the state, residents increasingly feared that Virginia's cities might fall prey to the social disorder found in the North.[6]

Virginians complained bitterly about immoral men and women who visited markets and grog shops and traveled for business on Sundays. One Sabbatarian society noted with disgust that "the influence of Sunday markets upon the morals of the towns where they exist . . . is such as to grieve the heart of every Christian."[7] Another Virginian proclaimed, "Never was the order of our city in a more deplorable condition. Vice and crime are walking rampant through our streets."[8] Thus, as Virginians celebrated commerce and competed to get ahead in the business world, they also worried that their increasingly fluid society would create a generation of confidence men who would undermine the state's moral and social order. This anxiety only worked to heighten the perceived need to shape men's character and behavior.

Seeking to stabilize their society through individual self-restraint and moral reform, evangelical whites in the South did not shy away from benevolence and moral reform efforts; in fact they embraced benevolent reform with the same passion as their northern counterparts.[9] In the 1820s and 1830s, white women in Virginia launched volunteer societies, Sunday schools, and orphanages to oversee public morals and provide help for the less fortunate. Virginia's cities were also home to branches of national and regional reform organizations, such as the Association for the Improvement of the Condition of the Poor, the Dorcas Society, the American Temperance Union, the American Colonization Society, and the General Union for Promoting Observance of the Christian Sabbath.[10]

However, as white poverty became an increasingly noticeable problem in Virginia's cities—recipients and inmates of the Richmond poorhouse, for example, were overwhelmingly white—city leaders sought to put the poor to work and "rid the city of pauperism" and "idle vagrants."[11] Like other middle-class and elite Americans in the 1840s and 1850s, Virginians increasingly associated crime and poverty with moral depravity. Richmond City Council minutes in 1842 stated that "it is well known to the City Council that the most fruitful source of pauperism, and ultimate causes of crime . . . have their origin in those departures from the code of morality which are mainly visited by only the censure of public opinion[,] a penalty which, all experience proves, is too feeble to suppress or cure."[12]

Ideas about poor relief shifted over the course of the antebellum period. Historian Bruce Dorsey explains that by the 1840s poverty became largely associated with male immorality, intemperance, and a general lack of self-discipline. Poor women who lost male support were viewed as victims of bad male behavior such as gambling, drinking, risky speculation, or poor business practices.[13] As a result, antebellum Virginians not only placed a growing emphasis on reforming men's character as the solution to the problem of poverty but also increasingly distinguished between the "worthy" and "unworthy" poor.

This shift significantly affected women's benevolent work. Many urban communities lost confidence in the effectiveness of women's charity and poor relief because they believed women's naturally soft and sympathetic nature had led them to give indiscriminately to men whose immoral conduct had brought pauperism on themselves. Thus, policy makers justified cutting public aid to the poor in favor of facilitating the work of private charities that explicitly sought to save men's souls and change their behavior.[14]

Moreover, in Virginia the growing visibility of white poverty thwarted proslavery arguments about the superiority of a slave society and challenged arguments about the benefit of slavery to all classes of whites. Proslavery advocates frequently boasted that northern white wage laborers faced a life of poverty, illness, poor living conditions, and dependence on charity. In a slave society, on the other hand, they claimed, all white men were equal, independent, and shielded from economic uncertainties.[15] Thus, slaveholders were eager to blame Virginia's growing white poverty on individual men's intemperate behavior and lapses in moral judgment rather than on the economic displacements wrought by the emerging market economy.

This perceived need to strengthen and improve white men's moral conduct and bolster civic virtue made secret fraternal orders increasingly popular. The fraternities claimed that their brotherly bonds, secret passwords, and fraternal rituals provided an effective means of policing white male conduct, and they also pointed out that fraternal sick and death benefits distributed financial help only to the worthy poor (fraternity members and their families). It was this unique system of male friendship and benefits, the orders argued, that made their fraternities more adept at cultivating and maintaining good moral character among men than other groups and institutions.

Just as women cultivated intimate female friendships during the early antebellum era, men too enjoyed close ties to one another in Virginia.[16] The lodge room was a place where male friendships developed and grew. Within Virginia's antebellum fraternal organizations men formed close bonds with one another. Samuel Myers of Richmond described his relationships with his lodge brothers as unique and affectionate friendships that gave birth to an "intimacy," "security," and "assurance" not easily found outside of the lodge.[17] Fraternal literature also repeatedly cited the friendship of Jonathan and David in the Old Testament as an example of genuine male friendship, a friendship marked by the men's enduring loyalty to one another, even in the face of mortal danger and family strife. The fraternities encouraged members to emulate the two men's bond of friendship and emphasized the importance of fidelity, mutual assistance, and harmony among lodge members.[18]

This intense brotherhood, the fraternities maintained, made their orders more effective at fighting male vice than other benevolent and reform associations. According to the orders other voluntary associations were no doubt enthusiastic about helping men reform their conduct but were unable to keep men from returning to their bad habits. The bonds cultivated in fraternal orders helped men avoid bad behavior and "restored" respectability to brothers who had temporarily lapsed.[19]

> When the siren voice of vice and guilty pleasure is luring him with its
> charms and bribing him with its fatal fascinations, virtuous resolution gives
> way, the strong man feels shorn of his strength, and is ready to yield himself
> a willing victim on the alter [sic] of vice and folly. 'Tis then, my brethren,
> the hand of Friendship rouses him from his delusions and plucks him as a
> brand from the burnings of sin and passion.[20]

Fraternity members who saw a brother "struggling manfully" against the temptation to drink, to act immorally, or to "abandon his position as a man of integrity" in business dealings were obligated to come to their brother's aid and remind him of his principles.[21]

This was particularly true when it came to drinking. The Sons of Temperance insisted that their order was more effective at promoting and sustaining total abstinence from alcohol among men than other temperance societies because their fraternal rituals created a "strong and permanent bond of union" among members.[22] Support, encouragement, and chiding from fraternity brothers when necessary helped men keep their temperance pledge. To illustrate this principle, Virginia Son of Temperance Alexander Martin recounted the story of a fraternity brother from Richmond who had fallen back into his old drinking habits to the horror of his family. His lodge brothers searched the city for him, and finally finding him in a bar, the men dragged their besotted brother away and sat with him for several days until he had recovered. The redeemed man was then accepted back into the lodge room with "brotherhood and human sympathy." Martin asks, "Now, had he been a member of one of the old societies; whose duty would it have been to take charge of his case, and endeavor to restore him to the position from which he had miserably fallen? . . . [W]ould a single hand have stretched forth to save him?"[23]

Moreover, despite women's antebellum role as men's moral counterweight, many men and women believed that only other men could understand these types of struggles against vice. The temptations that men faced in the rough-and-tumble public world, a world with which respectable white women were not supposed to be familiar, confronted them during business transactions, on public streets, and in taverns. In fact, the orders argued, women's "native modesty" would cause her to shrink from the "unpleasant labors" of fraternal orders, such as sitting with a sick man.[24]

Secret fraternal orders reinforced the nineteenth-century notion of "separate spheres" for men and women. This increasingly strict sexual division of labor promoted the idea that men and women inhabited two different worlds. According to this philosophy, the dissolute and fiercely competitive world of business and politics was too harrowing for women to withstand. Women, as "natural" paragons of virtue and morality, could best serve society by creating a nurturing, stable home for their families.[25]

Fraternity members claimed that, unlike men, women did not need to form social organizations to elevate their moral character and feel sisterly love and compassion for other members of their sex, because "her head is already attuned to every finer feeling, and every tender sympathy."[26] Women inherently possessed the characteristics that Masons, Odd Fellows, and Sons sought to command through fraternal orders. Men needed the powerful influences of group organization to bring out their philanthropic impulses. The collective efforts and intensity of the quasi-familial brotherhoods in fraternal orders caused members' hearts to become "open, tender and sympathetic" to "the distress of [their] fellow creatures."[27]

Although a man's sympathies could be cultivated, and he could be trained to carry out practical charity work, a woman's natural sympathies prevented her from sensibly conducting the work of public benevolence. A woman's soft heart, her undisciplined enthusiasm for moral reform, and her misguided zeal made her efforts ineffective.[28] "Woman is fashioned like the Æolian harp, which, when touched by the gentlest breath of summer's eve, sends forth strains of subduing melody and gushing tenderness." Man, on the other hand, "require[d] an artificial bond, and the cultivation of his moral and sympathetic powers," but once made aware of the suffering of his fellow man, he became "strong in virtue and prompt in deeds of benevolence and charity."[29]

Furthermore, the orders argued that benevolence was a manly responsibility. "The responsibility to do all the good he can, rests upon every man; and he who shrinks from its performance, because of the obstacles he may have to encounter, forfeits his claim to the dignity of manhood, and is unworthy [of] the confidence of his fellows."[30] "Females, children, the aged and the infirmed," despite their devotion to the temperance cause, had already proven inefficient and unable to secure permanent success.[31] Thus, as women's charities were increasingly characterized as indiscriminate, fraternal orders claimed that by contrast their charitable work was "systematic" "practical," "stable" and "uniform."[32]

Secret fraternal orders also boasted that they dispensed fraternal sick and death benefits judiciously and only to "worthy" members. The orders claimed that these benefits kept white men from relying on public charity and also insisted that their emphasis on temperance and good moral conduct attacked the root cause of white male poverty. Most importantly, the system of sick and death benefits shielded white men from the perceived shame of charity.[33]

In the post-Revolutionary era, the Freemasons had provided special money to help brothers in need, raised funds to educate Masonic orphans, and buried deceased brothers. "Friendly societies," which members paid a monthly fee to belong to and in return could receive weekly payments in times of sickness and provisions for burial, existed in many large American cities by the early national period. The Odd Fellows, however, were the first fraternal order to combine a centralized mutual benefit system with secret fraternal rituals in the late 1830s. The Masons and the Sons also created a centralized system for the collection and distribution of charitable funds during the antebellum period.[34]

Once accepted into a fraternity, new members were eligible to collect benefits after six months. The Virginia Sons and Odd Fellows paid six and a quarter cents per week (twenty-five cents per month) in dues and could expect to receive $3 a week if they became too sick to work, between $10 and $20 for burial of their wife, and from $15 to $30 to pay for their own burial.[35] The Masons created a similar system designed to distribute charity only to the worthy. The order regularly took up collections for brothers or their widows who were ill or in need.[36]

Members believed that they had a contractual relationship with their order. As brothers they were obligated to meet certain standards of conduct and pay their dues on time. In return, they were "entitled" to the benefits of membership, which included financial sick and death benefits, physical care when ill, and assistance when traveling in strange town or city.[37] Fraternity members claimed that their system of benefits was not an "indiscriminate charity" or "a reward for pauperism or idleness" because only "worthy" men who had paid their dues were eligible to receive these benefits. The men argued that they were also safeguarding the coffers of the republic by aiding only the worthy poor, widows and orphans, and men who became too ill to work.[38] In addition, the orders buoyed white men's independent status and their egos by stating that every member, rich or poor, was equally entitled to collect benefits.

The orders also made very clear that the money members received as benefits did not constitute charity or dependence. Raleigh Daniel explained to a crowd of Odd Fellows that the order's benefits were a right of Odd Fellowship.

> Benefits are bestowed upon all members rich and poor alike. Thus, the relief being drawn from a fund to which each has equally contributed, and is equally entitled, it is enjoyed as a right, not as an alms, and the proud and delicate mind escapes the most painful ordeal of distress—the keen consciousness that it is soliciting or receiving charity.[39]

Thus, members who encountered financial trouble would not need to submit themselves to the will of another or become obligated to a creditor. They could collect money to which they were rightfully entitled as contributing members of their order.

In a slave society, benefits such as these took on special meaning. White male poverty threatened to discredit proslavery claims that slavery was superior to the "wage slavery" of the North. Proslavery advocates boasted that slavery made all white men equal and prosperous. In reality this was not true, and many white men struggled to make ends meet, especially in times of illness. Fraternal benefits for southern white men helped to maintain the herrenvolk myth that even the poorest whites were above blacks economically and socially in a slave society.[40]

White male poverty was also a threat to a man's masculinity because it allegedly indicated a lack of moral character and dependency. The benefit system reinforced the ideals of restrained manhood emerging in Virginia by emphasizing upright moral character and the importance of a man's ability to support himself and his family. The orders mandated that benefits would not be paid to men whose inability to work was the result of intoxication or immoral behavior. Moreover, each of the orders only accepted men who were not "in any way incapacitated from earning a livelihood."[41] Men with disabilities, including those with physically deformed limbs and the blind, were not permitted to join the orders because it was assumed that their disability prevented them from supporting themselves.[42]

The fraternities sometimes made exceptions to these rules, further demonstrating the importance the orders placed on men's role as the family breadwinner. If a disabled man could prove that he was not dependent on the public or the will of others and if he would be able to participate fully in the brotherhood, the orders granted him membership. The Sons of Temperance, for example, agreed to admit a deaf-mute man to the order, provided he could participate in their rituals, communicate the order's secret signs, signals, and passwords, and pay his dues.[43] Similarly, when a man missing his left arm applied for membership to the Odd Fellows, the order decided that his disability "unless [it] disqualified [him] thereby from pursuing his business and supporting himself, is not sufficient reason for rejecting him."[44] However, the Freemasons declared a man with a metallic leg "clearly and positively in eligible [sic]" for membership, presumably because it interfered with his ability to support himself.[45]

If a man became disabled *after* he was already a fraternity member, he was then entitled to receive sick benefits. The orders made an important distinction between men who were candidates for membership and those who were worthy "brothers." When a Richmond Mason lost his hand in a gun accident, the master of his lodge wrote to the Grand Lodge of Virginia to inquire whether the man could be raised to the next degree. The grand lodge replied that because the man was a "brother" and not a "stranger," he was entitled to all of the "rights and benefits" of Freemasonry. His disability, the grand lodge stated, should have no bearing on his status within the order. "At each step the Lodge must be satisfied of the worthiness and qualification of [a member]," the grand lodge stated. "These are moral and not physical requisites."[46]

However, the orders would not dispense sick benefits to men who had a preexisting illness. For example, Brother William Gilmore of Madison Division of the Sons of Temperance applied for sick benefits on account of a problem with his leg that prevented him from working. The division refused his request, stating "[Gilmore] himself admitted that the sickness was caused by a sore on his leg which existed prior to his being initiated. . . . [He was afflicted with a disease] at the time of his initiation and we think not entitled to benefits according to the constitution."[47] The orders worried about men attempting to gain membership into their fraternities merely to take advantage of the benefits or other sources of funding. These unworthy men, they insisted, were "too lazy to pursue any profitable calling, and [we]re content to live upon the alms of their brethren."[48]

Brothers also could rest assured that if they were to become ill or die someone would help to provide for their family and take care of their family's business. Frequently a member from the deceased's lodge would be appointed to watch over his widow and make sure her needs were met and "attend to any business [her] sex may incapacitate [her] from attending to."[49] The government of the Sons, Masons, and Odd Fellows made extensive provisions for the support and protection of widows and orphans. In fact, the orders argued that their chief duty was to alleviate "human woes . . . by visiting the fatherless and widow in their affliction, and binding up the broken heart."[50] In countless speeches and publications, fraternity members boasted that drying the tears of the cheerless widow was one their most important obligations. Instead of lamenting his children's "famine pinched faces" or worrying that his wife would be "a broken-hearted widow, struggling single-handed against poverty," a fraternity member could "close his eyes in death with the sweet assurance that his family would be left in the care of brothers whose constant duty it is to 'protect the widow and educate the orphan.'"[51]

In the rapidly shifting antebellum world in which fraternity members lived, it was not unimaginable that a man could suddenly fall ill and not be able to provide for his family. Secret fraternal orders assisted sick men in maintaining their role as family breadwinner. Moreover, because fraternity members believed that the benefits were an entitlement and not charity, the benefit system drew an artificial line that characterized men who did solicit outside or public charity as dependent. The orders argued that fraternal benefits not only were good for their members but were also good for the whole community because they reduced taxes and crime by minimizing the number of men relying on the state for charity.[52] Members further claimed that in addition to reforming men's behavior, educating the orphans of deceased members, and assisting the worthy poor, they also helped to bolster civic virtue and safeguard society and the country's free institutions. These functions were believed to be largely women's social roles in the early antebellum era, but as fraternal orders became increasingly popular, fraternity members redefined masculine civic responsibilities and even claimed that their lodge work was a patriotic act.

According to fraternity members, the close bonds cultivated inside the lodge fostered the extension of both fraternal sympathy and patriotism outside of the lodge. James Lawson Kemper explained that "brotherly love, patriotism and philanthropy, all flow[ed] from the same fountains of affection."[53] Thus, to love one's brother *was* to love one's country.

We hesitate not to say, that the heart that feels most deeply for human wo [sic] and suffering, is most susceptible of patriotic devotion—the hand that has oftenest wiped away a tear from the eye of sorrow, will strike the hardest blows in defence of its country's honor—no blood that stained the battle-fields of Mexico, shone more brightly or flowed more freely than that of the Odd-Fellows.[54]

The cultivation of benevolence, sympathy, and charity among lodge members, they claimed, heightened a man's sense of patriotism and his willingness to defend his country. This new connection between fraternal benevolence and manly patriotism underscored the orders' important role in preserving republican principles.

Invented Lineage

Beginning in the antebellum era, Virginia's Masons, Odd Fellows, and Sons of Temperance adopted and standardized new ritual ceremonies that created the appearance of a continuity between "ancient" republican principles and contemporary antebellum fraternal republicanism.[55] Tying their goals and values to a rich historical tradition of republicanism, the fraternities argued that their orders operated as part of a larger, ongoing movement for human enlightenment and freedom that could be traced back through time.[56] This "invented lineage" was woven into the orders' repetitive rituals and consisted of exaggerated connections to historical figures and events. In many ways fraternities, like nations, endowed their symbols, rituals, and histories with deep cultural meanings in order to legitimize their authority and foster social respectability.[57]

The Masons asserted that their lodge government was and always had been a republican form of government. In fact, they claimed that their lodge's government was "the oldest Republic in the world."[58] Antebellum Freemasons stated that their organization began in ancient Israel with the building of King Solomon's temple, and they boasted a history that carried republican principles through ancient Greece and Rome, the Middle Ages, the Renaissance, and into the era of the American Revolution.

> Every Mason may justly exult over the fact, that his Fraternity originated, cherished and preserved this grand principle of republican liberty, which promises to revolutionize the world, and which has been modeled into the constitution of the great republic under which we live. . . . Let every free citizen of this happy land remember, that it was the Fraternity of Masons which, during the long night of the dark ages, during all the mutations and convulsions of thousands of years, preserved republican principles.[59]

The Odd Fellows maintained that Roman soldiers formed their order under the name "Fellow Citizens" during the reign of Nero in 55 AD. They claimed that Titus Caesar later renamed the fraternity the "Odd Fellows" after witnessing the soldiers' fervent friendship and fidelity to their country in 79 AD. According to the Odd Fellows' mythology, between the fifth and the eighteenth centuries Odd Fellowship spread throughout Spain, France, and Portugal, finally taking on a modern form in eighteenth-century Great Britain.[60] These creation myths made secret fraternal orders the time-honored stewards of republicanism and gave the impression that the Masons and Odd Fellows had always been patriotic organizations with republican values.

The Sons of Temperance also adopted complex fraternal rites, adapting the rituals of the Masons and Odd Fellows expressly for the purpose of combining brotherhood, ritual, and fidelity with collective reform.[61] Founded in the United States in 1842, the Sons of Temperance also tied their order to a sacred past, but in a different way from that of the Freemasons and the Odd Fellows. Instead of linking their fraternity to Greco-Roman republicanism, they made a connection between their order's goals and historical events that they claimed threw off the yoke of tyranny, such as the Protestant Reformation, the Glorious Revolution of 1688, and the American Revolution. William Roane Aylett argued that his fraternity brothers were like sixteenth-century Protestant reformers who sought "the improvement of man's social and moral condition, and the freedom of the human mind."[62]

Like the Masons and the Odd Fellows, the Sons of Temperance rooted their principles within a movement for liberty they believed to be grander than their own. The Sons asserted that they freed men from the tyranny, or slavery, of alcoholism and made temperance an essential republican value.[63] They also compared their orders' goals with those of the American Revolution.

> Be cheered with assurance that the same spirit which nerved the hearts of the "*Sons of Liberty*," in the days of our Revolution in their successful contest with European oppression, now animates the efforts of the *Sons of Temperance* of Virginia.[64]

Three other secret fraternal orders that existed in antebellum Virginia also connected the history of their orders to the Sons of Liberty and the Revolution: the Improved Order of Red Men, the United Order of American

Mechanics, and the Brotherhood of the Union. Each of these groups portrayed their orders as the direct ideological descendants of the founding fathers. Like the Sons of Temperance, these fraternities were founded in the United States, not Europe. Instead of contending that their orders had preserved and defended republican principles since antiquity, these American orders linked themselves to the moment when American liberty was born. The Red Men claimed to be the oldest secret society of American origin. They believed that the men who disguised themselves as Native Americans at the Boston Tea Party in 1773 were the original members of their fraternity.[65]

In reality, the Red Men were organized in early antebellum Baltimore and modeled their order after the Odd Fellows and the Masons. The fraternity only accepted free white adult men of "good moral standing." It provided sick and death benefits to members. It had regalia, and it banned political discussion within the "wigwam." Evidence of their existence in Virginia appears in state newspapers during the antebellum era, but almost no other local records of their lodges in Virginia exist.[66] The United Order of American Mechanics and the Brotherhood of the Union also claimed to be offshoots of the Sons of Liberty and embraced the rituals of the Freemasons, the Odd Fellows, and the Sons of Temperance in order to blend American and ancient republican traditions.[67]

Thus, Virginia's antebellum secret fraternal organizations used invented lineages to bolster their relationship to republicanism. They used their creation myths and their orders' purported connection to certain historical events to make themselves part of an ongoing struggle for republican freedom and to lend their orders prestige and legitimacy. Antebellum secret fraternal orders regarded themselves the unique and sacred stewards of American republicanism, responsible for preserving republican values for future generations.

Virginia's antebellum Freemasons also created an exaggerated connection to the founding fathers in order to portray themselves as the custodians of a specifically American republicanism. Mason R. B. Thomson boasted, "Who drew the Declaration of American Independence? A Mason."[68] Fraternity members haughtily asserted that George Washington, Benjamin Franklin, John Marshall, Nathanael Greene, Joseph Warren, and all the generals of American Revolution except one, Benedict Arnold the traitor, were Freemasons. Members also repeatedly bragged that "fifty-two of the fifty-six signers of the Declaration of Independence" and a majority of the framers of the U.S. Constitution were members of the Masonic fraternity.[69] What is significant about these claims is that they show that fraternity members linked themselves to the heroes of the Revolution, stressing their patriotism and character and distancing themselves from Benedict Arnold, in order to grant their organization added legitimacy and prestige. As Virginia Freemason John Bowie Strange asked, "Would men such as [Washington or Franklin] been found supporting an institution founded on any other than the best principles?"[70]

Yet the Masons' claims were not entirely accurate. First, although many of the men they named were indeed Freemasons, Thomas Jefferson was not, and he vehemently opposed exclusive societies and organizations. In addition, only nine of the signers of the Declaration of Independence and approximately half of the generals in the Continental army were Freemasons.[71] Moreover, both contemporary and subsequent documentation has proved with certainty that Benedict Arnold was a Freemason. Washington himself acknowledged Arnold's membership in the order.[72] Thus, the orders created a version of American history that suited their needs, connecting American patriotism with Masonic membership.

Fraternity members also incorrectly asserted that Revolutionary Masons had advocated white male equality, when many clearly had not. For example, in 1850, Freemason Robert G. Scott proudly boasted at a large public gathering that his "brother" George Washington had consistently been an "honest advocate of the equal and inalienable rights of man."[73] However, Washington, Franklin, and others had vigorously defended constitutional provisions that ensured that only "disinterested" men of some wealth, and not dependent laborers, would run the new nation. They also supported salary bans and freehold suffrage and office requirements.[74]

George Washington's membership in the Masonic order, in particular, further cultivated the idea among fraternity members that their orders were special stewards of republican principles. The fraternities admired Washington's reputation for neutrality in party politics and his supposed promotion of white male equality. During the mid-nineteenth century, Americans in general saw Washington as epitomizing Revolutionary ideals, and many believed he had played an important role in soothing factional strife during the debates to ratify the United States Constitution.[75] Washington's membership in the Freemasons was proof, the orders claimed, that fraternal principles such as brotherly love and white male equality were part of the founding fathers' original plan for the new republican nation. As a result, Virginia's fraternal orders often appropriated Washington's image to promote the unity of white men across class and partisan divisions.

Figure 5. Masonic membership certificate, 1856. Meade Family Papers, 1837–1981, sec. 9, Virginia Historical Society, Richmond.

Each of the orders strove to preserve Washington's memory. They marched in celebration of his birthday, erected elaborate monuments to him, and donated large marble blocks to the Washington National Monument in his honor. In addition, Virginia's Freemasons laid the cornerstone for the Washington National Monument and competed with the Mount Vernon Ladies Association for the purchase of Mount Vernon in the late 1850s.[76]

Virginia's Freemasons, Odd Fellows, and Sons of Temperance also claimed that their lodges served as a microcosm of an ideal republican society that had been passed down from antiquity. Each lodge, they contended, was a "miniature republic" where all white men were equal and had the right to vote.[77]

> We have ever clung to the principles of an unadulterated republican constitution. A fundamental rule in every Lodge is the absolute equality of all its members. No matter what distinctions the world may make[,] . . . [e]very

Figure 6. George Washington as Freemason, 1866. Library of Congress, Prints and Photographs Division, LC-DIG-pga-02796.

important office is purely elective, . . . [e]very brother equally exercises the right of suffrage. . . . The entire system is a beautiful example of a Republican Confederacy.[78]

Fraternity members boasted that their miniature republics set an example for the rest of society and that the white male equality they espoused was merely part of a larger movement for human freedom that dated back to antiquity and fulfilled the goals of the Revolutionary generation.

At the same time that the supposed republican past of the fraternal orders endowed all members with a special civic status as the guardians of republican virtue, it denied that women could play a significant social role. In fact, the invented lineage that the orders used to promote the timelessness of white male equality entailed the notion that throughout history physical weakness and frailty had prevented women from stepping into the public sphere. This fictive history of women's isolation from public life justified women's exclusion from their antebellum orders.

Mason Robert Enoch Withers asserted that women were not excluded from his fraternity because they were "unfaithful or unworthy" but simply because when the order was initially established women were not present. Masonic lore insisted that Freemasonry was founded during the building of King Solomon's temple in ancient Israel. The original members were supposedly stonemasons recruited to work on the temple by famed master builder Hiram Abiff.[79]

> Solomon employed in the construction of that Temple, only hale and hearty men and cunning workmen, so we, in imitation of that great exemplar, demand, as indispensable prerequisites to admission into our Order, that the candidate "shall be a man, free born, of good report, of lawful age" . . . As [women] wrought not at the temple, neither can they work with us.[80]

Invoking this historical precedent, fraternal orders argued that women's traditional absence from their order warranted their exclusion from the antebellum lodge room.

Furthermore, James Lawson Kemper argued that the Masons excluded women from membership for their own good. Women were "not made to contend with the ruder labors and stormier conflicts and hardships of life." Therefore, Kemper contended, it was the responsibility of Masons "to secure [for women] the effectual relief and active sympathy in distress, that her delicate and defenseless nature demands and deserves."[81]

Similarly, I. Randolph Finley declared women's natural piety, delicacy, and virtue made her unfit for the rigors of both public life *and* the lodge room.

> We esteem woman most highly in her own appropriate sphere. Woman . . .
> would be quite as much out of place, in the midst of our masculine employ-
> ments in the Lodge-room, as if she were to assume the politician's stand
> upon the hustings, don the Judge ermine, usurp the Minister's sacred office,
> or clad in the panoply of war, lead by a band of Amazons to carnage and
> conquest.[82]

This transhistorical subordination of women was presented as incontest-able evidence that women's confinement to the domestic sphere was natu-ral. Virginia's fraternal organizations argued that because women had been historically barred from politics and the public sphere, they should also be barred from their orders. An article in the *Independent Odd-Fellow*, for example, asserted that those who objected to women's exclusion from the order must also object to women's traditional exclusion from the "the jury box, the ballot box," and "the bench."[83]

Thus, women's exclusion from both the lodge room and politics was in many ways a vicious circle that rested on the common notion that neither was a "woman's place," nor had they ever been. Women, too frail to with-stand the work of fraternal orders and the demands of the public life, mem-bers argued, were best suited for "the domestic fireside."[84] Furthermore, by placing political and military service in the same category as fraternal membership, the orders made fraternalism an aspect of patriotic manhood, effectively redefining masculine civic responsibilities to include fraternal activities.

Therefore, reforming men's character and promoting brotherly love, the "masculine employments" of the lodge room, were men's civic responsi-bilities. As in politics and business, "stout hearts" and "strong arms" were needed to carry out men's duties in both the lodge and in a fraternal re-public.[85] Women were asked only to give men their gratitude and warmest blessings from the safety of the domestic sphere.

> But while we [men] go forth amid the perils of the field and flood—amid
> the deadly contagion of the chamber of disease and death, binding up the
> broken heart, and drying the weeping eye, may we not ask [women's] prayers
> to sustain, and your smiles to encourage? Believe me, among all this band

of brothers, there is not a true heart but beats in unison with your interests, and in the hour of peril not an arm here but will be outstretched in your defence.[86]

As the self-appointed guardians of republicanism, fraternal orders attempted to fix women's proper role in a republican society solidly in the domestic sphere. Using examples from the past, the fraternities even warned that women who stepped too far outside of the domestic sphere posed a threat to republican values and to the state itself. "When the Roman mother forgot and forsook the sphere she once moved in, the State felt shock, and her foundations of liberty and virtue were overthrown."[87] Thus, by the end of the antebellum era, Virginia's secret fraternal organizations had remade their public image. Relying on invented lineages to give their orders legitimacy, they constructed a mythological past for their fraternities that appropriated images of the founding fathers, justified women's exclusion from the lodge, and made lodge work a masculine civic responsibility. The fraternities carved out a unique role for themselves within Virginia's antebellum political culture as the friends and guardians of republican principles and the manly proponents of civic virtue.

Masculine Civic Responsibility

In addition to public benevolence, secret fraternal organizations promoted education as an important means of safeguarding republican principles and protecting their communities against vice and licentiousness. Education, they claimed, would prevent men from being seduced by unscrupulous partisan demagogues, teach them to be responsible citizens, and help them form enlightened opinions regarding a republican government. Quoting George Washington, Thomas Jefferson, and James Madison, secret fraternal orders predicted that intelligence and virtue would become "the stability of the times."[88]

Many antebellum Americans who fretted about the fragility of republican government saw education for both men and women as a key to maintaining the moral virtue of the republic's citizenry.[89] Secret fraternal orders' concern over education reflected a larger problem in antebellum Virginia. Despite efforts to establish a system of popular education, statewide public schools would not be established until after the Civil War. Throughout the antebellum period, children were educated by family members at home, by private tutors, or at private academies. Some poor children also received money for education from the state's literary fund.[90]

Virginia's secret fraternal orders believed that equal education for all white children was essential to the future of republicanism. The orders were adamant that both poor and rich children should have equal access to education. "We want no distinctions made either between a system for the rich and one for the poor, Mind is *mind*."[91] Pike Powers also declared that all classes of children must be educated to secure republican principles.

> The people must be educated—not the children of rich only, but the children of the poor man who is scarcely able to pay his taxes and entitle himself to a vote. Our country abounds in Colleges and Academies, but is yet deficient in a good system of primary education, accessible to the poorest citizen, fostering the talents of the humblest, and opening the door to usefulness, wealth and distinction alike to all.[92]

Consequently, the Sons, Odd Fellows, and Masons each made specific provisions within their orders not only to provide for the education of deceased members' children but also to subsidize local schools, donate space in their lodge buildings to serve as classrooms, and open their own academies and colleges.[93]

Each fraternity made provisions to pay for the education of deceased members' "orphans."[94] In 1841, the Grand Lodge of Virginia created the Special Grand Charity Fund for the education of Masonic orphans. The lodges collected money for the fund from members several times a year. The fund operated much like a Masonic scholarship. Each subordinate lodge sent in the name of a needy Masonic orphan to the grand lodge, which then awarded the funds. Once a year the grand lodge produced a list of students who had received aid. In 1846, for example, the fund paid for the education of forty-four Masonic orphans.[95]

The Sons and Odd Fellows also had school and orphans' funds that earmarked money for the education of deceased members' children. In both fraternities a specially elected committee oversaw educational fund-raising and the funds' distribution at the local level. Upon the death of a member, a visiting committee was assigned to the deceased's family. The committee appointed lodge members to look after the children and ensure that they attended school regularly and progressed in their education. The committee was also responsible for placing children in a nearby school and, in some cases, in a suitable trade or profession after the child graduated.[96] Sometimes local Odd Fellows lodges opened their own schools to educate members' children.[97] In Petersburg, for example, Appomattox Lodge, no.

16, established a "sinking fund" in 1847 to which every member contributed four dollars annually. The money was then allocated to support the "Odd fellows' School of the Town of Petersburg."[98]

Despite their success in supporting and establishing local schools, the orders' attempts to establish colleges and academies in Virginia proved to be an expensive and difficult undertaking. The Freemasons were the most successful, most likely because they had access to the kind of money needed to build and sustain a school. The fraternity established the Caldwell Masonic Institute in Blacksburg and the Higginbotham Male and Female Academy in Amherst County, and it received a charter from the general assembly for the Masonic School of Virginia in Staunton. In 1859, Masons in Danville also discussed building a Masonic male school but postponed their plans because of the Civil War.[99]

In 1848, the Sons, in addition to funding and overseeing individual orphans' education, proposed a Sons of Temperance college. The fraternity advocated opening a college because it believed that educated men not only fostered public virtue but were less likely to drink.[100] The Odd Fellows established Martha Washington Female College in 1853. Virginia's secret fraternal orders argued that improvements in women's education as well as men's would help secure republican principles. This attitude toward women's education was in keeping with an emerging concern for women's education throughout the state and the South. By the late 1840s and 1850s women's colleges and private academies had cropped up across Virginia and other southern states. In fact, by 1860, thirty-two of the country's thirty-nine female colleges were in the South.[101]

The new schools, however, brought several changes to women's education. Men, not women, overwhelmingly ran schools in the 1850s. Throughout the 1820s and 1830s, it was women who generally founded institutes of learning for young boys and for young women. Women ran their own schools and served as school supervisors. Teaching in early antebellum Virginia was an important source of income for women. Not only did single women support themselves with the money they made as teachers, they also profited from boarding students in their homes.[102]

Early in the antebellum era, some men in Virginia even found the occupation of teacher to be "disreputable" because of the large number of women teachers. In 1838, George W. Dame, master of Roman Eagle Lodge and principal of the Danville Female Academy, observed that "the occupation of the teacher is in low repute and a very few young men of Virginia who were qualified would engage in that occupation."[103] This began to change, however, during the 1840s, and by the 1850s more and more men—in the form of principals, presidents, boards of trustees, and professors—were running Virginia's new educational institutions. Although some schools had female "assistants," who frequently taught subjects such as embroidery, women were generally excluded from positions of authority. This stands in contrast to the Northeast, where the majority of schoolteachers were women until the Civil War.[104]

Martha Washington Female College in Abingdon was an example of the new male-run educational institutions of the 1850s. McCabe Lodge, no. 56, IOOF, ran and subsidized the college. The school's charter specified that the lodge annually elect twelve Odd Fellows to a board of trustees. The board, in turn, would elect a president and appoint the college's professors and assistants. The charter required that the college's president be an Odd Fellow who was married, at least thirty years old, and Protestant. The school's assistants could be either male or female, but the female assistants were required to be single and live on campus, and they were "responsible to the President for their demeanor."[105]

The new male-run schools of the late antebellum period also stressed teaching women "mental discipline."[106] As James D. McCabe explained, a woman's intellectual toughness would properly prepare her for her domestic duties. McCabe railed against what he believed to be the degraded state of women's education in other places. He claimed that training women only for the purpose of social intercourse had drawn them away from their important duties at home as wives and mothers.

> The present system of female education is defective—the great effort of the hot-bed systems of *fashionable* female education is to fit young ladies for society . . . [by giving them] a smattering of French and music . . . [and] a few fashionable novels. . . . The immortal mind is left without mental discipline—without knowledge of the holy mission God has committed to women. This system of education causes the domestic duties, when assumed, to be looked upon as merest drudgeries—as barriers to the proper enjoyment of life—household affairs are confused and neglected—duties to children are discharged by *proxy*.[107]

McCabe concluded that any female mind that received only a "fashionable" education would continue to expand with "unpruned wildness" and eventually acquire the elements of its own undoing.

A good education, the orders argued, would enable women to become good republican mothers. Fraternity members subscribed to a belief in what modern historians have termed "republican motherhood."[108] Republican motherhood was both women's designated social and political role away from the public sphere. It dictated that, as mothers, women were responsible for raising the next generation of virtuous republican politicians and community leaders. In a sense, they nurtured the nation's future. Thus, when a woman got married and raised her children to be good citizens, she fulfilled her obligations to society. Contemporaries took this responsibility quite seriously, and they believed that intelligent, chaste, virtuous American mothers would prevent society from spiraling into moral corruption and decay.[109]

With the important task of motherhood in mind, the members of Virginia's fraternal orders claimed that "while our daughters may not be educated for statesmen and philosophers, they should be fitted to train up statesmen and philosophers."[110] Fraternity members were careful to explain that a proper woman's education was meant "to provide instruction in the branches of a sound, thorough and practical education for woman, in her true and appropriate sphere."[111]

Thus, as the guardians of republicanism, Virginia's secret fraternal orders took up the cause of education. The orders clearly believed that an equal education for all whites was vital to securing republican values and that it was men, not women, who should carry the weight of this responsibility. Secret fraternal orders took an active part in establishing male-dominated schools, and their schools promoted a new style of female education that reinforced the idea that a republican woman's proper place was in the domestic sphere.

Secret fraternal orders diminished women's leadership roles not only in public benevolence and education but also in the mollification of partisan strife. Historian Elizabeth Varon has argued convincingly that white women's moral influence served to moderate Virginians' fierce partisan battles of the 1840s. Varon explains that both men and women in the early antebellum era believed that women's presence at political events would help men to understand the moral consequences of their actions and alleviate the anxiety of partisan competition. Thus in the 1830s through the mid-1840s, women were invited to attend partisan rallies and fund-raisers in the belief that their presence would restrain men's competition and divisive impulses.[112] By the 1850s, however, fewer women were attending partisan events. Many of the gains they had made in the public sphere, such as public speaking, "acquired a taint of radicalism." Increasingly, male proxies read women's speeches, while women, if in attendance, stayed seated as observers.[113]

Secret fraternal orders also served as partisan mediators. The orders claimed that they successfully subdued men's selfish and competitive impulses, obliging them to treat other men as brothers. "The waves of party and sectarian strife may beat high and angrily without; but when they reach the door of the Mason's fraternal retreat they have reached a bound they cannot pass."[114] Within the "calm seclusion" of the lodge room, away from the world of aggressive and competitive party politics, men had the opportunity to cultivate meaningful male friendships.[115] These friendships, which extended across class and party divisions, in turn, fostered a concern for their fellow man outside the lodge, unity among white men, and, ultimately, manly patriotism. Within the lodge walls, the orders contended, men met not as Democrats or Whigs but affectionate brothers.

> In Odd-Fellowship may be found the safeguard of our country, from civil commotion and strife. Nothing can be better calculated to hush the animosities which are prone to rise from conflicting religions, or political views and feelings. In Odd-Fellowship meet men of all sects and parties, and, they meet not simply as acquaintances, but, as friends and brothers.[116]

Virginia's Freemasons, Odd Fellows, and Sons of Temperance believed they were safeguarding republicanism by combating partisan strife. The constitutions of all three orders banned the discussion of politics within the lodge and penalized those who broke this rule with a heavy fine.[117]

Fraternity members were not opposed to the idea of party politics; in fact many of the most ardent Whigs and Democrats were members of a secret fraternal order. The fraternities, however, feared that overzealous partisanship would destroy men's relationships with one another and that it would inevitably lead to moral corruption and demagoguery.[118] Thus, the lodge, in addition to the home, became a moral counterweight to the aggressive world of politics and business. Fraternal orders' efforts to quell partisan conflict and restrain men's selfish impulses effectively marginalized women's moral influence in the public sphere. Like public benevolence and education, fraternal orders made subduing partisan strife a masculine civic responsibility.

Women's Reform

It was not a coincidence, then, that women's reform societies and church associations lost power in Virginia in the mid-1840s as new subdivisions of the Sons, Masons, and Odd Fellows mushroomed across the state. As Suzanne Lebsock notes with respect to Petersburg, after decades of leaving poor relief to women and women's organizations, men had, by 1850, taken up and taken over the cause. A great number of women's benevolent organizations also became auxiliaries to men's organizations, leaving women with very little say in how these associations were run. Lebsock claims that by 1859 a new structure of voluntary societies had emerged that put men at center stage and relegated women to supporting roles.[119]

Secret fraternal orders contributed to this shift not only by making public benevolence, education, and the quelling of party strife masculine civic responsibilities but also by establishing women's auxiliaries as the proper place for women, thereby circumscribing the boundaries of women's work and leadership roles in public. At the national level, the Masons, Odd Fellows, and Sons each established a women's auxiliary in the later antebellum era. The auxiliaries created a special "honorary degree" for female relatives of men who belonged to a subordinate lodge. The auxiliaries did not offer sick benefits to women, nor did they partake in the orders' rituals. In 1851, the Odd Fellows established an honorary degree for women, the Rebekah degree. Only the wives of Odd Fellows were eligible for the degree, and a woman's membership was wholly dependent on her husband's moral conduct and timely payment of dues.[120] In 1855, the Freemasons created their own women's auxiliary, the Order of the Eastern Star (OES). The Masons required that male officers oversee the OES's work.[121]

In Virginia, the Freemasons and Odd Fellows did not establish OES or Rebekah lodges until after the Civil War, but in 1856, after much debate, the Virginia Sons of Temperance began permitting subordinate lodges to admit "lady visitors."[122] Although a national antebellum female auxiliary to the Sons existed, the Daughters of Temperance, historian Jack Blocker suggests that the Daughters of Temperance were a part of the more radical "woman-centered" arm of the reform movement that emerged in the 1840s.[123] This appears to have been the case in western New York, where the Daughters, led by Susan B. Anthony, worked in conjunction with ultraist female reformers. Anthony, however, broke with the Daughters and formed the New York State Women's Temperance Society after men at a state Sons' meeting refused to let her speak in public.[124]

The Virginia Sons were careful to restrict the activities women undertook as visitors and were happy to oversee those women who supported the fraternity's work from their appropriate sphere. John A. Broadus, grand worthy patriarch of the Grand Division of Virginia Sons of Temperance, reported in his 1856 annual communication that it is both natural and proper that we should watchfully resist everything which tends towards female masculinity; the idea of admitting females to regular membership, to be formally initiated, to receive pass-words, to vote &c., is beyond all question highly objectionable. I would go as far as the farthest in opposing as resisting such a procedure. But to invite the ladies occasionally to attend a meeting as mere spectators . . . [with their] promise not to reveal the ceremonies, &c., what can there be in this inconsistent with female delicacy?[125]

Broadus's warning against "female masculinity" reveals how strongly fraternity members considered their lodge activities to be masculine work. Thus, secret fraternal orders successfully bolstered and endorsed trends in Virginia that limited women's public role in charity, benevolent reform, education, and partisan strife.

In promoting white male equality through the ideal of fraternal republicanism, Virginia's secret fraternal organizations also had a substantial impact on broader social transformations in the antebellum period. By asserting the significance of fraternal orders in preserving republicanism, the orders imparted to themselves the legitimacy and moral authority necessary to serve as the new public guardians of Virginia's civic virtue. This new fraternal republicanism helped unify white men across class lines by relying on an invented lineage that allegedly dated back to classical antiquity.

These developments also contributed to an important shift in women's public role in antebellum society. The fraternities claimed to have brought discretion, stability, and uniformity to public benevolence, which contrasted their efforts with women's indiscriminate charity work and unchecked sympathies. At the same time, they proclaimed the propriety and naturalness of women's confinement to the private sphere at public speeches, dinners, and other events, noting the potential danger to society when women did step outside of their domestic boundaries.

Suzanne Lebsock has suggested that although the motives behind men's taking over of "so many women's causes in the 1850s" cannot "be assigned with any confidence," the effect "was the same as if there had been a deliberate campiagn to compensate for women's growing autonomy." Despite the absence of organized feminism and gender consciousness in antebellum Virginia, Lebsock demonstrates that female-led benevolent associations, poor-relief activities, and social reform efforts resulted in greater personal autonomy for women in the 1840s. Lebsock argues that the gains women had made sparked a "backlash" against what was perceived to be their inappropriate intrusion into the public sphere.[126]

Whether or not fraternal orders consciously or intentionally supplanted women's work in the public sphere because they felt women had overstepped their bounds, the end result was the same: they greatly diminished the importance of women's role as the guardians of public virtue, and they marginalized women's *public* work in benevolence, education, and partisan harmony. In doing so, secret fraternal orders aided in the contraction of women's "appropriate" sphere and stifled any argument that would connect white women's domestic influence and maternal duties to a more positive public or political role.

FIVE

Civic Brotherhood

On February 22, 1850, Freemason Joseph Mayo participated in the cornerstone-laying ceremony for the equestrian statue of George Washington in Richmond's Capitol Square. In what was surely one of the highlights of his public life, Mayo stood beside the state's most influential men and introduced President Zachary Taylor to a crowd of almost three thousand people who had come to watch the Masonic ceremony.[1] The cornerstone-laying ceremony symbolized the beginning of a new era of white male control of public space. Elite and nonelite white men from all over the city and state had marched in unison that day to honor founding father and Freemason George Washington.

Only sixteen years later in 1866, Mayo, then the city's mayor, fought desperately to reinstitute the city's pre–Civil War pass and curfew system that had controlled black access to public space. Unsuccessful, he and other white Richmonders watched in horror and disbelief as newly freed African Americans paraded through the city's main streets and flooded into Capitol Square in celebration of Washington's birthday and the Fourth of July.[2] In fact, white Virginians contended that they would rather abolish Washington's birthday and Independence Day celebrations altogether than watch former slaves take "complete possession of the day and the city," which whites believed was theirs alone.[3]

Both episodes clearly demonstrate, although in different ways, the important power that controlling public space conveyed in antebellum Virginia. Participation in public festivals, parades, and celebrations conferred legitimacy on those that inhabited public space, and served as an important measure of white male citizenship. During the antebellum era, Virginia's secret fraternal orders turned out in large numbers to march in public parades and ceremonies alongside the militia, voluntary fire associations, and prominent politicians. At these events, the fraternities publicly positioned themselves among other masculine groups whose duty, both literally and figuratively, was to protect their community. Moreover, the orders physically modified the urban landscape by establishing prominently positioned lodge buildings in between other important civic institutions such as courthouses, schools, and churches.

By the mid-1850s, Virginia's secret fraternal organizations occupied a highly visible place in urban public space. The orders conducted public ceremonies for hall dedications, funerals, national holidays, anniversary parades, and the laying of cornerstones. The fraternities' colorful parades and newly constructed buildings confirmed the orders' role as protectors of civic virtue and reinforced the notion that charity, benevolence, and partisan harmony were male civic responsibilities not unlike military service or volunteer firefighting. Furthermore, the joint participation of white men from different economic backgrounds at these public commemorations softened class distinctions, creating a civic brotherhood among white men.

Public Space and Fraternal Celebrations

In addition to creating tension between middle- and working-class men, the advent of slave hiring in Virginia's urban centers also affected the relationship of blacks and whites. Race relations rapidly declined in the late 1840s and 1850s as free blacks and hired slaves filled skilled and unskilled jobs in the state's urban centers. Many whites believed that the increase in urban slavery had fostered the growth of black impudence, crime, and insubordination.[4]

Slave hiring had led to important changes in the way free blacks and slaves occupied public space and spent their free time. The majority of hired slaves were brought to cities and towns from farms and plantations in the countryside. In order to cut costs, employers often paid urban slaves a weekly stipend to find their own housing, clothing, and food, a practice referred to as "living out." Slaves who lived out were free from the direct supervision of both their masters and the whites who employed them during working hours.[5]

Hired out slaves gained added opportunities to earn cash and increase their mobility by hiring themselves out for extra work or by participating in "overwork." Whites complained that blacks spent their extra money on new clothes, alcohol, and other luxuries. They also reported seeing slaves and free blacks riding in carriages and promenading down the public streets wearing extravagant clothes, smoking cigars, and carrying canes. In effect, they saw slaves exercising privileges they believed were reserved for whites only.[6]

As a result, many municipalities passed new laws that restricted black mobility and privileges.[7] The Freemasons, Sons of Temperance, and Odd Fellows also played an important role in conveying to all Virginians that unfettered access to public space was solely a white male privilege. The fraternities' elaborate public events almost always involved a parade, complete with colorful banners, a band, and glittering regalia, through the town squares and main streets of their communities where black movement was tightly controlled. These celebrations not only demonstrated the power of white male unity but also reinforced the notion that even the poorest white man remained above blacks within Virginia's social hierarchy.

During the 1840s and 1850s, Virginia's fraternal organizations were an integral part of most public civic celebrations. The fraternities turned out for the Fourth of July, George Washington's birthday, funerals, monument dedications, and cornerstone-laying ceremonies for churches, schools, and other public buildings. According to historian Mary P. Ryan, these well-ordered parades were the result of a period of growth and change in public celebrations during the antebellum period. Between approximately 1825 and 1850, public ceremonies became increasingly organized, going from carnivalesque celebrations to careful cultural performances.[8] These new ceremonies further reflected the shift in antebellum culture that gradually downplayed class identity and instead underscored republican manhood and universal white male citizenship. Thus, the trade and occupational associations that dominated parades in the 1820s gradually disappeared and were replaced in the 1840s and 1850s by fraternal organizations, militia companies, and voluntary fire associations. As Ryan suggests, the participation of these preconstituted white male associations in civic performances conferred "ceremonial citizenship" on the members of these groups as individuals and organizations.[9]

Public celebrations, then, brought prestige and cultural authority to the members of Virginia's secret fraternal orders. Participation in parades legitimized fraternity members' role as protectors of the community's civic virtue, regardless of their economic status. In marching with the literal guardians of their neighborhoods—firemen and the militia—fraternal orders carved out a place for themselves among the public defenders of the state. In addition, the Odd Fellows, the Sons of Temperance, and the Freemasons loudly proclaimed their ideal of brotherly love and their commitment to providing mutual assistance and aid for widows and orphans. This bolstered the notion that charity and benevolence were masculine civic responsibilities as important as military service and firefighting.

By the late 1850s, public ceremonies also increasingly excluded white women. Earlier in the nineteenth century, some of Virginia's female associations and teachers had participated in Fourth of July and other public patriotic celebrations in Richmond, Norfolk, and other cities and towns.[10] During the 1840s, Whig women adopted the notion that women ought to be partisans in order to raise loyal, politically informed sons. The Ladies Association for Erecting a Statue of Henry Clay, for example, had even played a limited role in Virginia party politics.[11]

At the same time secret fraternal orders were attempting to legitimize their own public role, social conservatives were worrying that women's activities in the public sphere had exceeded the boundaries of female propriety. Newspaper articles reflected Virginians' fears that women had forsaken "all their characteristic delicacy and gentleness for the assumption of those harsher duties and occupations which have always, heretofore, been regarded as the province of men."[12] In response to a rumor in Danville that a "lady preacher" had come to town, one man proclaimed,

> Some hundreds are right uneasy about their wives. They are afraid that some
> of them women's rights folks from the N[orth], are travelling among us, and
> that some wives are encouraging them. We would rather have an abolitionist
> among us. . . . One would spoil our negroes, but the other would spoil our
> wives and sweethearts, and either, would be made bad pieces of property.[13]

Women's public behavior, in particular, concerned them. Several articles warned that women might someday be found on the public streets engaging in such manly activities as chewing tobacco, drinking whiskey, and wearing pants. One man wondered, "Are we ever to see some sweet lady-friend twirling a cane down Main street?"[14] Even women themselves protested that dandified white men, who feared getting their boots muddy, no longer stepped off the public sidewalk as women passed by. One woman declared that if becoming a "woman's right's woman" meant she would have to step off the sidewalk for men and dirty her shoes, she was not interested.[15]

By the 1850s, then, despite some Virginians' true willingness to accept women's party affiliations, the majority of men invited women to partisan events only to boast of women's approval, demonstrate men's "respectability," and symbolically reinforce the legitimacy of separate spheres. Whig womanhood remained fettered to women's roles as mothers and homemakers. According to Mary Ryan, women's participation in partisan events "lured women closer to the public sphere, but along duplicitous, dependent, and manipulative avenues, and then only to a center of discourse still dominated by men."[16] Consequently, women's public celebrations, partisan or not, began to emphasize women's association with the family and domesticity, and by the outbreak of the Civil War, women's role in the public sphere had become more and more circumscribed.[17]

As fraternity members made their orders an increasingly visible part of the urban landscape, they closed off formalized public spaces to women.[18] Prior to the 1840s, Virginia's Masons and Odd Fellows often met in taverns or private homes. By the early 1850s, however, buildings owned by the exclusively male orders occupied a prominent position among other important public institutions such as courthouses, schools, and churches. In Lynchburg in the 1840s, for example, the Ladies Association for Erecting a Statue of Henry Clay continued to meet in private homes and various local churches, while the Odd Fellows, Freemasons, and Sons each completed their own halls. These fraternal buildings conveyed the order's social integrity and helped establish their legitimacy among other public institutions that protected liberty and cultivated civic virtue. Moreover, the Lynchburg Freemasons' lodge became an important public meeting space and the "center for many of the most significant happenings in town."[19]

Those lodges that did lease space until they could raise enough money to build their own hall often rented rooms in the building of another fraternal organization or from a fraternity member who owned a business. They sometimes even shared space with the local county courts, and in at least one case, the Freemasons lent out space in their lodge to a government body. When a new Hustings court displaced the town council from its building in Danville, Virginia, the Masons temporarily rented space in their lodge building to the town council for court purposes. The town council then suggested that its body unite with the Masons in the erection of another building in a different location.[20]

The importance fraternity members attached to owning their own hall should not be underestimated. At the very first meeting of the Sons of Temperance's Covington Division, for example, the new members noted that their top priority was to acquire a hall and regalia. Fraternity members correctly believed that owning a lodge building not only would endow their order with prestige but also would help further their principles and attract new members.[21] After the cornerstone-laying ceremony for Marshall Lodge's new Masonic hall in Lynchburg, membership in the fraternity skyrocketed to ninety-six members, the most brothers the lodge had ever had. Masonic Historian William Moseley Brown notes that

> there is no doubt of the fact that the erection of the new Hall had contributed largely to this result and had aroused more interest in the community generally than at any time in the Lodge's history of more than fifty years up to that date.[22]

An elaborate fraternal hall drew white men to the order because they recognized that owning a piece of public space meant the organization possessed a certain amount of public authority. The political meaning of owning property was not lost on one Son of Temperance from Rockingham County. Daniel Watkins's lodge, Mount Crawford Division, no. 19, met in a space his division rented from fellow lodge member Peter S. Roller. Although the order had successfully transformed the room above Roller's store into an appropriate meeting hall, the division began discussing the possibility of building its own hall in 1850. Watkins, a forty-three-year-old hatter listed on the 1850 census as owning neither property nor slaves, suggested that the division buy "a peace [sic] of Land to mak [sic] us Freeholders."[23] Perhaps Watkins did not mean to suggest that the lodge's collective ownership of a hall could literally grant individual nonfreeholders the right to vote. Yet the association he made between owning a lodge building and political power further reinforced the notion that the power to control civic space was a chief means by which one could influence antebellum political culture.[24]

Members also emphasized that owning a building aided them in their charity work. At the dedication of his order's new lodge in downtown Richmond on December 14, 1841, Odd Fellow D. D. Smith insisted that the new hall would help the men to more effectively alleviate the "widow's moan" and the "orphan's cry."

> A day of rejoicing has arrived! The members of the Independent Order of Odd-Fellows of the city of Richmond have realized their hopes in the

completion of a building, erected ... by the agency of their own industry, charity, prudent foresight, and proper devotion to the principles they love and revere. Within its sacred walls they will be able ... to assemble, and discuss and adopt such measures as will aid in the advancement of benevolence and truth.[25]

The new lodge building would help to fulfill the benevolent and charitable aims of the order by attracting worthy men to their cause. One of the day's other speakers challenged "all good, virtuous and intelligent men" to join the order under their new roof.[26]

The Odd Fellows' glittering procession to the new hall's dedication ceremony called further attention to the charitable works of the fraternity. The *Richmond Enquirer* described the procession in detail, noting the striking appearance of the Odd Fellows' colorful sashes, banners, and regalia. "This long-expected and much-talked of event came off yesterday. ... [The order] made a fine display, and the whole effect of the waving banners, unique symbols, and rich insignia was very grand and imposing."[27] The different-colored banners the order carried bore a variety of words and phrases, including "Friendship, Love, & Truth," "Benevolence," and "Faith, Hope, & Charity."[28] Other banners bore symbols and emblems. Some had biblical themes (the lamb, the dove, the cross), while others emphasized principles of the order, such as genuine brotherhood (heart in hand, three links), charity (three pillars, horn of plenty), unity (bundle of rods), and the equality of men within the order (scale and sword). According to orator D. D. Smith, the Odd Fellows carried the banners to advertise the fraternity's principles to the community and to remind fraternity members of their "obligations and duties."[29] In addition, and perhaps more importantly, the banners and symbols, combined with the sight of fraternity members formally possessing the space of the public streets, worked to connect the notions of masculinity, civic duty, charity, and benevolence in the minds of spectators.

Furthermore, the new lodge hall, "a handsome and substantial building," seemed to announce the success of Odd Fellowship in Richmond.[30] The hall was a three-story brick and granite building at the corner of Mayo and Franklin streets in downtown Richmond. The order used the upper stories of the building for lodge meetings and as a space for large celebrations. The second floor of the new Odd Fellows' Hall was built to accommodate very large fraternity meetings. It could also be rented out for concerts, balls, and other social gatherings.[31]

Three storefronts also flanked the first floor of the new building. Like lodge halls owned by other antebellum fraternities, this building was used for more than just the order's meetings. Fraternities typically would rent out the lower rooms of their halls to generate revenue. The Odd Fellows' hall, erected only five blocks from the city's main Masonic hall, was also in the center of Richmond's slave trade district, which the order capitalized on in 1860, when it rented out one of the first floor storefronts to Davis, Deupree and Co., "for the purpose of SELLING NEGROES, At Private and Public Sale, on Commission."[32] Thus, the building also reminded passersby of the potential for all white men to become masters.

After the dedication ceremony the public returned home, and fraternity members attended an "elegant," but alcohol-free, catered dinner held at the Exchange Hotel.[33] In all, the new building and dedication ceremony helped to strengthen the masculine reputation of the order and solidify the growing public power of the nonelite white men who were its members.

Funerals

Of all the public processions in which Virginia's secret fraternal organizations participated, funerals were the most common. Fraternal funeral processions and ceremonies served three different and important functions. When a fraternity member died, his lodge brothers not only honored his memory by gathering as a group but also coordinated the arrangements for his funeral, carried his remains to the graveyard, and performed the actual funeral ceremony. Funerals dramatically and publicly illustrated that fraternity members believed that true men were not just "masters and statesmen."[34] True men also contributed to their community and took care of their fellow man.

Lodge members gathered together as quickly as possible when one of their brothers died. The orders appointed between six and eight brothers to serve as pallbearers or marshals in the funeral procession and made arrangements for the ceremony. If necessary, a brother would also be sent to the deceased's home to sit up with, or "watch," the corpse.[35]

The funeral ceremony was more than an opportunity for fraternity brothers to pay their last respects to their deceased lodge brother. The faithful care of a brother's remains, the orders claimed, was proof that the brotherly love and friendship they shared was genuine. Each of the fraternities' funeral ceremonies stressed that the performance of this last ritual was the mark of true devotion and friendship.[36] At the end of the Sons of Temperance ceremony, for example, the worthy patriarchy announced to the fraternity that "this last act of our kindness [made] our pledge of friendship true." The brothers then solemnly circled around the grave and tossed emblems of the order onto the coffin while singing, "We in mournful accents breathe ov'r him, 'Our pledge of Friendship's true.'"[37]

On the morning of the funeral, the lodges were formally opened to note the beginning of a sacred time, and members were expected to maintain proper fraternal conduct as defined by the orders' bylaws. From the lodge room, members marched in somber procession to the home of the deceased to "meet" or "receive" the corpse. After the lodge received the body of their late brother, they began a solemn and slow march to the graveyard.[38] Interestingly, during the antebellum period women increasingly did not attend the burial ceremony or walk with the body to the gravesite, despite the fact that they had traditionally prepared the bodies of loved ones for burial. The glorification of the home and domesticity in the 1820s and 1830s placed death and mourning rituals squarely within women's responsibilities to their families (at least in New England).[39] By the mid-nineteenth century, however, women competed with the funeral industry, which had become more and more professionalized, and perhaps with fraternal organizations. It is unclear who prepared the body for burial in fraternal ceremonies—the family, lodge members, or an undertaker.[40]

In the antebellum era, the amount of pomp at a person's funeral often indicated the class status of the deceased. In urban areas, for example, the poor were forced to rely on their city government or a local church agency for burial. These ceremonies were bereft of the rituals and embellishments of private funerals.[41] Membership in a fraternal organization, however, entitled every member to a funeral marked by pageantry and ostentatious display regardless of his economic status. Thus, fraternity members with little money or property not only could rest assured that their family would never need to rely on the government for their funeral but also could be confident that they would be remembered as a valued member of the community.

For example, Son of Temperance Austin Blackerly, listed in the 1850 federal census as a fifty-year-old "laborer" with no real estate and no slaves, could expect that his fraternity brothers would make arrangements and participate in his funeral when he died. Moreover, the men who would march at Blackerly's funeral included not just other laborers but fellow lodge members, like tailor William McAtee, blacksmith Simon Switzer, and farmer Robert Grattan, who owned $45,000 in real estate.[42]

The number of mourners involved in the funeral procession also could be an indicator of status. All lodge members were required to participate in a brother's funeral. The constitutions and bylaws of the Freemasons, Odd Fellows, and Sons of Temperance made funeral attendance for all lodge brothers mandatory. Any member who did not attend a brother's funeral risked a fine and the scorn of his lodge.[43] When Chesley Kinney, a local lawyer and member of Staunton Lodge, no. 13, died unexpectedly in February 1851, his fraternal brothers honored him with an elaborate Masonic funeral. The newspaper that announced his death noted that Kinney "shared largely the esteem and good will of all who knew him, as was testified by the large procession of mourning friends who followed him to the grave."[44]

This worked both ways. Not only did Kinney gain prestige, even in death, from his membership in a fraternal order, his lodge brothers also attained a certain level of social prominence as participants in Kinney's funeral procession. A sampling of Staunton Lodge members reveals that men from varying economic backgrounds—such as poor confectioner Charles Ball, middling merchant David Huffman, and wealthy coppersmith Benjamin Points—would have marched as brothers to deposit Kinney's remains into his grave.[45] The participation of both elite and nonelite white men in each others' antebellum funeral ceremonies conferred greater social status on nonelite white men and offered a display of public unity among white men that did not exist decades earlier.

Funeral ceremonies and published eulogies also often defined the ideals of society. According to secret fraternal organizations, a good man not only cared for and supported his family but also contributed to his community. In an 1854 eulogy for Freemason Edmund Pendleton Hunter, orator J. A. Leitch identified four different types of deceased men: men whose death was a relief to their community; men who would be scarcely missed after death; men who would be missed from the places they worthily filled; and men whose death constituted a loss to their entire community. The eulogy described the ideal man as honest and upright as well as "benevolent and useful." Thus, according to Leitch, a true man went beyond just taking care of his friends and family; he at the same time worked to better his community. Interestingly the men whom Leitch leveled the most scathing criticism against were not "evil" men but men who he claimed had "lived selfishly."[46]

> They have had no interests beyond the little circle of kindred that gathered about them—exerted no cheerful or beneficent influences for the general good. They have contributed nothing except what, in securing their own selfish ends they could not avoid, to the welfare of society. . . . It is hard to

say why a community should mourn the death of such men. It has suffered no loss.

For those men who made a contribution to their community, however, he predicted that mournful wails would be heard well "beyond the family."[47] Leitch's categories provide a valuable insight into how antebellum fraternities measured the value of a man's life and reveal just how important they regarded men's civic responsibilities to be.

The eulogy also helps explain the importance of the public death announcement and resolutions that antebellum fraternities published in local newspapers. In addition to making the arrangements for the funeral ceremony, the orders appointed a committee to prepare a preamble and a set of resolutions regarding the loss of their brother. The statements expressed the lodge's profound loss, noting that the deceased had been a "good and faithful" fraternity brother, an "upright and honest citizen," and a valuable member of the community. The preamble and resolutions were sent to local newspapers for publication, and a copy was sent to the deceased's family.[48] These resolutions were written as part of the funeral process for every brother that died. This public statement of a brother's character reminded the lodge's community that fraternal organizations were important benevolent and civic institutions. It also depicted all members, regardless of economic status, as fulfilling their masculine responsibilities in life to their family, their polity, and their community.

The lack of respect for deceased free blacks in antebellum Virginia stands in shocking contrast to the treatment of deceased white fraternity members. In the 1840s, professors at the University of Virginia and Hampden-Sydney College found themselves with a shortage of human cadavers for medical research. White Virginians were very often unwilling to donate their bodies for scientific research after they had died, and strict laws regulated the internment and gravesites of white bodies. To make up for the dearth in cadavers, some professors surreptitiously collaborated with unscrupulous men in the cities of Norfolk, Alexandria, Richmond, and Petersburg to snatch recently buried free black bodies from their graves. The bodies of free blacks were more suitable candidates for body snatching because white gravesites were more closely guarded and citizens would surely have demanded prosecution of anyone tampering with whites' graves. Despite public knowledge of black body snatching, legal authorities made no attempt to stop it.[49]

The lack of respect for black funeral rituals and black bodies further highlighted the status the orders' elaborate funeral ceremonies imparted to members, living and dead. Fraternity funeral processions, public resolutions, and ceremonies publicly displayed the new confidence white men had in one another, effectively softening class distinctions. They also signaled the importance of charity work to the redefinition of white manhood in antebellum Virginia.

Anniversary Celebrations

Another important event on the fraternity calendar was a lodge's anniversary celebration. The Masons, Odd Fellows, and Sons of Temperance each held an annual celebration to promote the principles of their order and to note the longevity of their lodge. Anniversary celebrations also provided an opportunity for members to invite friends, family, and the general public to interact with and learn about their fraternity. These celebrations generally involved three key events: a large and colorful procession, a speech, and a public dinner.

The entire lodge became involved in the planning several months in advance. The members had very specific tasks to complete such as sending out invitations to the public and other local lodges (they often invited other nearby lodges from their order and other fraternal organizations to participate in their ceremonies), securing a speaker and a band, washing the regalia, and making arrangements for the dinner.[50]

For example, on May 12, 1851, Mount Crawford Division, no. 19, of the Sons of Temperance hosted an elaborate public celebration for its fifth anniversary. The celebration began with a procession through the main streets of town. The Mount Crawford band led the parade, and the local Sons and the neighboring Worth and Brownsville Divisions marched behind it. The parade ended in the backyard of a local store where a crowd of "bretherin [sic] and a very large assembrige [sic] of Ladies and Gentleman" who were not connected to the order sang temperance odes, listened to the band, and listened to the addresses of brothers L. D. Harris and Daniel Feete. Later that evening, the Sons formed in procession again, marched to a local church, and listened to additional addresses given by brothers Josiah Roller and William Reed. After the speeches, members of the fraternity then waited on the "the ladies," serving them "lemmon aid," "candis," raisins, and cake.[51]

Like funerals and hall dedication ceremonies, anniversary celebrations involved white fraternity members of varying economic backgrounds

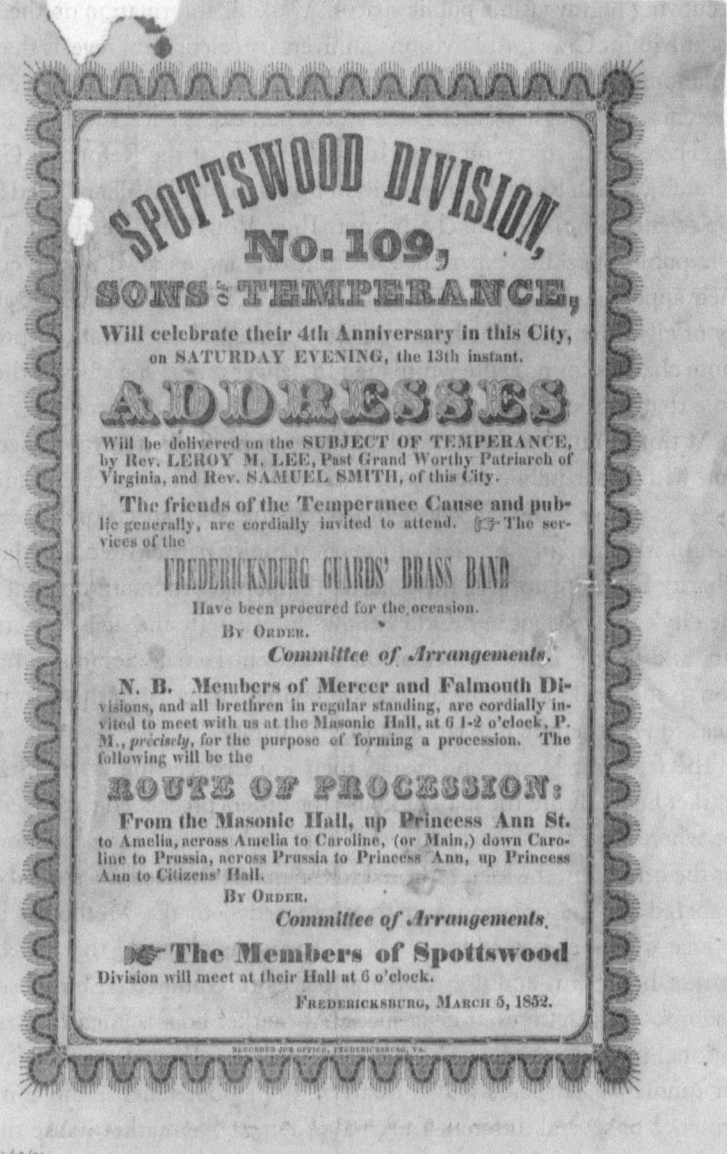

Figure 7. Sons of Temperance broadside, 1852. Broadside 1852:4, Virginia Historical Society, Richmond.

occupying highly visible public spaces. Available information on the speakers at Mount Crawford Division's anniversary celebration reveals that these ceremonies also gave nonelite white men the opportunity to give public speeches. Although Daniel Feete surely had experience speaking in public (Feete was a thirty-nine-year-old clergyman at the Reformed German Church), Josiah Roller (farmer, age twenty-eight) and William Reed (joiner, age twenty-nine) most likely did not. Thus, Roller and Reed gained valuable public speaking experience in front of a large crowd of citizens, and their appearing in such a prominent position reinforced the public authority of all white men. Furthermore, secret fraternal organizations provided more chances for nonelite white men to deliver public speeches at the same time that public speaking opportunities for women were declining.[52]

At times fraternal orders would also combine their anniversary celebration with other public events, such as cornerstone-laying ceremonies. On these occasions fraternal orders joined together for a special public celebration in which a large portion of the community participated. In May 1850, Charity Division, no. 6, of the Sons of Temperance in Staunton joined with the city's Freemasons and Odd Fellows to celebrate the division's anniversary and lay the cornerstone for the Wesleyan Female Seminary. In addition to the local lodges, the orders also invited lodges from the surrounding areas to join them in one large and lavish parade.[53]

The fraternities met and began their joint procession at the Staunton market house. From the market house the orders proceeded to the seminary lot, where the Freemasons performed the cornerstone-laying ceremony. After the ceremony, the men returned to the market house for a special dinner prepared for the occasion and then proceeded to the Methodist church to hear a temperance address.[54] Mary Ryan has observed that antebellum market houses, in addition to being places of commercial business, were also important fixtures of civic space. At market houses, men held organizational meetings and acted "in public interest." They also used the space for municipal purposes and for carrying out poor relief.[55] The combined presence of several different fraternal orders at the market house that day further accentuated the important civic role secret fraternal organizations played in antebellum Virginia.

The records of Charity Division, no. 6, indicate that 225 men attended the temperance dinner alone.[56] Included among the members of these three lodges were some of Staunton's most prominent politicians and public figures, such as state representatives Hugh W. Sheffey and John Imboden, former mayor Levi L. Stevenson, and merchants Nicholas K. Trout, Jacob

Pollitz, and Thomas P. Eskridge. However, the bulk of the men who belonged to these lodges were merchants, lawyers, plasterers, harness makers, carpenters, house painters, bricklayers, and laborers of varying economic positions.[57] The united appearance of these men at the marketplace, the church, the seminary, and on the streets of downtown Staunton unquestionably demonstrated the public authority of white civic brotherhood. It also visually conveyed to the community that all white men, regardless of status, not only had access to public space but also controlled it.

Community Celebrations

In addition to participating in the orders' internal celebrations, such as hall dedications, members' funerals, and anniversary celebrations, Virginia's secret fraternal organizations took part in a community-wide public celebrations and civic events. Like internal celebrations, external public ceremonies also softened class distinctions among white men and emphasized the orders' benevolent goals. Community-wide celebrations, however, differed from internal celebrations because public celebrations like the Fourth of July, Washington's birthday, and state funerals positioned fraternal orders among the protectors of the community.

Virginia's fraternal organizations joined with the general public to mourn the deaths of national political figures. In towns and cities across Virginia, the Odd Fellows, Freemasons, and Sons of Temperance marched through the streets with the militia and other organizations in mock funeral ceremonies to commemorate the deaths of Andrew Jackson, James Polk, Zachary Taylor, and Henry Clay. The ceremonies took on added significance because Jackson, Clay, and Polk were all at one time active Freemasons. Thus, members of the order referred to the deceased politicians as "brother" and performed the same funeral rituals they would have used if a member of their own lodge had died.[58]

The Freemasons played a key role in the organization and planning of the local funeral ceremonies for the national figures. For example, the Masonic lodges in Petersburg created a joint committee with local citizens to make arrangements "for a public demonstration of respect for the memory and private virtues of our eminent Brother the late Ex-President of the United States James K. Polk."[59] The order hired a band, wore mourning dress, and announced the events in the newspaper in advance. Petersburg's two Masonic lodges joined the local Sons of Temperance divisions, Odd Fellow lodges, civil authorities, and militia companies in the funeral procession. On August 4, 1849, spectators lined the streets of downtown Petersburg to watch the procession. The community then gathered in a densely crowded auditorium to hear Masonic past master Richard K. Meade deliver Polk's eulogy.[60] Events such as these clearly reinforced the prominence of all fraternity members, no matter what their occupation. The men who participated in these political funerals demonstrated the elevated place fraternities occupied in political culture.

Similarly, antebellum Independence Day celebrations involved elaborate processions through town, a patriotic address, and the reading of the Declaration of Independence. Usually a public dinner then followed, complete with many scripted and spontaneous toasts. In the early national period, the primary participants in these processions were elite community leaders and militia members. "Ordinary people" demonstrated their patriotism by holding their own smaller celebrations or by breaking the windows of the wealthy citizens who had not placed candles in them as proof of their patriotism. By the 1840s, however, Virginia's secret fraternal organizations and other white male organizations had commandeered national patriotic holidays such as the Fourth of July and Washington's birthday.[61]

In 1850, the Covington Division of the Sons of Temperance made arrangements for an elaborate Fourth of July celebration. The final plans for the celebration outlined a fifteen-point order of events planned down to the smallest detail. The day's celebration included a parade through town, a church ceremony at which attendees heard a temperance address and witnessed a Bible and banner presentation, a public dinner, several patriotic addresses, the reading of the Declaration of Independence, and nonalcoholic toasts. The Sons also invited both the Freemasons and the Odd Fellows and local citizens to join them.[62]

One year earlier, the Odd Fellows from McCabe Lodge, no. 56, in Abingdon made the short trip across the state border to celebrate the Fourth of July with citizens and fraternity brothers in Rogersville, Tennessee. In his address, speaker of the day James D. McCabe noted the appropriateness of jointly celebrating the benevolent principles of Odd Fellowship and the patriotic ideals of the founding fathers, asserting that the fraternity was "a dispenser of local and national blessings."[63] In closing his speech, McCabe encouraged fraternity members to fuse the symbols of the Odd Fellowship and Independence Day mentally and physically as they formed in procession.

> Brethren, go on—unfurl the white banner of your Order—give it proudly to the breeze—let its triumphant folds intertwine, and become blended with

the stars and stripes of the freeman's hope and home; till oppression breaks his sceptre, war lies crushed on his harness—"till man is bound in brotherhood to man."[64]

Moreover, McCabe positioned his fraternity brothers among the defenders of the community by comparing the order's regalia to a "military costume" that separated "the solider from the civilian."[65] As these statements clearly indicate, fraternity members increasingly blurred together their manly responsibilities as citizens, brothers, and patriots.

Virginia's fraternities also played an important role in the commemoration of George Washington's birthday. In 1851, Staunton's community leaders held a meeting at the county courthouse two weeks before Washington's birthday to plan the town's celebration. They chose several prominent citizens to give patriotic speeches and read Washington's Farewell Address. They also determined to issue formal invitations to the military companies, the people of Augusta County, and "all the divisions of the Sons of Temperance, and Masonic and Odd-Fellows lodges specially."[66]

The most impressive fraternal celebration of Washington's birthday, however, took place in Richmond in 1850. On February 22, Richmond's Freemasons, Sons of Temperance, and Odd Fellows participated in the cornerstone-laying ceremony of the city's new equestrian statue of George Washington in Capitol Square. Virginia's fraternal orders took their role in the creation and dedication of Washington's statue very seriously. The statue's commissioners (three of whom were Freemasons) and Virginia's governor, John B. Floyd (both a Freemason and an Odd Fellow), chose a Bronze equestrian statue to memorialize Washington. According to the *Richmond Enquirer*, the committee and other Virginians felt that an equestrian statue would be the most appropriate way to honor Washington's legacy because "to the military spirit of George Washington we are indebted for our liberties."[67]

The governor and committee also specifically chose Capitol Square as the location for the statue because, as the site of the governor's mansion and Thomas Jefferson's impressive Greco-Roman state legislature building, the square was one of the most significant public spaces in Richmond. For black Virginians, however, Capitol Square had a more sinister meaning. Capitol Square was the place where the state publicly punished and executed rebellious slaves, for the express purpose of frightening and controlling the black population.[68] Further, municipal law forbade slaves and free blacks from entering the areas surrounding the governor's mansion and the legislature building without white permission. The grand welcoming of white fraternity members, alongside the militia, the city's firemen, and some of the most important men in the state, then, signified the public's confidence in the orders and, by extension, in white men's ability to uphold social order.

The day's ceremonies began with a large parade, which started at the city's courthouse and wound its way through the principal streets of downtown Richmond. All members of the Odd Fellows, Sons of Temperance, Masons, and other secret fraternal orders were invited to join in the procession.[69] In all, seven of the city's secret fraternal orders marched in the parade, which was over a mile long. Along with the governor of Virginia, President Zachary Taylor, former president John Tyler, and the Virginia General Assembly all joined the fraternal orders, local officials, the militia, and the city's firemen in the march toward the square. Local newspapers reported that thirty thousand people jammed the sidewalks, doors, and windows lining the parade route to see the grand procession. They also estimated that almost twenty-five hundred people crowded around the staging area where the cornerstone ceremony was performed.[70]

As the conductors of the cornerstone-laying ceremony, the Freemasons played a pivotal role in all of the day's events. James Points, most worthy grand master of the Grand Lodge of Virginia Freemasons, and other officers of the state's grand lodge sat with the governor and the president near the staging area. The other Freemasons who attended the day's festivities had the privilege of standing around the large hole where the cornerstone was to be laid. At the appropriate time, Points and the officers descended into the hole, while several Masons guarded the area above them with drawn swords. After several minutes, the governor descended into the hole and declared the stone well laid. The surrounding Masons then broke into song: "Hail! Mysterious Hail! Glorious Masonry, that makes us ever great and free."[71]

The orator of the day, Virginia Freemason and politician Robert G. Scott, then delivered an address. In his speech, Scott praised the service of his "illustrious brother" Washington to the country, noting his bravery, selflessness, and wisdom. He not only was a great patriot who advocated white male equality, Scott claimed, but also was a "bright and spotless example" of Freemasonry. Scott reveled in Washington's connection with the order, even pausing during his speech to hold up Washington's original Masonic apron, sash, and gavel, which drew a reaction from the crowd.

Figure 8. Unveiling of statue of George Washington in Capitol Square, 1852. Library of
Congress, Prints and Photographs Division, LC-USZ62-20438.

> An honest advocate of the equal and inalienable rights of man, [Washington] became satisfied that Masonry had at all times, and under the harshest trials, been the unfaltering supporter of just and free principles.... [O]ur Washington found Masonry true and steadfast in advancing the intellectual and moral improvement of the masses, and the elevation to that condition of equality and happiness that now blesses more than twenty millions of American freemen.[72]

Virginia's fraternal orders frequently appropriated the images and ideals of the Revolutionary generation to promote antebellum white male equality at public events. The civic brotherhood these fraternal orders displayed, both as the hosts of and participants in antebellum civic celebrations, positioned elite and nonelite fraternity members among the protectors of the republican state.

After Scott spoke, Governor Floyd gave an address, and Joseph Mayo, future mayor of Richmond, introduced President Zachary Taylor, who made a few remarks. After the ceremony, the Masons held a lavish dinner, and that evening fireworks were sent off over the capitol building. Capping off the evening was a Masonic ball at the Union Hotel, attended by President Taylor, which reportedly lasted until four o'clock in the morning.[73]

Thus, at numerous public events and civic ceremonies, politicians, businessmen, artisans, mechanics, and laborers stood united in fraternal regalia in some of the city's most highly visible areas. The joint participation of white men from different economic backgrounds in the public festivities surrounding the erection of Washington's statue created a civic brotherhood among white men. Participation in these types of community-wide commemorations imparted legitimacy to Virginia's secret fraternal organizations and served as an important measure of white male citizenship. Furthermore, the fraternities publicly positioned themselves among other masculine groups whose duty was to protect and guide their community, redefining the scope of men's civic duties to include benevolence and charity.

Undoubtedly, control of public space was intimately connected to control of public power in antebellum Virginia. Beginning in the 1840s, the state's secret fraternal organizations played a decisive and central role in public celebrations. In the face of the social and economic forces that pulled white men apart, secret fraternal orders established a new era of white male solidarity. Only eight months after the cornerstone-laying ceremony in Capitol

Square, representatives at the state constitutional convention eliminated freehold voting requirements for white men, finally ushering in universal white male suffrage in the Old Dominion.

Fraternal orders played a key role in uniting white men from all classes and establishing the community's confidence in these men to guide and protect the state. Public celebrations, including funeral processions, national holidays, and hall dedications, clearly reinforced fraternity members' public authority and social prestige. By possessing and controlling public space in new buildings and carefully scripted celebrations, fraternal orders constantly reminded other Virginians that they were the worthy guardians of public virtue and civic responsibilities. In thousands of ceremonies that excluded women and blacks, yet gave equal billing to even the lowest white male, fraternal orders left no doubt about their influential role as protectors and leaders of their communities.

Conclusion

In the final years before the Civil War, the nation's secret fraternal orders, like other national organizations, fell prey to sectional tensions. Virginia's fraternal leaders strove to hold their orders together across the Mason-Dixon Line, but as rumors of war spread, membership declined.[1] As political animosity outside the lodge became unavoidable, the orders struggled to convince members that the "calm seclusion of the lodge" would protect them from sectional strife.[2] The fraternities reminded members that political arguments would not be tolerated within the lodge room.

> We must be rigid in guarding, even from the suspicion of taint, that *cherished neutrality* on questions which divide the political and religious world, by demanding of our members, that in their actions in Lodges, they shall stand upon our common platform ungoverned in their conduct by influences, which are excluded as dangerous by the express words of our ritual.[3]

Virginia's Freemasons even attempted to keep sectional lines of communication open in the late 1850s by traveling to visit their Masonic brothers in Massachusetts and then hosting Boston Masons in Virginia.[4]

Just as Virginia's fraternity members struggled to consider their northern fraternal counterparts brothers to the bitter end, so too did the state's voting public. Virginia did not rush into secession shortly after Lincoln's election like the states of the lower South. Constitutional Unionist John Bell not only carried the state's electoral votes in 1860 with 44 percent of the popular vote but also secured a large number of urban votes. In urban areas, two-thirds of white men cast their vote for Bell or for northern popular sovereignty advocate Stephen Douglas.[5] It was not until Virginians realized that Lincoln was willing to use military force to prevent the South from seceding that the same men who had held their position as Unionists until as late as March 1861 became fervent Confederates. Virginians approved an ordinance of secession almost immediately after the firing on Fort Sumter in April 1861.[6]

During the war, the Sons of Temperance, Odd Fellows, and Freemasons broke off relations with northern lodges and refused to attend national annual meetings. Virginia's Freemasons argued that both the grand lodge's decision to end communications with their northern brothers and Virginia's decision to secede from the United States were justified. The Grand Lodge of Virginia claimed that it had not violated any Masonic principles in its support of secession.

> This duty as Masons we honestly perform by adhering to the sovereign
> power of our own State. It is under our State government we hold all our
> rights as husbands, fathers, and owners of property. . . . We think it behooves
> us to put this vindication of ourselves as men and citizens on our records
> and permit it to go down to our successors. For while Masonry has nothing
> to do with war or politics, the vindication of our characters as honest men
> and good citizens is dear to us.[7]

Thus, fraternity members contended that Virginia deserved their allegiance because it was the state and not the federal government that defined their public manhood and independent status as heads of their households and protectors of social dependents, including slaves.

After the war, American fraternalism once again experienced a significant rebirth. The postbellum orders served an important function in reunifying the North and the South, and rumors of fraternal recognition on the battlefield during the war grew into legends of fraternity brother helping fraternity brother despite their political differences.[8] A full-scale examination of the role fraternal manhood played in the process of reunion and Reconstruction has yet to be undertaken.

Although the orders were not able to prevent their members from succumbing to sectional animosity, they had played an important role in transforming Virginia's antebellum masculine culture. In the 1830s, Nat Turner's rebellion, the expansion of slave hiring, and the growing number of non-agricultural workers created significant tensions among white men. By the 1840s, burgeoning urbanization and industrialization, combined with the new living arrangements of urban slaves, led white Virginians to believe that the social order as they knew it was rapidly disintegrating. The state's secret fraternal orders helped Virginians adjust to these considerable cultural, economic, and political changes by cultivating harmony among white men across class and partisan divisions. In addition, the orders reinforced and legitimized the values of restrained manhood that promoted self-discipline, upright moral conduct, temperance, and success at work.

Fraternal orders' internal workings helped assuage the strained relationship between white middle- and working-class men. The fictive kinship members cultivated in the lodge room and the heavy emphasis they placed on white male solidarity created a refuge from the cutthroat public world of business and politics. In addition, the collective effect of fraternal rituals, the careful screening of new members, and the policing of the lodge members' behavior created a masculine code of conduct that validated members' independence and respectability as well as helped establish networks of "worthy" men outside of the lodge. Lodge brotherhoods also justified the fraternities' role as the guardians of moral order and protectors of social dependents. The fraternities' exclusion of women and blacks and their system of sick and death benefits allowed a large number of white men from different classes to establish themselves as a group as the defenders of Virginia's dependents and the community in general.

The orders also believed that they had a special duty to protect the nation's republican principles. The orders argued that their ideals of white male equality were part of a time-honored natural social order, offering as evidence the fact that fraternal heritage and rituals could be traced to classical Greco-Roman traditions and the patriotism of the American Revolution. The social hierarchy this invented lineage codified in turn sanctioned the exclusion of women from both fraternal orders and public life. As the special stewards of public virtue, then, the fraternities made charity, benevolence, education, and the quelling of partisan conflict men's exclusive civic responsibilities.

Finally, white men showcased their interclass bonds and new roles as public protectors by participating in parades, commemorations, building dedications, and other public celebrations. Fraternal events and meeting spaces formed a very visible part of the urban public landscape in antebellum Virginia. Thus, as fraternity members filled the public streets alongside politicians, firefighters, and the militia at important civic events, they reinforced the validity of a broader white male claim to political power.

The study of antebellum secret fraternal orders helps elucidate the process by which nonelite white men legitimized their status as independents and shored up new definitions of white manhood. Virginia's secret fraternal orders played an important role in bringing together white men in the 1840s and 1850s. Collectively, these factors also helped to bolster public confidence in nonelite whites, an important precondition to securing universal white male suffrage.

A closer examination of men's organizations also illustrates the interconnectedness of men's and women's social relationships in history. In her book on women in Petersburg, Virginia, historian Suzanne Lebsock tracks the development of a women's culture in antebellum Virginia, noting in her last chapter on women's organizational life that a dearth of comparable information on men's organizations leaves us with no clear idea of how much gender really mattered to the growth and development of the voluntary associations that characterized the first half of the nineteenth century.[9] This study has shown that gender did matter in both women's and men's organizations. Secret fraternal orders fostered a powerful white male solidarity based not just on whiteness but also on a common conception of southern fraternal manhood that defined life beyond the lodge room and affected the lives of both women and men in antebellum Virginia.

APPENDIX

A Note on Terms and Calculations

I have classified fraternity members according to their occupations. Over-whelmingly, fraternity members were artisans or craftsmen and middle-class professionals or businessmen. My term "artisan/craftsman" relies on Ira Berlin and Herbert Gutman's definition of the term "skilled working-men" as a group comprising bricklayers, carpenters, painters, plasterers, stonemasons, and bakers, blacksmiths, butchers, carriage makers, shoemak-ers, printers, jewelers, tailors, tanners, wheelwrights, and clock makers.[1] For middle-class businessmen, I have employed Jonathan Daniel Wells's standards for defining the professional and commercial occupations, a cat-egory that includes grocers, druggists, clerks, merchants, innkeepers, agents, storekeepers, traders, lawyers, doctors, dentists, manufacturers, teachers, en-gineers, and clergymen.[2] I also use the terms "laborer" and "farmer/planter" (listed in the 1850 federal census or in lodge records as a laborer or farmer or planter) and "government/miscellaneous" to describe political and state jobs, such as constable, mayor, clerk of county court, and jobs that didn't fit other categories, such as flour inspector.

I gathered information about fraternity members using lodge rosters from 1850 or from as close to 1850 as possible. Lodge rosters are available in published organizational records or lodge minute books. In the absence of lodge rosters, I used the names of men who attended their order's state meetings as representatives of their local lodge and officers' names that were published in the newspapers.

To calculate the percentages I present as evidence in chapter 2, I first counted the number of men in each lodge for which I had reliable census information. Then I tallied the number of men in each occupational cat-egory and determined what percentage of lodge members belonged to each occupational group. Therefore, the data in chapter 2 represents information about only those men for whom I could find reliable data and not the entire lodge. For example, for Rockingham Union Lodge, no. 27, Masonic lodge, forty-four members were listed on the lodge's 1850 roster. I was able to find reliable census data on only thirty-three of the forty-four men. I have listed them below by occupation:

1 brick mason
1 confectioner
1 "none"
1 mayor of Harrisonburg
1 tavern keeper
1 clerk of the state supreme court
1 dentist
1 physician
1 editor
1 cabinetmaker
1 saddler
5 carpenters
9 merchants
8 farmers

Based on these numbers, I determined that over half the lodge's members held nonagricultural jobs, which were primarily in the commercial, professional, or skilled-labor sectors (table A1). In addition, I found that twenty-one of thirty-three men were also listed as slave owners on the federal slave schedule for Rockingham County, making the percentage of slaveholders in lodge 65.6 percent.

TABLE A1. The Occupational Distribution of Rockingham Union Lodge, No. 27, Freemasons, 1850.

n = 32	Raw number	Percent of lodge
Artisan/craftsman	9	28.1
Professional/commercial	12	37.5
Laborer	0	0
Farmer/planter	8	25
Government/miscellaneous	3	9.4

NOTES

Abbreviations

FM Proceedings *Proceedings of the Grand Annual Communication of the Grand Lodge of Virginia*, Freemasons

OF Proceedings *Journal of the Right Worthy Grand Lodge of Virginia*, 100F (1837–59)

ST Proceedings *Minutes of the Grand Division of the Sons of Temperance of the State of Virginia*

Introduction

1. June 22 and 29, 1847, minute book, Records of Marshall Division; "Initiation," in *Blue Book*, 11–17 (quote on 17).

2. "Initiation," in *Blue Book*, 17–24 (quotes on 21 and 24).

3. Daniel, "Oration," 6.

4. For a good explanation of the market revolution in America, see Stokes, introduction, in *The Market Revolution in America*; Paul E. Johnson, "The Market Revolution," 545–53.

5. For a impressive overview of young men's changing perspectives in the 1850s, see Carmichael, *The Last Generation*, 5–50.

6. See, for example, Genovese, *Roll, Jordan, Roll*, and Merrill, "Cash Is Good to Eat."

7. Watson, "Slavery and the Development in a Dual Economy"; Egerton, "Markets without a Market Revolution"; Johnson, "Market Revolution," 556; Sellers, *The Market Revolution*, 396–427; Hahn, *The Roots of Southern Populism*; Cecil-Fronsman, *Common Whites*. For an alternative interpretation see Escott, "Yeoman Independence and the Market."

8. Freehling, *The Road to Disunion*, 17–24.

9. Towers, *The Urban South*; Wells, *The Origins of the Southern Middle Class*; Lockley, *Welfare and Charity in the Antebellum South*; Byrne, *Becoming Bourgeois*; Gillespie, *Free Labor in an Unfree World*; Barnes, *Artisan Workers in the Upper South*.

10. Engerman, "Southern Industrialization"; Wells, *The Origins of the Southern Middle Class*, 7–8.

11. Majewski, *A House Dividing*; Adams, *Old Dominion, Industrial Commonwealth*; Towers, *The Urban South*; Wells, *The Origins of the Southern Middle Class*; Delfino and Gillespie, eds., *Global Perspectives on Industrial Transformation in the American South*.

12. For examples of this new historical scholarship, see Crofts, "Late Antebellum Virginia Reconsidered"; Kimball, *American City, Southern Place*; Noe,

Southwest Virginia's Railroad; Takagi, *"Rearing Wolves to Our Own Destruction"*; Shade, *Democratizing the Old Dominion*; Tarter, "The New Virginia Bookshelf"; Crofts, *Reluctant Confederates*; Schlotterbeck, "The 'Social Economy' of an Upper South Community"; and Carmichael, *The Last Generation.*

13. Carmichael, *The Last Generation*, 10–18 (quote on 10 and 11).

14. Friend and Glover, "Rethinking Southern Masculinity." For scholarship that links southern manhood to a culture of honor and violence, see Bertram Brown, *Southern Honor*; Kenneth S. Greenberg, *Honor and Slavery*; Gorn, "'Gouge and Bite, Pull Hair and Scratch'"; Ayers, *Vengeance and Justice*; and Proctor, *Bathed in Blood*. For scholarship that examines southern manhood from a new perspective, see Friend and Glover, eds., *Southern Manhood*; Carmichael, *The Last Generation*; Sheehan-Dean, *Why Confederates Fought*; Jabour, "Male Friendship and the Early National South."

15. Amy S. Greenberg, *Manifest Manhood*, 10–12. See also Dorsey, *Reforming Men and Women*, 20–21, 27, 103–8, 124–31.

16. Greenberg, *Manifest Manhood*, 11–12.

17. Important exceptions (although the primary focus of these works is not specifically antebellum fraternalism) include Bullock, *Revolutionary Brotherhood*; Clawson, *Constructing Brotherhood*; Carnes, *Secret Ritual and Manhood in Victorian America*; Brian Greenberg, "Free Labor Fraternalism," 89–101; and Lipson, *Freemasonry in Federalist Connecticut*. The majority of scholarship on the fraternal orders has focused on the history of Freemasonry in the late nineteenth and twentieth centuries, although several important studies examine the history of other orders. See Dumenil, *Freemasonry and American Culture*; Karpeil, "Mystic Ties of Brotherhood"; Beito, *From Mutual Aid to the Welfare State*; Emery and Emery, *A Young Man's Benefit*; Fahey, *Temperance and Racism*; and Jason Kaufman, *For the Common Good*. In addition, several fascinating studies have recently been published that look at Freemasonry outside of the United States. See Jacob, *Living the Enlightenment*; Harland-Jacobs, *Builders of Empire*; Stefan-Ludwig Hoffman, *The Politics of Sociability*; Weisberger, McLeod, and Morris, eds., *Freemasonry on Both Sides of the Atlantic*; and Downes, "Freemasonry in Barbados Before 1914."

18. Gilkeson, *Middle-Class Providence*, 151–55; Deal, "The Forgotten Southerner," 89–80, 154–57, 164–66, 188–89, 198; Blumin, *The Emergence of the Middle-Class*, 192–229; Doyle, "The Social Functions of Voluntary Associations in a Nineteenth-Century American Town"; Click, *The Spirit of the Times*, 75–82; Blocker, *American Temperance Movements*.

19. Wells, *The Origins of the Southern Middle Class*, 6–16, 238; Bledstein, "Introduction: Storytellers to the Middle-Class." For an interesting discussion of southern class formations, also see Goloboy, "Success to Trade," 5–8, 70–80.

20. Wells, *The Origins of the Southern Middle Class*, 12.

21. Barnes, *Artisan Workers in the Upper South*, 66–113; Gillespie, *Free Labor in*

an Unfree World, xvii–xxii, 97–134, 170–71. See also Laurie, "'We are Not Afraid to Work.'"

22. Emery and Emery, *A Young Man's Benefit*, 6–7.

Chapter One. White Male Political Culture in Antebellum Virginia

1. Nicholas, "The Freehold Suffrage Defended," 395; Bruce, *The Rhetoric of Conservatism*, 89–92. For other examples of conservative rhetoric that claimed that natural equality, if taken literally, would bring social chaos and lead to voting rights for women and possibly slaves, see the speeches of Abel Parker Upshur and Benjamin Watkins Leigh, *Richmond Enquirer*, October 29, 1829.

2. Bruce, *The Rhetoric of Conservatism*, 2, 66; Shade, *Democratizing the Old Dominion*, 65–77.

3. Sutton, *Revolution to Secession*, 124–28, 135–38; Link, *The Roots of Secession*, 25–26.

4. Sutton, *Revolution to Secession*, 62–71; Shade, *Democratizing the Old Dominion*, 264.

5. Shade, *Democratizing the Old Dominion*, 66–77; Bruce, *The Rhetoric of Conservatism*, 66, 75–76; Leigh, "Power and Property," 336; Philip Barbour, *Richmond Enquirer*, October 29, 1829; Randolph, "Randolph on the Federal Issue," 352.

6. Leigh, "Power and Property," 337, 343; Eaton, "Southern Senators and the Right of Instruction," 312.

7. Eaton, "Southern Senators and the Right of Instruction," 312; Ambler, *Sectionalism in Virginia*, 167.

8. "Non-Freeholders' Memorial," 378, 382.

9. Doddridge, "Doddridge in Rebuttal," 336.

10. Morgan, "The Reformers' Rebuttal," 408–9. See also Summers, "Summers on the Gordon Plan," 377. After the convention, Morgan went on to become the superintendent of the Virginia penitentiary, a position he held for most of the antebellum era.

11. George M. Frederickson first used the word "herrenvolk," meaning "master race," to describe race relations in the American South. In theory, a herrenvolk democracy was a society in which all whites, regardless of class, were superior to all blacks (Frederickson, *The Black Image in the White Mind*, 61–70). See also McCurry, *Masters of Small Worlds*, 93, 232, 240, 251; Ford, "Making the 'White Man's Country' White," 735–37; Roediger, *The Wages of Whiteness*, 59–60; and Ashworth, *Commerce and Compromise*, 210–15, 231.

12. Freehling, *Drift Toward Dissolution*, 1–6.

13. Freehling, *Drift Toward Dissolution*, 125, 145–48; Shade, *Democratizing the Old Dominion*, 196–203. Although one Quaker petition to the legislature advocated the complete and immediate abolition of slavery and the restoration of natural rights to blacks, the majority of those in favor of ending slavery in Virginia were

not racial egalitarians and supported gradual emancipation or colonization. Four basic positions emerged out of the debates: that free blacks be removed from the state; that slaves be gradually emancipated and then colonized; that they be emancipated and the slave owners compensated; and that they remain enslaved.

14. Ashworth, *Commerce and Compromise*, 216–20. See also Oakes, *The Ruling Race*, xi–xiii, 192–217. A number of the most prominent proslavery thinkers of the antebellum period were Virginians. Thomas Dew, Abel Parker Upshur, Thornton Stringfellow, Alfred Bledsoe, Edmund Ruffin, and George Fitzhugh were all Virginians.

15. Upshur, "Domestic Slavery," 678, 683–85. Upshur, however, also operated under the faulty assumption that Virginia's slaves were content with their position at the bottom of the social ladder.

16. Upshur, "Domestic Slavery," 680.

17. Shade, *Democratizing the Old Dominion*, 34–35

18. Shade, *Democratizing the Old Dominion*, 41–43; Goldfield, *Urban Growth in the Age of Sectionalism*, 9–12, 183–89.

19. Shade, *Democratizing the Old Dominion*, 41–43; Goldfield, *Urban Growth in the Age of Sectionalism*, 9–12, 183–89; Crofts, "Late Antebellum Virginia Reconsidered," 256; Noe, *Southwest Virginia's Railroad*, 15–30; Siegel, *The Roots of Southern Distinctiveness*, 52–57; Schlotterbeck, "The 'Social Economy' of an Upper South Community," 21–22; Lebsock, *The Free Women of Petersburg*, 10–15; Kimball, *American City, Southern Place*, 16–21; Tripp, *Yankee Town, Southern City*, 7, 9–11; Barnes, *Artisan Workers in the Upper South*, 12, 26–7.

20. Schlotterbeck, "The 'Social Economy' of an Upper South Community," 21–22; Carmichael, *The Last Generation*, 37. See also Wells, *The Origins of the Southern Middle Class*, 19–39, and Byrne, *Becoming Bourgeois*, 25–35.

21. Barnes, *Artisan Workers in the Upper South*, 8, 40, 49–54, 68–75.

22. Shade, *Democratizing the Old Dominion*, 31; Siegel, *The Roots of Southern Distinctiveness*, 104–6; Goldfield, *Urban Growth in the Age of Sectionalism*, 3.

23. Goldfield, *Urban Growth in the Age of Sectionalism*, xv; Crofts, "Late Antebellum Virginia Reconsidered," 256–57; Shade, *Democratizing the Old Dominion*, 36–37; Barnes, *Artisan Workers in the Upper South*, 23–36.

24. Shade, *Democratizing the Old Dominion*, 32–33; Noe, *Virginia's Southwestern Railroad*, 35–39; Siegel, *The Roots of Southern Distinctiveness*, 47–57, 100–106, 120–30; Takagi, "*Rearing Wolves to Our Own Destruction*," 71.

25. Noe, *Southwest Virginia's Railroad*, 48–52; Schlotterbeck, "The 'Social Economy' of an Upper South Community," 14–16; Berlin and Gutman, "Natives and Immigrants, Free Men and Slaves," 1191; Siegel, *The Roots of Southern Distinctiveness*, 114–15.

26. Robert W. Ransone to Thomas Armistead Coleman, February 13, 1845, in Robins Family Papers, sec. 77.

27. Barnes, *Artisan Workers in the Upper South*, 32, 215; Steger, "'United to Support, But Not Combined to Injure,'" 77; Berlin and Gutman, "Natives and Immigrants, Free Men and Slaves," 1177–87; Schlotterbeck, "The 'Social Economy' of an Upper South Community," 14–16, 21–22; Goldfield, *Urban Growth in the Age of Sectionalism*, 97–109.

28. Shade, *Democratizing the Old Dominion*, 34–35, 49. For a statistical breakdown of the occupations of free men over the age of fifteen in Virginia from the 1850 federal census, see also DeBow, *Statistical View of the United States*, 128.

29. Carmichael, *The Last Generation*, 22–30; see also Byrne, *Becoming Bourgeois*, 4, 11–12, and Wells, *The Origins of the Southern Middle Class*, 15–16.

30. Schlotterbeck, "The 'Social Economy' of an Upper South Community," 14–16, 21–22; Kimball, *American City, Southern Place*, 167–71; Noe, *Southwest Virginia's Railroad*, 43–52, 70–83; Siegel, *The Roots of Southern Distinctiveness*, 130–37; Takagi, *"Rearing Wolves to Our Own Destruction,"* 82–87.

31. See especially Steger, "'United to Support, But Not Combined to Injure,'" 109, 113–16, 123–28, 139, and Wells, *The Origins of the Southern Middle Class*, 180–82, 185–89, 191.

32. Martin, *Divided Mastery*, 1–13; Zaborney, "Slaves for Rent"; Takagi, *"Rearing Wolves to Our Own Destruction,"* 1–2, 72.

33. Noe, *Southwest Virginia's Railroad*, 82–83.

34. Freehling, *Road to Disunion*, 23–24; Deyle, *Carry Me Back*, 4–7; Walter Johnson, *Soul by Soul*, 214–16.

35. Martin, *Divided Mastery*, 1–13; Zaborney, "Slaves for Rent," 205–13. This has also prompted fascinating new historical research on the slave insurance industry. See Murphy, "Securing Human Property."

36. Martin, *Divided Mastery*, 164–73, 183–87; Siegel, *The Roots of Southern Distinctiveness*, 136; Tripp, *Yankee Town, Southern City*, 12–15, 18–21; Takagi, *"Rearing Wolves to Our Own Destruction,"* 72, 114–15.

37. Noe, *Southwest Virginia's Railroad*, 82–83; Zaborney, "Slaves for Rent," 206; Steger, "'United to Support, But Not Combined to Injure,'" 114–18.

38. Wells, *The Origins of the Southern Middle Class*, 185–89; Schechter, "Free and Slave Labor in the Old South," 173. Schechter and Wells also note the existence of similar tensions between white workers and slave laborers in other southern cities, such as Baltimore, Savannah, Birmingham, and Charleston.

39. Wells, *The Origins of the Southern Middle Class*, 189.

40. Schechter, "Free and Slave Labor in the Old South," 165–86; Kimball, *American City, Southern Place*, 167–71; Takagi, *"Rearing Wolves to Our Own Destruction,"* 82–87; Wells, *The Origins of the Southern Middle Class*, 185–89.

41. Bean, "The Ruffner Pamphlet of 1847," 265–67; Peyton, *History of Augusta County, Virginia*, 220–21; *Lexington Gazette*, February 25, 1847, quoted in Bean, "The Ruffner Pamphlet of 1847," 267.

42. Bean, "The Ruffner Pamphlet of 1847," 268, 270–71. It is important to note that Ruffner was far from being a racial egalitarian. His condemnation of slavery arose from his belief that slavery was damaging to white society.

43. Shade, *Democratizing the Old Dominion*, 96–97, 170; Sutton, *Revolution to Secession*, 103–21; Bean, "The Ruffner Pamphlet of 1847," 265–67; Steger, "'United to Support, But Not Injure,'" 108–9. See also "Convention Bill," *Richmond Enquirer*, October 9, 1846, and "A State Convention," *Richmond Enquirer*, December 4, 1849.

44. Simpson, "Political Compromise and the Protection of Slavery." See also Gaines, "The Virginia Constitutional Convention of 1850–51," 153–60; Sutton, *Revolution to Secession*, 103–41; and Link, *The Roots of Secession*, 11–27.

45. Link, *The Roots of Secession*, 13–26; Sutton, *Revolution to Secession*, 128–35.

46. Link, *The Roots of Secession*, 128–35.

47. Simpson, "Political Compromise and the Protection of Slavery," 392.

48. Faulkner, *Speech of C. J. Faulkner*, 6–7.

49. Gaines, "The Virginia Convention of 1850–51," 247; Pulliam, *The Constitutional Conventions of Virginia*, 94.

50. *Richmond Enquirer*, November 11, 1851, quoted in Link, *The Roots of Secession*, 26.

51. Naragon, "Ballets, Bullets, and Blood," 154, 169–71; *Presidential Elections*, 92–93; Link, *The Roots of Secession*, 132–36; Bladek, "'Virginia Is Middle Ground,'" 59.

52. "A Statement Shewing the Number of White Males and White Females, n.p.; *ST Proceedings*, January 1852, 258; *OF Proceedings*, 1851, 664; *FM Proceedings*, 1851, 59–95.

53. "A Statement Shewing the Number of White Males and White Females." For membership statistics of Richmond Lodges (including Manchester), see *ST Proceedings*, July 1850, 202–13; *OF Proceedings*, 1851, 662–64; and *FM Proceedings*, 1851, 59–95. Richmond had 4,404 free white adult men in 1850, and the lodges collectively had a membership of 1,780 men (100F, 690; Masons, 266; Sons, 824).

54. See *Richmond Daily Dispatch*, January 19, 1852, March 24, 1852, July 28, 1856; *Staunton Spectator*, February 23, 1853, February 8, 1855; and Cherry, *The Improved Order of Red Men in Virginia*.

Chapter Two. Secret Fraternal Orders in Antebellum Virginia

1. Syrett, *The Company He Keeps*, 51–78.

2. Barnes, *Artisan Workers in the Upper South*, 37–65.

3. Lockley, *Welfare and Charity in the Antebellum South*, 132–40; Green, *This Business of Relief*, 49–50; "First Annual Report of the Gentlemen's Benevolent Society," *Richmond Enquirer*, November 21, 1845; Duke, "The Richmond Home for Boys."

4. Varon, *We Mean to Be Counted*, 86–88.

5. Kimball, *American City, Southern Place*, 183–214; Amy S. Greenberg, *Cause for*

Alarm, 11–17, 41–66. See also *Constitution and By-Laws of the Petersburg, Virginia Fire Company*, in Spotswood Family Papers, sec. 4.

6. Kimball, *American City, Southern Place*, 191–93; Greenberg, *Cause for Alarm*, 15–16.

7. Stevens, ed., *The Cyclopedia of Fraternities*, vii.

8. Jacob, *Living the Enlightenment*, 34–36; Bullock, *Revolutionary Brotherhood*, 9–49; Lipson, *Freemasonry in Federalist Connecticut*, 13–45; Rutyna and Stewart, *The History of Freemasonry in Virginia*, 3–10, 29–30.

9. See Bullock, *Revolutionary Brotherhood*, 137–38, 150–53; Wood, *The Radicalism of the American Revolution*, 223–24; Travers, "'In the Greatest Solemn Dignity'"; Curl, "The Capitol in Washington, D.C., and Its Freemasonic Connections"; Brooke, "Ancient Lodges and Self-Created Societies"; and Lipson, *Freemasonry in Federalist Connecticut*.

10. Bullock, *Revolutionary Brotherhood*, 207–13, 222–25.

11. Carnes, *Secret Ritual and Manhood in Victorian America*, 22–24; Rutyna and Stewart, *The History of Freemasonry in Virginia*, 290–92; Lipson, *Freemasonry in Federalist Connecticut*, 260–64.

12. Heitmann, *A History and Manual of the Independent Order of Odd Fellows*, 14–15, 18–22. See also Grosh, *The Odd-Fellow's Manual*, 25–52.

13. Bullock, *Revolutionary Brotherhood*, 277–78; Vaughn, *The Antimasonic Party in the United States*, 1–6; Tabbert, *American Freemasons*, 58–59.

14. Vaughn, *The Antimasonic Party in the United States*, 2, Bullock, *Revolutionary Brotherhood*, 296–98; Tabbert, *American Freemasons*, 59–61; "Hon. Edward Evert's Opinion of Secret Societies."

15. Bullock, *Revolutionary Brotherhood*, 277–307; Vaughn, *The Antimasonic Party in the United States*, 3–20; Tabbert, *American Freemasons*, 62–64; Rutyna and Stewart, *The History of Freemasonry in Virginia*, 253–63, 433.

16. Stevens, ed., *Cyclopedia of Fraternities*, vii, 238–45, 254–58, 284–86, 290, 311–15, 403, 409–10. The fraternal orders that are more well known today—such as the Knights of Pythias, the Grand Army of the Republic, the Loyal Order of Moose, the Shriners, the Benevolent and Protective Order of Elks, the Fraternal Order of Eagles, and the Woodmen of the World—were all established after the Civil War.

17. Carnes, *Secret Ritual and Manhood in Victorian America*, 23–24, 26–27, 31–33.

18. Carnes, *Secret Ritual and Manhood in Victorian America*, 27–36, 51–65; Bullock, *Revolutionary Brotherhood*, 242, 316–19.

19. See Bullock, *Revolutionary Brotherhood*, 188–98; *By-Laws for the Government of Richmond Lodge*, 5–6.

20. Clawson, *Constructing Brotherhood*, 118; Beito, *From Mutual Aid to the Welfare State*, 9–11; Carnes, *Secret Ritual and Manhood in Victorian America*, 26; Bullock *Revolutionary Brotherhood*, 194. For more information regarding the Odd Fellows' benefits in the late nineteenth and early twentieth centuries, see Emery and Emery, *A Young Man's Benefit*.

21. I use the word "lodge" generically throughout the book to refer to the each fraternity's most basic subordinate lodges. Most of the other orders, however, referred to their subordinate lodges according to the organizational theme of their fraternity. For example the Sons of Temperance called their subordinate lodges "divisions," the Red Men used "tribes," the Order of United American Mechanics "councils," and the Druids "groves."

22. Rutyna and Stewart, *The History of Freemasonry in Virginia*, 269.

23. Rutyna and Stewart, *The History of Freemasonry in Virginia*, 269–70; Carnes, *Secret Ritual and Manhood in Victorian America*, 28–29.

24. *FM Proceedings*, 1851, 59–94.

25. Heitmann, *A History and Manual of the Independent Order of Odd Fellow*, 101–2; *OF Proceedings*, April 1840, 167; *OF Proceedings*, 1850, 588–90. The Grand Lodge of Virginia met twice a year until 1844, after which it met annually.

26. Blocker, *American Temperance Movements*, 39.

27. Blocker, *American Temperance Movements*, 1–29, 39. See also Raymond Pulley, "General Cocke and the Temperance Crusade"; Varon, *We Mean to Be Counted*, 30–37; Hewitt, *Women's Activism and Social Change*, 99–113; Walters, *American Reformers*, 123–30.

28. Blocker, *American Temperance Movements*, 35–39; Tyrrell, "Drink and Temperance in the Antebellum South," 490; Walters, *American Reformers*, 131.

29. Blocker, *American Temperance Movements*, 48–50; Tyrrell, *Sobering Up*, 203–12.

30. Varon, *We Mean to Be Counted*, 31–34; Pearson and Hendricks, *Liquor and Anti-Liquor in Virginia*, 58–61.

31. Evans, ed., *A Digest of the Resolutions and Decisions of the National Division of the Sons of Temperance*, 5.

32. *ST Proceedings*, April 1850, 156–65; Tyrrell, "Drink and Temperance in the Antebellum South," 491.

33. Evans, ed., *A Digest of the Resolutions and Decisions of the National Division of the Sons of Temperance*, 2.

34. Martin, *Prize Essay on the Principles and Operations of the Order of the Sons of Temperance*, 12.

35. Powers, *Address Delivered before the Sons of Temperance*, 12–13; Martin, *Prize Essay on the Principles and Operations of the Order of the Sons of Temperance*, 13–14.

36. *By-Laws for the Government of Richmond Lodge*, 5–6; *Constitution, By-Laws and Rules of Order of Old Dominion Lodge*, 12; June 28, 1851, minute book, Records of Madison Division.

37. Dove, *The Masonic Textbook*, 83–86; *Constitution and By-Laws of Micajah Pendleton Division*, 6–7; *Constitution, By-Laws, and Rules of Order of Old Dominion Lodge*, 8; *By-Laws for the Government of Richmond Lodge*, 4–5.

38. *Constitution and By-Laws of Micajah Pendleton Division*, 3.

39. Phillip I. Barziza to Charles W. Montague, October 8, 1850, Montague Family Papers, sec. 2.

40. Grosh, *The Odd-Fellow's Manual*, 211–14; Withers, *An Address, Delivered at Masonic Hall*, 15–16; July 16, 1844, minute book, Records of Marshall Division.

41. Dove, *The Masonic Textbook*, 83–86; *Constitution and By-Laws of Micajah Pendleton Division*, 6–7; *Constitution, By-Laws and Rules of Old Dominion Lodge*, 8; *By-Laws for the Government of Richmond Lodge*, 4–5.

42. Strange, *Address Delivered at the Dedication of the New Masonic Hall*, 10.

43. McCabe, *Address before Hawkins Lodge*, 19.

44. Myers, *Address Delivered by W. Samuel H. Myers*, 6; Caldwell, *Masonry Its Own Defence*, 12.

45. "Odd-fellowship," 82.

46. Scott, "Address," *FM Proceedings*, 1845, 56.

47. Powers, *Address Delivered before the Sons of Temperance*, 13; Taylor, *Temperance Address, before the Lexington Division*, 6.

48. "Odd-fellowship," 82.

49. "Odd-fellowship," 75.

50. See Carnes, *Secret Ritual and Manhood in Victorian America*, 26–29, 31–35; Clawson, *Constructing Brotherhood*, 119–20; Click, *The Spirit of the Times*, 75–82; Gilkeson, *Middle-Class Providence*, 151–55; Brian Greenberg, "Free Labor Fraternalism," 89–101; Ryan, *Cradle of the Middle Class*, 105–44; Deal, "The Forgotten Southerner," 89–90, 154–57, 164–66, 188–89, 198; Blumin, *The Emergence of the Middle Class*, 150–65, 166–89; Doyle, "The Social Functions of Voluntary Associations," 336, 339–43; Rorabaugh, "The Sons of Temperance in Antebellum Jasper County," 266–68; Carlson, "'Drinks He to His Own Undoing,'" 668–69; Eslinger, "Antebellum Liquor Reform in Lexington, Virginia," 168–69; Tyrrell, "Drink and Temperance in the Antebellum South," 492–94; and Quist, *Restless Visionaries*, 220–27, 261–64, 286, 290.

51. Membership rosters from Richmond lodges Nos. 10, 19, 36, 51, and 53 and Rockingham Union Lodge, no. 27, are found in *FM Proceedings*, 1850. Occupational data was obtained from U.S. Census Office, Seventh Census of the United States, 1850, Virginia, Free Population Schedules, Henrico, Rockingham, and Appomattox Counties. Please see the appendix for more information regarding these calculations.

52. *OF Proceedings*, 1849, 1853; *Richmond Daily Dispatch*, January 15, 1852, March 26, 1852, April 1, 2, 1852; *Richmond Enquirer*, February 22, 1850; Records of Chesapeake Lodge; Records of Marshall Lodge (n.b.: record incorrectly labels order as the "International Order of Odd Fellows"); U.S. Census Office, Seventh Census of the United States, 1850, Virginia, Free Population Schedules, Henrico and Mathews Counties. Some lodge rosters from 1857 are also found in the *Proceedings of the Right Worthy Grand Lodge of Virginia*, 65–99.

53. *ST Proceedings*, July 1848, October 1849, October 1850, January 1852; *Richmond Daily Dispatch*, January 19, 1852, March 26, 1852, April 4, 1852, June 3, 4, 5, 15, 1852; *Richmond Enquirer*, February 22, 1850; Records of Marshall Division; Records of Mount Crawford Division; Records of Mount Hermon Division; Hill, "Sons of Temperance"; U.S. Census Office, Seventh Census of the United States, 1850, Virginia, Free Population Schedules, Henrico and Rockingham Counties. See also Tyrrell, "Drink and Temperance in the Antebellum South," 492–94, and Eslinger, "Antebellum Liquor Reform in Lexington, Virginia," 163–64.

54. Slave-owning data obtained from U.S. Census Office, Seventh Census of the United States, 1850, Virginia, Slave Population Schedules, Henrico, Buckingham, Rockingham, Appomattox, and Mathews Counties. For membership rosters, see *FM Proceedings*, 1851; *OF Proceedings*, 1849, 1853; *ST Proceedings*, July 1848, October 1849, October 1850, January 1852; *Richmond Daily Dispatch*, January 15, 19, 1852, March 26, 1852, April 1, 2, 4, 1852, June 3, 4, 5, 15, 1852; *Richmond Enquirer*, February 22, 1850; Records of Marshall Division; Records of Mount Crawford Division; and Records of Chesapeake Lodge. The percentage of slaveholders for the Odd Fellows could be slightly higher than average. I had to use the names of the officers and grand representatives owing to the scarcity of lodge rosters, and these may have been some of the wealthier members of the order who could afford to do more traveling and be away from their businesses more frequently than other members. Unfortunately, there are no other studies of other southern Odd Fellows or Freemasons with which to compare this data.

55. See Blocker, *American Temperance Movements*, 50–51; Rorabaugh, "The Sons of Temperance in Antebellum Jasper County"; Quist, *Restless Visionaries*; Carlson, "'Drinks He to His Own Undoing'"; Tyrrell, "Drink and Temperance in the Antebellum South." There were more slave owners among Sons in Georgia, Alabama, and South Carolina, and a higher percentage of them were involved in agriculture.

56. Carlson, "'Drinks He to His Own Undoing,'" 659–63; Tyrrell, "Drink and Temperance in the Antebellum South," 485–510; Eslinger, "Antebellum Liquor Reform in Lexington, Virginia," 163–86; Rorabaugh, "The Sons of Temperance in Antebellum Jasper County," 263–79; Quist, *Restless Visionaries*, 220.

57. Blocker, *American Temperance Movements*, 50; Carlson, "'Drinks He to His Own Undoing,'" 681–82, 687–89; Eslinger, "Antebellum Liquor Reform in Lexington, Virginia," 165–73; Quist, *Restless Visionaries*, 303, 306–7, 337–38. See also Parsons, *Manhood Lost*, 55–68.

58. Berlin, *Slaves without Masters*, 308–15; Palmer, "Negro Secret Societies," 209.

59. Butler, "Black Fraternal and Benevolent Societies in Nineteenth-Century America," 85–88; Skocpol and Oser, "Organization despite Adversity," 392–97; Walker, "'The Freemasonry of the Race,'" 167–69; Brooks, *The Official History and Manual of the Grand United Order of Odd Fellows in America*, 94–110. See also Fahey, *Temperance and Racism*, 105–25.

60. Bullock, *Revolutionary Brotherhood*, 158–59; Walker, "The Freemasonry of the Race," 42–45, 74.

61. Bullock, *Revolutionary Brotherhood*, 159–60; Freehling, *Drift Toward Dissolution*, 82–83; Walker, "'The Freemasonry of Race,'" 145.

62. *Norfolk American Beacon*, September 5, 1852.

63. In 1846, the city of Alexandria was retroceded to Virginia, and if Universal Lodge had been legally established in the District of Columbia, it became illegal under Virginia law.

64. *Norfolk American Beacon*, September 1, 1852. See also *Norfolk American Beacon*, September 5, 1852.

65. Prince Hall, "History of the Prince Hall Masons in Virginia"; Walker, "'The Freemasonry of Race,'" 167–69.

66. Dove, *The Masonic Textbook*, 83, 87.

67. "Report of the Foreign Correspondence Committee," in *FM Proceedings*, 1846, 24–26; "Report of the Foreign Correspondence Committee," in *FM Proceedings*, 1847, 21. See also Loretta J. Williams, *Black Freemasonry and Middle-Class Realities*.

68. "Report of the Foreign Correspondence Committee," in *FM Proceedings*, 1846, 22–26.

69. Brooks, *The Official History and Manual of the Grand United Order of Odd Fellows in America*, 12–31.

70. Brooks, *The Grand United Order of Odd Fellows in America*, 18–31, 32; *Proceedings of the National Division of the Sons of Temperance*, 18–21; Blocker, *American Temperance Movements*, 50; Carlson, "'Drinks He to His Own Undoing,'" 668.

71. *Rules of Order, Constitution, and General Laws, of the R.W. Grand Lodge of Virginia*, 55. For example, see *Constitution, By-Laws, and Rules of Order of Old Dominion Lodge*, 8.

72. OF *Proceedings*, 1858, 962–64; OF *Proceedings*, 1859, 1003–6.

73. OF *Proceedings*, 1858, 962–64; OF *Proceedings*, 1859, 1003–6, 1004.

74. Fahey, *Temperance and Racism*, 105.

75. *ST Proceedings*, July 1850, 176; *ST Proceedings*, October 1851, 217.

76. "Sons of Temperance: Disbandment of Southport Division," *Liberator*, September 6, 1850.

77. *ST Proceedings*, July 1850, 176.

78. *ST Proceedings*, October 1851, 217.

79. Pearson and Hendricks, *Liquor and Anti-Liquor in Virginia*, 117.

80. Pearson and Hendricks, *Liquor and Anti-Liquor in Virginia*, 27–28.

81. Eslinger, "Antebellum Liquor Reform in Lexington, Virginia," 169–71, 173, 178.

82. Williams, Minor, Willey, Preston, and Cross, *Address to the People of Virginia, by the State Temperance Convention*, 7–8.

Chapter Three. Keeping Out the Unworthy

1. "Cornerstone of Odd Fellows Hall," 4–5; Daniel, "Oration," 6–7, 11.

2. Jefferson Wallace to Charles Blair, November 27, 1854, quoted in Kimball, *American City, Southern Place*, 15.

3. Halttunen, *Confidence Men and Painted Women*, 33–44, 192–94.

4. Rooker, *Oration before the Independent Order of Odd Fellows*, 8–9.

5. Rooker, *Oration before the Independent Order of Odd Fellows*, 9–10.

6. Rooker, *Oration before the Independent Order of Odd Fellows*, 9–11.

7. Withers, *An Address, Delivered at Masonic Hall*, 16.

8. Byrne, *Becoming Bourgeois*, 27–30. See also Eelman, *Entrepreneurs in the Southern Upcountry*.

9. Adam W. Plecker to Peter S. Roller, April 27, 1848, Roller Family Papers, box 2. Both Plecker and Roller were active members of the Mount Crawford Division, no. 19, of the Sons of Temperance. "Skelton" may be a reference to lodge brother and blacksmith George Skelton.

10. John H. Blakemore to Peter S. Roller, January 15, 1847, Roller Family Papers, box 1.

11. Accounts, 1848–54, Records of Randolph Lodge.

12. March 31, 1849, minutes, Records of Madison Division.

13. *Independent Odd-Fellow* (September 1841): 95. Odd Fellows in New England published a similar directory. See *The Symbol and Odd Fellows's Magazine* 4 (December 1845): 564.

14. Hyneman, ed., *Universal Masonic Record and Directory*.

15. For examples, see *FM Proceedings*, 1851, *ST Proceedings*, July 1847, and "Notice of Rejections, Suspensions, Expulsions," 1850–57, Records of Chesapeake Lodge.

16. *ST Proceedings*, July 1847.

17. These black books are very difficult to find and are not identified as such in archival records and databases. See for example the black book for Virginia Sons of Temperance, Mount Crawford Division, no. 19, listed as "Alphabet of Divisions" among the bound volumes in the records of Mount Crawford Division at UVA. A black book created by multiple Odd Fellows' lodges in antebellum Massachusetts and identified as "B.B." is in the private collection of Michael P. Musick, Harpers Ferry, West Virginia.

18. *ST Proceedings*, January 1848, 14.

19. "To All Odd-Fellows and Others throughout the World," 92.

20. "To All Odd-Fellows and Others throughout the World," 92–93. See also see "Beware of the Swindler!" *Staunton Spectator*, June 13, 1849, and "Look Out for Swindler!" 865.

21. Byrne, *Becoming Bourgeois*, 33–35; Wells, *The Origins of the Southern Middle Class*, 62–63.

22. Caldwell, *Masonry Its Own Defence*, 14 (his emphasis).

23. Mandell, "Celebration in Fredericksburg," 283.

24. "Charles Stedom, or the Wealthy Odd Fellow," *Abingdon Virginian*, February 12, 26, 1853.

25. Mandell, "Celebration in Fredericksburg," 283.

26. *Constitution, By-Laws and Rules of Order, of Springfield Division*, 17; *By-Laws and Rules of Order of Appomattox Lodge*, 24; Caldwell, *Masonry Its Own Defence*, 9; Shaver, *An Address Delivered before Lebanon Lodge*, 12. They also sat with the bodies of deceased members during the time between death and burial.

27. Albert D. Clarke to Rodolpus Clarke, April 17, 1843, Albert D. Clarke, Personal Papers Collection.

28. Kemper, *An Address, Delivered at Standardsville, Virginia*, 3.

29. Strange, *Address Delivered at the Dedication of the New Masonic Hall*, 8–9.

30. "Quid Nunc?" 32; Taliaferro, *An Address, Delivered before the Masonic Fraternity of Williamsburg, Virginia*, 26; Daniel, "Oration," 12.

31. Bullock, *Revolutionary Brotherhood*, 64–65, 259–60.

32. For a detailed analysis of fraternal rituals after the Civil War see Carnes, *Secret Ritual and Manhood in Victorian America*.

33. See Halttunen, *Confidence Men and Painted Women*, 102–9, for the rituals involved in entering the parlor.

34. Caldwell, *Masonry Its Own Defence*, 20.

35. *By-Laws and Rules of Order of Union Lodge*, 21.

36. McCabe, *Address before Hawkins Lodge*, 22. On processions, see also chapter 5.

37. "Regalia," in *Blue Book*, 43–44.

38. Powers, *Address Delivered before the Sons of Temperance*, 12; Rooker, *Oration before the Independent Order of Odd Fellows*, 9.

39. "Initiation," in *Blue Book*, 25. For an example of a password, see "Traveling Password and Explanation," December 17, 1855, in Asa Holland Papers, and "Key," in *Blue Book*, 45.

40. "Inside Sentinel Card," in Records of the Mount Hermon Division, fol. 7; "Initiation," in *Blue Book*, 25.

41. Thomson, *An Address Delivered before Benevolentia Lodge*, 12.

42. Caldwell, *Masonry Its Own Defence*, 12.

43. Rooker, *Oration before the Independent Order of Odd Fellows*, 10.

44. Finley, *An Address Delivered before Naval Lodge*, 7.

45. McCabe, *Address before Hawkins Lodge*, 19–22.

46. Taylor, *Temperance Address, before the Lexington Division*, 2.

47. "General Laws: For the Government of Subordinate Lodges, Working under Charter from the Grand Lodge of Virginia, IOOF," in *OF Proceedings*, 1837, 25–28; *Constitution and By-Laws of Micajah Pendleton Division*, 15; Dove, *The Masonic Textbook*, 95–96.

48. October 22, 1851, November 14, 1851, minute book, Records of Mossy Creek Division.

49. Withers, *An Address, Delivered at Masonic Hall*, 17. See also Shaver, *An Address Delivered before Lebanon Lodge*, 4.

50. *FM Proceedings*, 1846, 14.

51. Shaver, *An Address Delivered before Lebanon Lodge*, 11.

52. December 20, 1850, April 19, 1851, April 27, 1851, minute book, Records of Mount Crawford Division.

53. McCabe, *Address before Hawkins Lodge*, 19; Myers, *Address Delivered by W. Samuel H. Myers*, 8.

54. Strange, *Address Delivered at the Dedication of the New Masonic Hall*, 12

55. December 19, 1851, minute book, Records of Covington Division.

56. "Notice of Rejections, Suspensions, Expulsions," 1850–57, Records of Chesapeake Lodge.

57. N.d. [April 1848], April 29, 1848, minute book, Records of Mount Crawford Division.

58. N.d. [April 1848], April 29, 1848, minute book, Records of Mount Crawford Division.

59. Pfifer may have found Smith's offer to be particularly insulting because it had a racial connotation. Very often slaves were forced to supplement their diet with small game animals in order to provide enough food for themselves and their families. Muskrat, along with opossum and skunk, was sometimes eaten when no other food could be obtained. Perhaps, then, Smith was offering Pfifer what they both considered to be "slave" food. See Proctor, *Bathed in Blood*, 150–51.

60. April 29, 1848, minute book, Records of Mount Crawford Division .

61. April 29, 1848, minute book, Records of Mount Crawford Division; "Roster Book of Expulsions, 1846–1860," Records of Mount Crawford Division, box 1, 2.

62. *OF Proceedings*, 1846, 356–59.

63. *OF Proceedings*, 1846, 359.

Chapter Four. Securing the Republic

1. Kammen, *A Season of Youth*, 49–51; Kruman, "The Second Party System and the Transformation of Revolutionary Republicanism," 510, 521–25; Wood, *The Radicalism of the American Revolution*, 230–31; Steven Mintz, *Moralists and Modernizers*, xiii–xv.

2. McCabe, *Address before Hawkins Lodge*, 7–24 (quotes on 7–8 and 19). For other examples of this fear of moral deterioration and fraternal solutions, see McElroy, *An Address Delivered before a Convention of Masons*, 8–11; Powers, *Address Delivered before the Sons of Temperance*, 7–8.

3. Campbell, *Slavery on Trial*, 44.

4. Goldfield, *Urban Growth in the Age of Sectionalism*, 142–46; Campbell, *Slavery on Trial*, 41–49, 61–68; Kimball, *American City, Southern Place*, 46–48; Eslinger, "Antebellum Liquor Reform in Lexington, Virginia," 170–75; Tripp, *Yankee City, Southern Town*, 71–77 (discusses late 1850s).

5. "Morals of the Country," *Danville Reporter*, June 24, 1842.

6. Kimball, *American City, Southern Place*, xix.

7. Virginia Society, 1834 annual report, quoted in Forrest L. Marion, "'All That Is Pure in Religion and Valuable in Society,'" 201.

8. *Norfolk Southern Argus*, June 18, 1850, quoted in Goldfield, *Urban Growth in the Age of Sectionalism*, 143.

9. Quist, *Restless Visionaries*, 7, 19–101; Lockley, *Welfare and Charity*, 60–114; Green, *This Business of Relief*, 46–48; Varon, *We Mean to Be Counted*, 23–35; Lebsock, *Free Women of Petersburg*, 212–16. See also Bellows, *Benevolence among Slaveholders*.

10. Varon, *We Mean to Be Counted*, 10–40; Lebsock, *Free Women of Petersburg*, 195–236; Green, *This Business of Relief*, 46–50; Marion, "'All That Is Pure in Religion and Valuable in Society,'" 192, 198–216.

11. Green, *This Business of Relief*, 55–56, 60–61, 222 (table 4); Lebsock, *Free Women of Petersburg*, 213–15; Lockley, *Welfare and Charity*, 28, 30–47.

12. Green, *This Business of Relief*, 44–47; Lockley, *Welfare and Charity*, 97–102; Dorsey, *Reforming Men and Women*, 74–75, 79–85; minutes, Richmond City Council, 1842, quoted in Green, *This Business of Relief*, 53.

13. Green, *This Business of Relief*, 44–46, 53; Lockley, *Welfare and Charity*, 98; Dorsey, *Reforming Men and Women*, 63.

14. Lockley, *Welfare and Charity*, 98; Dorsey, *Reforming Men and Women*, 63, 73–89.

15. See especially Ruffin, *The Political Economy of Slavery*.

16. See Jabour, "Male Friendship and the Early National South," 83–111; Buza, "'Pledges of Our Love,'" 10–11, 14–16, 29–30; Yacovone, "Abolitionists and 'The Language of Fraternal Love,'" 85–95; Watson, "Flexible Gender Roles during the Market Revolution," 81–107. Although not primarily a study of U.S. Masonry, Stefan-Ludwig Hoffman, "Civility, Male Friendship, and Masonic Sociability in Nineteenth-Century Germany," touches on the important theme of political culture and Masonic friendships.

17. Myers, *Address Delivered by W. Samuel H. Myers*, 9.

18. OF Proceedings, 1847, 388. See also Shaver, *An Address Delivered before Lebanon Lodge*, 11–12; McCabe, *Address before Hawkins Lodge*, 31; "Quid Nunc?" 55.

19. Martin, *Prize Essay on the Principles and Operations of the Order of the Sons of Temperance*, 13.

20. Anderson, "Friendship, Love, and Truth," 26–27.

21. Anderson, "Friendship, Love, and Truth," 26–27; for similar sentiments, see also Thomson, *An Address Delivered before Benevolentia Lodge*, 11–12, and Lee, *Prize Essay on the Principles and Operations of the Order of the Sons of Temperance*, 8, 11.

22. Powers, *Address Delivered before the Sons of Temperance*, 12–13; Martin, *Prize Essay on the Principles and Operations of the Order of the Sons of Temperance*, 13–14.

23. Martin, *Prize Essay on the Principles and Operations of the Order of the Sons of Temperance*, 13.

24. Smith, "Oration," 183.

25. See Stanley, "Home Life and the Morality of the Market"; Kerber, "Separate Spheres, Female Worlds, Woman's Place."

26. Hamilton, "Address," 98.

27. Hamilton, "Address," 98; McCabe, "Address," 116; "A Short Essay on Odd-fellowship," 53; Disney, "Address," 102; Rooker, *Oration before the Independent Order of Odd Fellows*, 10 and 15.

28. Martin, *Prize Essay on the Principles and Operations of the Order of the Sons of Temperance*, 9.

29. Thomson, *An Address Delivered before Benevolentia Lodge*, 15.

30. "To Our Patrons," 1.

31. Martin, *Prize Essay on the Principles and Operations of the Order of the Sons of Temperance*, 9.

32. Lockley, *Welfare and Charity*, 8; Dorsey, *Reforming Men and Women*, 63, 73–89; McCabe, *Address before Hawkins Lodge*, 16; Martin, *Prize Essay on the Principles and Operations of the Order of the Sons of Temperance*, 2; Lee, *Prize Essay on the Principles and Operations of the Order of the Sons of Temperance*, 12; Smith, "Oration," 174; Anderson, "Friendship, Love, and Truth," 29.

33. Green, *This Business of Relief*, 44–46, 53; Lockley, *Welfare and Charity*, 98; Dorsey, *Reforming Men and Women*, 63; Martin, *Prize Essay on the Principles and Operations of the Order of the Sons of Temperance*, 10; McCabe, *Address before Hawkins Lodge*, 16.

34. See Bullock, *Revolutionary Brotherhood*, 188–98; *By-Laws for the Government of Richmond Lodge*, 5–6; Clawson, *Constructing Brotherhood*, 118; Beito, *From Mutual Aid to the Welfare State*, 9–11; and Carnes, *Secret Ritual and Manhood in Victorian America*, 26.

35. *Constitution, By-Laws and Rules of Order of Old Dominion Lodge*, 14–15; June 28, 1851, minute book, Records of Madison Division.

36. Tabbert, *American Freemasons*, 106–12.

37. Caldwell, *Masonry Its Own Defence*, 14; Smith, "Oration," 173; Mandell, "Celebration in Fredericksburg," 283.

38. Martin, *Prize Essay on the Principles and Operations of the Order of the Sons of Temperance*, 10; McCabe, *Address before Hawkins Lodge*, 16; Raleigh, "Oration," 10–11.

39. Raleigh, "Oration," 11.

40. Lockley, *Welfare and Charity*, 214.

41. The quote is from the 1844 constitution of Marshall Division, no. 3, Sons of Temperance, but almost identical requirements can be found in the constitutions of any of the other subordinate lodges and divisions.

42. Grosh, *The Odd-Fellow's Manual*, 65–67; Dove, *The Masonic Textbook*, 83, 87.

43. Evans, ed., *A Digest of Resolutions and Decisions*, 49–51.

44. *OF Proceedings*, 1857, 917. See also *OF Proceedings*, 1858, 962 and 972.

45. *FM Proceedings*, 1853, 35; *FM Proceedings*, 1855, 40.

46. *FM Proceedings*, 1860, 22–24. See also Raleigh, "Oration," 10–11.

47. April 19, 1851, minute book, Records of Madison Division.

48. "Impostors," 116–17. For a similar complaint among the Freemasons, see committee to W. R. Weisiger, August 30, 1852, in Records of Manchester Lodge, box 4.

49. Shaver, *An Address Delivered before Lebanon Lodge*, 14.

50. Strange, *Address Delivered at the Dedication of the New Masonic Hall*, 9.

51. McCabe, *Address before Hawkins Lodge*, 18–19; Scott, "Oration," in *FM Proceedings*, 1845, 64–66.

52. Powers, *Address Delivered before the Sons of Temperance*, 11–12.

53. Kemper, *An Address, Delivered at Standardsville, Virginia*, 15.

54. McCabe, *Address before Hawkins Lodge*, 16–20 (quote on 20).

55. Bullock, *Revolutionary Brotherhood*, 239–41; Carnes, *Secret Ritual and Manhood in Victorian America*, 14, 24–29.

56. Bullock, *Revolutionary Brotherhood*, 64–65, 239–41, 259–60; Carnes, *Secret Ritual and Manhood in Victorian America*, 14, 24–29; Nelson, *National Manhood*, 182–85.

57. My thinking here has been greatly influenced by Eric Hobsbawm's idea of "invented tradition." See Hobsbawm, "Introduction: Invented Traditions."

58. Kemper, *An Address, Delivered at Standardsville, Virginia*, 11.

59. Kemper, *An Address, Delivered at Standardsville, Virginia*, 13. For similar themes and claims also see: Thomson, *An Address Delivered before Benevolentia Lodge*, 5–11; Scott, "Address," in *FM Proceedings*, 1845, 57–65; and Withers, *An Address, Delivered at Masonic Hall*.

60. Heitmann, *A History and Manual of the Independent Order of Odd Fellows*, 13; Shaver, *An Address Delivered before Lebanon Lodge*, 7–8; Raleigh, "Oration," 9.

61. Blocker, *American Temperance Movements*, 48; *ST Proceedings*, October 1849, 15–16; William S. White, *Total Abstinence from Intoxicating Drinks as a Beverage Expedient*, 6; Powers, *Address Delivered before the Sons of Temperance*, 12–14.

62. Minor, "The Temperance Reformation in Virginia," 436; "Report of the Grand Worthy Patriarch," in *ST Proceedings*, October 1854, 10; Aylett, "1852 Temperance Speech," 5–6, in Aylett Family Papers.

63. Carlson, "'Drinks He to His Own Undoing,'" 684–86.

64. "Report of the Grand Worthy Patriarch," in *ST Proceedings*, January 1854, 501–2.

65. Stevens, ed., *The Cyclopedia of Fraternities*, 311–17.

66. Lindsay et al., *The Official History of the Improved Order of Red Men*, 17–22, 275–76, 508; Stevens, ed., *The Cyclopaedia of Fraternities*, 238; *Richmond Enquirer*, February 26, 1850; *Staunton Spectator*, February 2, 1853. The Red Men had a handful

of lodges in Virginia's cities during the antebellum period. Membership peaked at approximately 950 members statewide during the mid-1850s. Lodges, or "tribes," initially sprung up in cities, such as Wheeling, Alexandria, and Harper's Ferry, but by 1851 tribes existed in Richmond, Petersburg, Lynchburg, and Norfolk. Just prior to the Civil War, the tribes in Richmond and Petersburg boasted almost 100 members each. The Virginia state records for the Improved Order of Red Men were destroyed by fire in Richmond during the Civil War. The Virginia council's speeches, records, and other documents regarding this order are necessarily based on statistics from the national journal of the order, secondary sources, and newspaper accounts. See *Richmond Enquirer*, February 26, 1850; *Staunton Spectator*, February 2, 1853; *Staunton Spectator*, February 23, 1853; and *Richmond Daily Dispatch*, January 19, 1852.

67. "Order of United American Mechanics," 311–17; *Richmond Enquirer*, February 26, 1850; *Richmond Daily Dispatch*, January 19, 1852; Reynolds, *George Lippard*, 19–21; *White Banner* 1 (1851): 141–42; *Staunton Spectator*, February 23, 1853.

68. Thomson, *An Address Delivered before Benevolentia Lodge*, 11.

69. Strange, *Address Delivered at the Dedication of the New Masonic Hall*, 14; Finley, *An Address Delivered before Naval Lodge*, 11; Taliaferro, *An Address, Delivered before the Masonic Fraternity of Williamsburg, Virginia*, 26–27; Thomson, *An Address Delivered before Benevolentia Lodge*, 11; Caldwell, *The Grand Secret Out*, 15; Kemper, *An Address, Delivered at Standardsville, Virginia*, 13. In a similar speech five years earlier, Scott also claimed that "fifty at least of those who signed the Declaration of Independence were Masons" (*FM Proceedings*, 1845, 65).

70. Strange, *Address Delivered at the Dedication of the New Masonic Hall*, 14.

71. Tabbert, *American Freemasons*, 40–41. The nine signers of the Declaration of Independence who were Freemasons were William Ellery, Benjamin Franklin, John Hancock, Joseph Hewes, William Hooper, Robert Treat Paine, Richard Stockton, George Walton, William Whipple, and Ronald Heaton. See Tabbert, *American Freemasons*, 224 n. 27.

72. Thomas Jefferson to James Madison, December 28, 1794, in *The Life and Selected Writings of Thomas Jefferson*, 485–86; "Benedict Arnold, A Freemason, and His Escape Caused by Freemasonry," 99; Heron, *Historical Sketch of Fredericksburg Lodge*, 23; Tabbert, *American Freemasons*, 41.

73. *Richmond Enquirer*, February 26, 1850.

74. Wood, *The Radicalism of the American Revolution*, 289–94.

75. Albanese, *Sons of the Fathers*, 159–67; Zelinsky, *Nation into State*, 34; Kimball, *American City, Southern Place*, 203; Peterson, *The Jefferson Image in the American Mind*, 149, 164–66, 171–73, 178.

76. "Celebration of the 22nd," *Staunton Spectator*, February 12, 1851; Heron, *Historical Sketch of Fredericksburg Lodge*, 10, 14; *Richmond Dispatch*, January 14, 1852; *OF Proceedings*, 1851, 632; Rutnya and Stewart, *The History of Freemasonry in Virginia*, 279–80; Walthall, *History of Richmond Lodge*, 125; William Moseley Brown,

Marshall Lodge, 235; *Richmond Daily Dispatch*, January 14, 1852; *ST Proceedings*, October 1850, 54–55.

77. Thomson, *An Address Delivered before Benevolentia Lodge*, 10. See also "Odd-fellowship," 82, and "Installation," in *Constitution and By-Laws of the Charles City Division*, 16.

78. Kemper, *An Address, Delivered at Standardsville, Virginia*, 11–12.

79. Dove, *The Masonic Textbook*, 4–8; Dove, *A History of the Grand Lodge of Virginia*, 8.

80. Withers, *An Address, Delivered at Masonic Hall*, 21–22.

81. Kemper, *An Address, Delivered at Standardsville, Virginia*, 16.

82. Finley, *An Address Delivered before Naval Lodge*, 13.

83. Disney, "Address," 102. See also "Odd-Fellows' Celebration," *Richmond Enquirer*, December 21, 1841.

84. Disney, "Address," 103.

85. Finley, *An Address Delivered before Naval Lodge*, 13; McCabe, "Oration," 35–36.

86. McCabe, "Oration," 35–36.

87. Thomson, *An Address Delivered before Benevolentia Lodge*, 14–15. See also McCabe, "Oration," 35–36.

88. "A Special Communication of Staunton Lodge, No. 13," February 21, 1845, in correspondence of Pittsylvania Lodge, 1833–42, Records of Pittsylvania Lodge; McCabe, *Address before Hawkins Lodge*, 9–11; McElroy, *An Address Delivered before a Convention of Masons*, 8–11.

89. Kaestle, *Pillars of the Republic*, 79–84. For a more extensive explanation of antebellum educational trends, see chapters four, five and six of *Pillars of the Republic*.

90. Dabney, *Virginia*, 245–51; Maddox, *The Free School Idea in Virginia before the Civil War*, 126–53.

91. "Education," 72.

92. Powers, *An Address Delivered before the Sons of Temperance*, 9.

93. The Odd Fellows and Sons explicitly indicated that they would provide money for both girls and boys, but whether or not the Masons intended to pay for the education of girls from their Grand Charity Fund cannot be determined with certainty. They did open the Higginbotham Male and Female Academy in Amherst County.

94. When a lodge member died, members referred to his children as orphans even if their mother was still living.

95. Rutnya and Stewart, *The History of Freemasonry in Virginia*, 294–96.

96. *Constitution and By-Laws of the Lafayette Division*, 10–11; *Constitution, By-laws and Rules of Order of Springfield Division*, 16–17; June 2, 1849, minute book, Records of Madison Division; "Report of the Widows and Orphans' Fund," March 20, 1847, minute book, Records of Marshall Division.

97. *Constitution, By-Laws and Rules of Order of Old Dominion Lodge*, 23–24.

98. *By-Laws and Rules of Order of Appomattox Lodge*, 11–12.

99. Rutnya and Stewart, *The History of Freemasonry in Virginia*, 296; William Moseley Brown, *Freemasonry in Staunton, Virginia*, 68–69; Dame, *A Historical Sketch of Roman Eagle Lodge*, 47; William Moseley Brown, *Freemasonry in Virginia*, 106–8.

100. *ST Proceedings*, July 1848, 117–21.

101. Jabour, "'Grown Girls, Highly Cultivated,'" 26, 64; Farnham, *The Education of the Southern Belle*, 18, 58. At least four of these colleges were run by Odd Fellows, one in Virginia (Martha Washington Female College), one in North Carolina, and two in Tennessee.

102. Farnham, *The Education of the Southern Belle*, 57; Lebsock, *Free Women of Petersburg*, 172–76.

103. Dame, *A Historical Sketch of Roman Eagle Lodge*, 10–11, 28, 80–81; Dame quoted in Maddox, *The Free School Idea in Virginia before the Civil War*, 109.

104. Lebsock, *Free Women of Petersburg*, 172–76; Farnham, *The Education of the Southern Belle*, 57; Mintz, *Moralists and Modernizers*, 111.

105. "The Independent Order of Odd Fellows Establishes Martha Washington Female College at Abingdon, Virginia, 1853." It is not known if there was a connection between James D. McCabe and this lodge. McCabe was originally from Fredericksburg and later moved to Richmond, and he was not a member of McCabe Lodge during the 1850s. It is possible that the lodge was named after him in honor of his long and active participation in the order, which began in the late 1830s.

106. Jabour, "'Grown Girls, Highly Cultivated,'" 26; Farnham, *The Education of the Southern Belle*, 25–28; Lebsock, *Free Women of Petersburg*, 175.

107. McCabe, *Address before Hawkins Lodge*, 14.

108. See Kerber, *Women of the Republic*, and Varon, *We Mean to Be Counted*, 5, 11–12, 18–20, 85–86, 93–96.

109. Kerber, "The Republican Mother," 42–43; Norton, "The Evolution of White Women's Experience in America," 608, 618; Kann, *The Gendering of American Politics*, 49–67.

110. *OF Proceedings*, 1856, 892. See also McCabe, *Address before Hawkins Lodge*.

111. *OF Proceedings*, 1855, 829.

112. Varon, *We Mean to Be Counted*, 78–86.

113. Varon, *We Mean to Be Counted*, 96–102.

114. Caldwell, *Masonry Its Own Defence*, 12.

115. Taliaferro, *An Address, Delivered before the Masonic Fraternity in Williamsburg, Virginia*, 30.

116. Mandell, "Celebration in Fredericksburg," 285. See also Caldwell, *Masonry Its Own Defence*, 12, and Taylor, *Temperance Address, before the Lexington Division*, 2.

117. Powers, *Address Delivered before the Sons of Temperance*, 13; Dove, *The Masonic*

Textbook, 254; Constitution, By-Laws and Rules of Order of Old Dominion Lodge, 9; Constitution and By-Laws of the Lafayette Division, 12.

118. McElroy, An Address Delivered before a Convention of Masons, 10; Powers, Address Delivered before the Sons of Temperance, 8; "Public Celebration," 41.

119. Lebsock, Free Women of Petersburg, 198, 215–16, 225–26, 230, 236.

120. Heitmann, History and Manual of Independent Order of Odd Fellows, 36–37, 62–63; Grosh, The Odd-Fellow's Manual, 170–78; OF Proceedings, 1851, 676.

121. Burke, "Leaving the Enlightenment," 255–57; Voorhis, The Eastern Star, 7–9; Tabbert, American Freemasons, 79–80.

122. Voorhis, Eastern Star, 41–45; Heitmann, History and Manual of Independent Order of Odd Fellows, 62–63. One "Sisters of Temperance" group was reportedly established in Richmond, but it is unclear how they may have been related to the Sons of Temperance. See Pearson and Hendricks, Liquor and Anti-Liquor in Virginia, 98n.

123. Blocker, American Temperance Movements, 49.

124. Hewitt, Women's Activism and Social Change, 160–61. "Ultraist" female reformers were some of the most radical reformers. They advocated complete legal, social, and economic equality for women. See Hewitt, Women's Activism and Social Change, 40.

125. ST Proceedings, April, 1856, 133.

126. Lebsock, Free Women of Petersburg, 236, 226–27, 230, and esp. 234–36. See also Varon, We Mean to Be Counted, 101–2; Ginzburg, Women and the Work of Benevolence, 98–132; and Lockley, Welfare and Charity, 143.

Chapter Five. Civic Brotherhood

1. Richmond Enquirer, February 26, 1850.

2. Elsa Barkley Brown and Kimball, "Mapping the Terrain of Black Richmond," 305; Naragon, "Ballots, Bullets, and Blood," 350–71. For more information on African American public space, see White, "'It was a Proud Day'"; Walker, "'The Freemasonry of the Race'"; Van Zelm, "Virginia Women as Public Citizens"; Dailey, Before Jim Crow, 103–13; Elsa Barkley Brown, "Negotiating and Transforming the Public Sphere"; Higginbotham, Righteous Discontent, 7–13; and Kelley, "'We are not what we seem.'"

3. Richmond Dispatch, July 6, 1866, quoted in Brown and Kimball, "Mapping the Terrain of Black Richmond," 305; Naragon, "Ballots, Bullets, and Blood," 356–71.

4. Takagi, "Rearing Wolves to Our Own Destruction," 1–2, 72, 112–14; Tripp, Yankee City, Southern Town, 12–15, 18–21; Martin, Divided Mastery, 1–10, 18–19, 103.

5. Martin, Divided Mastery, 168–73; Siegel, The Roots of Southern Distinctiveness, 136–37.

6. Takagi, "Rearing Wolves to Our Own Destruction," 72, 112–15; Martin, Divided Mastery, 171–73; Tripp, Yankee Town, Southern City, 12–15, 18–21; Bogger, Free Blacks in Norfolk, Virginia, 132, 153–55, 158–60.

7. Kimball, *American City, Southern Place*, 71–72; Goldfield, *Urban Growth in the Age of Sectionalism*, 143–45; Takagi, "*Rearing Wolves to Our Own Destruction*," 115; Martin, *Divided Mastery*, 168; Siegel, *The Roots of Southern Distinctiveness*, 136–37; Bogger, *Free Blacks in Norfolk, Virginia*, 134–35, 159–62; Lebsock, *Free Women of Petersburg*, 94.

8. Ryan, *Women in Public*, 20–23.

9. Ryan, "The American Parade," 132–34, 137–43, 148; Ryan, *Civic Wars*, 60, 71–75. For more information regarding early American public culture and nationalism and the creation of patriotic holidays, see Purcell, *Sealed with Blood*; Waldstreicher, *In the Midst of Perpetual Fetes*; Newman, *Parades and the Politics of the Street*, 83–119; Travers, *Celebrating the Fourth*; Zelinsky, *Nation into State*, 69–74; and Burnstein, *America's Jubilee*.

10. Lebsock, *Free Women of Petersburg*, 214–26; Varon, *We Mean to Be Counted*, 24.

11. Varon, *We Mean to Be Counted*, pp. 88–95.

12. "The Destiny of Women," *Richmond Daily Dispatch*, February 4, 1852.

13. *Danville Republican*, January 17, 1854, quoted in Siegel, *The Roots of Southern Distinctiveness*, 113–14.

14. *Danville Republican*, January 17, 1854, quoted in Siegel, *The Roots of Southern Distinctiveness*, 113–14; "Bloomerism Unadorned," *Richmond Daily Dispatch*, January 23, 1852; "The Destiny of Women," *Richmond Daily Dispatch*, February 4, 1852.

15. *Staunton Spectator and General Advertiser*, March 9, 16, 1853.

16. Ryan, *Women in Public*, 31–32; Varon, *We Mean to Be Counted*, 71–79; Ryan, "Gender and Public Access," 271.

17. Ryan, *Women in Public*, 37–42.

18. Ryan, *Women in Public*, 67–68; Ryan, *Civic Wars*, 36–37.

19. Varon, *We Mean to Be Counted*, 89; *Lynchburg Virginian*, January 2, 13, 20, 1845; William Moseley Brown, *Marshall Lodge*, 177, 198, 197–212, 216; *Lynchburg Virginian*, October 15, 1846.

20. For example, see July 13, 1849, minute book, Records of Covington Division; June 3, 1848, minute book, Records of Mount Crawford Division; January 21, 1850, June 17, 1850, minute book, Records of Charity Division; and Dame, *A Historical Sketch of Roman Eagle Lodge*, 28.

21. June 29, 30, 1849, July 13, 1849, February 14, 1851, minute book, Records of Covington Division; Smith, "Oration," 173–74.

22. Brown, *Marshall Lodge*, 204.

23. June 3, 1848, May 24, 1850, minute book, Records of Mount Crawford Division. Roller, who owned $10,000 of property and seven slaves, amended Watkins's motion to state "a pease [sic] sufficiently large to build on."

24. Ryan, *Civic Wars*, 15, 36–37, 60; Ryan, "The American Parade," 132–38; Durrill, "A Tale of Two Courthouses," 659–66; Baker, *Affairs of Party*, 267–68. White men owning fifty acres of unimproved property, twenty-five acres of cultivated

property, a house on a lot in town, or a five-year lease on a home in town qualified them to vote under the Virginia Constitution of 1830. See Bruce, *The Rhetoric of Conservatism*, 2, 66, and Peterson, "The Virginia Convention of 1829-1830: Introduction," in Peterson, ed, *Democracy, Liberty, and Property*, 280–81.

25. Smith, "Oration," 173–74.

26. Slade, "Introductory Address."

27. *Richmond Enquirer*, December 21, 1841.

28. *Richmond Enquirer*, December 21, 1841.

29. Smith, "Oration," 176.

30. Smith, "Oration," 176.

31. "Odd-Fellows' Hall in Richmond."

32. "Odd-Fellows' Hall in Richmond"; Brown and Kimball, "Mapping the Terrain of Black Richmond," 297–98; Kimball, *American City, Southern Place*, 40; Davis et al., *Auction and Commission House*.

33. *Richmond Enquirer*, December 21, 1841.

34. See Kenneth S. Greenberg, *Masters and Statesmen*.

35. See, for example, *By-Laws and Rules of Order of Appomattox Lodge*, 14–15; *Constitution, By-Laws and Rules of Order of Springfield Division*, 17–18; and Laderman, *Sacred Remains*, 31.

36. Dove, *The Masonic Textbook*, 242. See also Grosh, *The Odd-Fellow's Manual*, 365–70, 376, and Evans, ed., *A Digest of the Resolutions and Decisions of the National Division of the Sons of Temperance*, 75–76.

37. Evans, ed., *A Digest of the Resolution and Decisions of the National Division of the Sons of Temperance*, 75–76.

38. Dove, *The Masonic Textbook*, 242; Grosh, *The Odd-Fellow's Manual*, 365–70, 376; Evans, ed., *A Digest of the Resolutions and Decisions of the National Division of the Sons of Temperance*, 75–76; death of John H. Greenway, June 17, 18, 1855, minute book, McCabe Lodge; death of John L. Robinson, March 23, 1850, minute book, Records of Covington Division; death of Valentine Switzer, August 1, 5, 1848, minute book, Records of Mount Crawford Division; death of Matthew Miller, October 8, 9, 14, 1845, minute book, Records of Marshall Division; death of R. A. Carrington, March 25, 1855, death of A. Millspaugh, November 19, 1857, minute book, Records of Randolph Lodge; death of James N. Rawls, July 22, 1854, minute book, Records of Somerton Lodge.

39. Laderman, *Sacred Remains*, 42–43; Lipson, *Freemasonry in Federalist Connecticut*, 170–73; Smith-Rosenberg, "The Female World of Love and Ritual," 383; Laderman, *Sacred Remains*, 30.

40. Gary Laderman suggests that in the early nineteenth century women had begun to turn the process of laying bodies out for burial into their own business, similar to midwifery. By the 1850s, however, the commercialization of funerals and the privatization of rural cemeteries helped make the business of death a male professional role in urban areas (30, 45–50). In the city of Richmond, at least one

fraternity member, Freemason John G. Turpin, was listed on the 1850 federal census as an undertaker. Several fraternity members were also deeply involved in the creation of Richmond's first rural cemetery, Hollywood Cemetery. The orders also established their own Odd Fellows, Masonic, and Sons of Temperance cemeteries in some places.

41. Laderman, *Sacred Remains*, 41–43.

42. Records of Mount Crawford Division; U.S. Census Office, Seventh Census of the United States, 1850, Virginia, Free Population Schedules, Rockingham County.

43. *Constitution and By-Laws of Holston Division*, 22; *By-Laws and Rules of Order of Appomattox Lodge*, 18.

44. "Sudden Death," *Staunton Spectator*, February 12, 1851.

45. This information comes from the lodge roster of Staunton Lodge, no. 13, in *FM Proceedings*, 1850, and U.S. Census Office, Seventh Census of the United States, 1850, Virginia, Free Population Schedules, Augusta County. The dollar amount is the value of each man's real and personal property as listed on the census.

46. "Eulogy," in *FM Proceedings*, 1854, 8–12.

47. "Eulogy," in *FM Proceedings*, 1854, 9–10.

48. "Sudden Death," *Staunton Spectator*, February 12, 1851; "Extract from the Minutes of Lynchburg Lodge, No. 17, IOOF," *Lynchburg Virginian*, November 16, 1846; William Mosely Brown, *Blandford Lodge*, 241–43; death of John H. Greenway, June 17, 18, 1855, death of Cyrus King, March 23, 24 1855, death of Samuel Logan, July 15, 16, 1855, minute book, McCabe Lodge; death of John L. Robinson, March 23, 1850, minute book, Records of Covington Division; death of Valentine Switzer, August 1, 5, 1848, death of J. W. Smith, October 10, 1849, minute book, Records of Mount Crawford Division; death of Matthew Miller, October 8, 9, 14, 1845, minute book, Records of Marshall Division.

49. Bogger, *Free Blacks in Norfolk, Virginia*, 129–30; Laderman, *Sacred Remains*, 82–83. See also Breeden, "Body Snatchers and Anatomy Professors," 321–45. Apparently the work required monitoring the funerals of free blacks and quickly digging up the bodies before decomposition had set in. The bodies were then packed in crates or barrels and sent to the schools. Although these activities were known to many people, the body snatchers did try to cover their tracks by refilling the grave with dirt and leaving the funeral flowers and so forth the way they had found them. Another example of this practice is the disinterment of infamous New York prostitute Helen Jewett. See Cohen, *The Murder of Helen Jewett*, 300.

50. May 13, 1848, May 12, 1851, minute book, Records of Mount Crawford Division; May 1, 1849, April 29, 1850, May 1, 13, 1850, minute book, Records of Charity Division; "Public Procession," *Staunton Spectator and General Advertiser*, June 8, 1853, Rady, *History of Richmond Randolph Lodge*, 33; Rutnya and Stewart, *Freemasonry in Virginia*, 3; Dove, *A History of the Grand Lodge of Virginia*, 53–55;

Walthall, *History of Richmond Lodge*, 121; Withers, *An Address, Delivered at Masonic Hall*, 4–5.

51. May 12, 1851, minute book, Records of Mount Crawford Division.

52. December 20, 1850, minute book, Records of Mount Crawford Division; U.S. Census Office, Seventh Census of the United States, 1850, Virginia, Free Population Schedules, Rockingham County.

53. April 15, 29, 1850, May 1, 1850, minute book, Records of Charity Division.

54. May 1, 1850, minute book, Records of Charity Division.

55. Ryan, *Civic Wars*, 36–37, 76.

56. May 1, 1850, minute book, Records of Charity Division. The previous year, in a celebration featuring Staunton's Odd Fellows and Sons of Temperance, the local newspaper claimed that approximately 100 Odd Fellows and 150 Sons participated in the procession. See "The Procession," *Staunton Spectator and General Advertiser*, May 9, 1849.

57. *FM Proceedings*, 1850, 61–62; minute book, Records of Charity Division; *Staunton Spectator*, April 18, 1849; U.S. Census Office, Seventh Census of the United States, 1850, Virginia, Free Population Schedules, Augusta County. Unfortunately, membership rosters for Staunton Lodge, no. 45, IOOF, are not available for the early 1850s. Several names, however, are listed in affiliation with the order in the *Staunton Spectator*.

58. "Last Hours of Mr. Polk," *Staunton Spectator*, July 4, 1849; Rutnya and Stewart, *Freemasonry in Virginia*, 300; Walthall, *History of Richmond Lodge*, 112; Brown, *Marshall Lodge*, 214, 223; Brown, *Blandford Lodge*, 196–98.

59. Quoted in Brown, *Blandford Lodge*, 196.

60. Brown, *Blandford Lodge*, 196–97.

61. "Celebration at Middlebrook," *Staunton Spectator*, July 12, 1848; Newman, *Parades and Politics of the Street*, 85–88; Ryan, *Women in Public*, 23, 30.

62. June 21, 1850, July 1, 1850, minute book, Records of Covington Division. See also May 30, 1851, June 20, 27, 1851, July 4, 1851, minute book, Records of Covington Division, for details of a similar celebration.

63. McCabe, *Address before Hawkins Lodge*, 7–8, 16.

64. McCabe, *Address before Hawkins Lodge*, 24.

65. McCabe, *Address before Hawkins Lodge*, 22.

66. "Celebration of the 22nd," *Staunton Spectator*, February 12, 1851.

67. "History of the Monument," in *FM Proceedings*, special grand communication, 1858, 41–43; *Richmond Enquirer*, February 15, 1850.

68. Kimball, *American City, Southern Place*, 7; Naragon, "Ballots, Bullets and Blood," 90–91, 357–59.

69. *Richmond Enquirer*, February 22, 1850.

70. *Richmond Enquirer*, February 19, 26, 1850; *Richmond Times*, February 25, 1850.

71. *Richmond Enquirer*, February 26, 1850; *FM Proceedings*, special grand communication, 1850, 32–33.

72. *Richmond Enquirer*, February 26, 1850.

73. *Richmond Enquirer*, February 26, 1850.

Conclusion

1. In Virginia, state membership in the Sons of Temperance dropped from approximately 13,000 in 1853, to 6,500 in 1856 (*ST Proceedings*, July 1853, April 1856). Similarly, in 1853, membership in the Virginia Odd Fellows stood at around 6,800 men, but by 1858, only 5,500 remained (*OF Proceedings*, 1853, 1858). In 1854, the Virginia Masons had 4,152 members. By 1859, the order had 5,465 members (*FM Proceedings*, 1854, 1859). Interestingly, membership in the Masons grew during the late 1850s. This is most likely because the Freemasons never instituted a Grand Lodge of the United States. Thus, the order never faced the organizational bureaucratic dilemmas that confronted the Odd Fellows and Sons in the late 1850s.

2. Taliaferro, *An Address, Delivered before the Masonic Fraternity of Williamsburg, Virginia*, 30; *OF Proceedings*, 1855, 821; *OF Proceedings*, 1856, 868; *OF Proceedings*, 1857, 917; *ST Proceedings*, April 1859, 314; "The Sons of Temperance and Slavery," in *Virginia Conductor*, June 1858, 2:57–58.

3. *OF Proceedings*, 1855, 821.

4. See *Memoir of the Pilgrimage to Virginia*.

5. Link, *The Roots of Secession*, 208–28; Shade, *Democratizing the Old Dominion*, 286–91.

6. Link, *The Roots of Secession*, 232–41.

7. Grand Lodge of Virginia, *Free Masonry and the War*, 12.

8. For examples of such legends, see Roberts, *House Undivided*, and Munn, *Freemasons at Gettysburg*. Munn's work celebrates the completion of the Friend to Friend Masonic Memorial in the Gettysburg National Cemetery, which depicts a Union and Confederate soldier embracing each other in Masonic brotherhood as one of the soldiers lies dying.

9. Lebsock, *Free Women of Petersburg*, 197.

Appendix

1. See Berlin and Gutman, "Natives and Immigrants, Free Men and Slaves," 1178.

2. See Wells, *The Origins of the Southern Middle Class*, 238.

BIBLIOGRAPHY

Libraries and Archives

Duke   Rare, Book, Manuscript, and Special Collections Library, Duke University, Durham, N.C.

GLVA   Grand Lodge of Virginia, Allen E. Roberts Masonic Library and Museum, Richmond, Va.

JMU   Special Collections, Carrier Library, James Madison University, Harrisonburg, Va.

LVA   Library of Virginia, Richmond, Va.

UVA   Albert and Shirley Small Special Collections Department, University of Virginia Library, Charlottesville, Va.

VHS   Virginia Historical Society, Richmond, Va.

W&M   Special Collections Research Center, Swem Library, College of William and Mary, Williamsburg, Va.

Primary Sources

NEWSPAPERS

Abingdon Virginian, 1849–56
Danville Register, 1848
Danville Reporter, 1836, 1837, 1840, 1842
Danville Republican, 1853, 1854, 1856, 1857
Fredericksburg Weekly Advertiser, 1853–54
Hampton News and Advertiser, 1854
Independent Odd Fellow, 1841–44
Liberator, 1850
Lynchburg Virginian, 1844–47, 1851–52
Masonic Olive Branch, 1837
Norfolk American Beacon, 1852.
Norfolk and Portsmouth Herald, 1852
Odd-Fellows' Magazine, 1839–40
Richmond Daily Dispatch, 1852, 1856
Richmond Enquirer, 1844–46, 1849–51
Rockingham Register and Valley Advertiser, 1847, 1849, 1854
Staunton Spectator, 1848–51, 1852
Staunton Spectator and General Advertiser, 1852–53
Staunton True American, 1855–57
Virginia Conductor, 1857–60

UNPUBLISHED MANUSCRIPT RECORDS

Aylett Family Papers, 1851–96. Ms 110, box 4, UVA.

Albert D. Clarke, Personal Papers Collection, 1843. Accession no. 39662, LVA.

Asa Holland Papers. Duke.

Holladay Family Papers. VHS.

Minute Book, Central Lodge, no. 39, 1849–55. Freemasons. GLVA.

Minute Book, McCabe Lodge, no 56. IOOF. Private collection.

Montague Family Papers, 1808–1939. VHS.

Records of Charity Division, no. 6, 1848–50. Sons of Temperance of North
America, Grand Division of Virginia. Accession no. 11691, UVA.

Records of Chesapeake Lodge, no. 89. IOOF. Accession no. 24667, Business
Records Collection, LVA.

Records of Covington Division, no. 244, 1849–52. Sons of Temperance of North
America, Grand Division of Virginia. Duke.

Records of Madison Division, no. 36, 1849–53. Sons of Temperance of North
America, Grand Division of Virginia. Mss Ms V Mi 18, W&M.

Records of Manchester Lodge, no. 14. Freemasons. VHS.

Records of Marshall Division, no. 3, 1844–48. Sons of Temperance of North
America, Grand Division of Virginia. JMU.

Records of Marshall Lodge, no. 44, 1848–54. IOOF. Robins Family Papers.

Records of Monguy Division, no. 226, 1848–55. Sons of Temperance of North
America, Grand Division of Virginia. VHS.

Records of Mossy Creek Division, no. 466, 1851–53. Sons of Temperance of North
American, Grand Division of Virginia. Mss Ms V Mi 17, W&M.

Records of Mount Crawford Division, no. 19, 1815–92. Sons of Temperance of
North America, Grand Division of Virginia. Accession no. 1014, UVA.

Records of Mount Hermon Division, no. 348, 1850–56. Sons of Temperance of
North America, Grand Division of Virginia. Holladay Family Papers, sec. 171.

Records of Pittsylvania Lodge, no. 24, 1833–42. Freemasons, Grand Lodge of
Virginia. Special Collections, sec. A, Duke.

Records of Randolph Lodge, no. 19, 1852–55. Freemasons. VHS.

Records of Somerton Lodge, no. 99, 1853–58. Freemasons. GLVA.

Records of University Division, no. 74, 1847–57. Sons of Temperance of North
America, Grand Division of Virginia. Accession no. 1995, UVA.

Robins Family Papers, 1784–1939. VHS.

Roller Family Papers, 1837–1911. VHS.

Spotswood Family Papers, 1760–1900. VHS.

PUBLISHED PAMPHLETS, SPEECHES, AND PRIMARY SOURCE DOCUMENTS

Anderson, William E. "Friendship, Love, and Truth." *Independent Odd-Fellow* 3
(May 1843): 25–31.

Address to the People of West Virginia, Shewing That Slavery Is Injurious to the Public Welfare, and That It May Be Gradually Abolished, without Detriment to the Rights and Interests of Slaveholders. Lexington: R. C. Noel, 1847. VHS.

"Benedict Arnold, a Freemason, and His Escape Caused by Freemasonry." In *A Collection of Letters on Freemasonry in Chronological Order*, 99–102. Boston: T. R. Martin, 1849.

Blue Book for the Use of Subordinate Divisions of the Order of the Sons of Temperance. Cincinnati: Ben Franklin Printing, 1853.

By-Laws and Rules of Order of Appomattox Lodge, No. 16, IOOF. Petersburg: J. M. H. Brunet, 1847. VHS.

By-Laws for the Government of Richmond Lodge, No. X, Revised May 1849. Richmond: John Warrock, 1849. Duke.

By-Laws and Rules of Order of Union Lodge, No. VII, IOOF. Richmond: William H. Clemmitt, 1858. UVA.

Caldwell, David. *Masonry Its Own Defence; or, The Freemason's Apology for Loving His Order, June 24, 1844.* Lynchburg: Toler, Townley and Statham, 1844. Duke.

———. *The Grand Secret Out; or, Masonry in Its Principles.* Norfolk: Broughton, 1846. Duke.

Constitution and By-Laws of the Charles City Division, No. 135 of the Sons of Temperance. Richmond: Banner of Temperance Printing Office, 1848. VHS.

Constitution and By-Laws of Holston Division, No. 120 of the Sons of Temperance of Marion, Virginia. Abingdon: Coale and Barr, 1854. UVA.

Constitution and By-Laws of the Lafayette Division, No. 25 of the Sons of Temperance. Richmond: L. K. Coonley, 1846. Duke.

Constitution and By-Laws of Micajah Pendleton Division, No. 410, Sons of Temperance. Lynchburg: Johnson and Woolfolk, 1851. VHS.

Constitution and By-Laws of the University Division, No. LXXIV, Sons of Temperance, Adopted October 22, 1847. Charlottesville: James Alexander, 1847. UVA.

Constitution, By-Laws and Rules of Order of Old Dominion Lodge, No. V, of the IO of OF of the State of Virginia. Portsmouth: D. D. Fiske, 1852. VHS.

Constitution, By-Laws and Rules of Order of Springfield Division, No. 167, Sons of Temperance. Richmond: Lewellen and Drinkard, 1850. UVA.

"Cornerstone of Odd Fellows Hall." *Independent Odd Fellow* 1 (June 1841): 4–5.

Davis, R. H., et al. *Auction and Commission House, Odd-Fellows' Hall . . . , June 4, 1860.* Richmond: Wynne Printer, 1860. VHS.

Debow, J. D. B. *Statistical View of the United States, Embracing Its Territory, Population—White, Free, Colored, and Slave—Moral and Social Conditions, Industry, Property and Revenue, the Detailed Statistics of Cities, Towns and Counties, Being a Compendium of the Seventh Census.* Washington, 1854.

Disney, David. "Address," *Independent Odd-Fellow* 1 (October 1841): 101–2.

Doddridge, Philip. "Doddridge in Rebuttal." In Peterson, ed., *Democracy, Liberty, and Property*, 331–37.

Dove, John. *A History of the Grand Lodge of Virginia: Its Progress and Mode of Development, in Two Lectures*. Richmond: Clemmitt and Fore, 1854.

————. *The Masonic Textbook, Containing a History of Masonry, and Masonic Grand Lodges, from the Earliest Times, Together with the Constitution of Masonry, or "Ahiman Rezon," and a Digest of the Laws, Rules and Regulations of the Grand Lodge of Virginia*. Richmond: Shepard and Colin, 1847. vhs.

"Education." *Independent Odd-Fellow* 1 (August 1841): 71–72.

Evans, Thomas J., ed. *A Digest of the Resolutions and Decisions of the National Division of the Sons of Temperance of the United States and the Grand Division of Virginia*. Richmond: H. K. Ellyson, 1847. vhs.

Faulkner, Charles J. *Speech of C. J. Faulkner, Esq., of Berkeley, in Committee of the Whole, on the Basis Question, Delivered in the Virginia Reform Convention, on Wednesday and Thursday, March 26th and 27th, 1851*. Richmond: R. H. Gallaher, 1851. uva.

Finley, I. Randolph. *An Address Delivered before Naval Lodge, No. 100, Portsmouth, Virginia, on the occasion of the Public Installation of Officers on the Anniversary of St. John the Baptist, June 24th, ad 1857, al 5857*. Portsmouth: *Daily Transcript* Steam Book and Job Printing, 1857.

Grand Lodge of Virginia. *Free Masonry and the War: Report of the Committee under the Resolutions of 1862, Grand Lodge of Virginia in Reference to Our Relations as Masonic Bodies and as Masons, in the North and South, Growing out of the Manner in Which the Present War Has Been Prosecuted*. Richmond: Chas H. Wynne, 1865.

Grosh, Aaron B. *The Odd-Fellow's Manual, Illustrating the History, Principles, and Government of the Order, and the Instructions and Duties of Every Degree, Station and Office in Odd Fellowship*. Philadelphia: Theodore Bliss, 1868.

Hamilton, James. "Address." *Masonic Olive Branch* 1 (July 1, 1837): 97–99.

"Hon. Edward Evert's Opinion of Secret Societies." In *A Collection of Letters on Freemasonry in Chronological Order*, 102–3. Boston: T.R. Martin, 1849.

Hyneman, Leon, ed. *Universal Masonic Record and Directory*. Philadelphia, 1860.

"Impostors." *Independent Odd-Fellow* 2 (September 1842): 116–17.

"The Independent Order of Odd Fellows Establishes Martha Washington Female College at Abingdon, Virginia, 1853." In *A Documentary History of Education in the South Before 1860*. Vol. 4 of *Private and Denominational Efforts*, ed. Edgar W. Knight, 412–15. Chapel Hill: University of North Carolina Press, 1953.

Journal of the Right Worthy Grand Lodge of Virginia, IOOF, 1837–1859. Richmond: MacFarland and Fergusson, 1860.

Lee, Leroy M. *Prize Essay on the Principles and Operations of the Order of the Sons of Temperance*. Richmond: H. K. Ellyson, 1852. uva.

Leigh, Benjamin Watkins. "Power and Property." In Peterson, ed., *Democracy, Liberty, Property*, 337–51.

"Look Out for Swindler!" *IOOF Proceedings of the R. W. Grand Lodge of the State of Wisconsin*. Kenosha, Wisc., 1861.

Kemper, James Lawson. *An Address, Delivered at Standardsville, Virginia, June 24th, 1854, by James L. Kemper, upon the Celebration of the Anniversary of St. John the Baptist, by the Piedmont Lodge of Free Masons.* Richmond: C. H. Wynne, 1854. VHS.

Mandell, D. J. "Celebration in Fredericksburg." *Odd-Fellows' Magazine* 1 (March 1840): 277–87. LVA.

Martin, Alexander. *Prize Essay on the Principles and Operations of the Order of the Sons of Temperance.* Richmond: H. K. Ellyson, 1851. VHS.

McCabe, James D. "Address." *Masonic Olive Branch* 1 (August 1, 1837): 115–17.

———. *Address before Hawkins Lodge, No. 41, IOOF, and the Citizens of Rogersville, Tenn., on the 4th Day of July, 1849, at the Laying the Corner-stone of the Odd-Fellows' Female Institute.* Abingdon: Coale and Barr, 1849. Duke.

———. "Oration." *Independent Odd-Fellow* 1 (July 1841): 25–38.

McElroy, James. *An Address Delivered before a Convention of Masons.* Staunton: Vincent E. Geiger, 1845. Duke.

Memoir of the Pilgrimage to Virginia of the Knights Templar of Massachusetts and Rhode Island, May 1859. Boston: A. Williams, 1859.

Minor, Lucian. "The Temperance Reformation in Virginia." *Southern Literary Messenger* 16 (July 1850): 432–38.

Minutes of the Grand Division of the Sons of Temperance of the State of Virginia. Richmond: 1845–59.

Minutes of the Grand Division of the Sons of Temperance of the State of Virginia at Their Regular Quarterly Session, Held July 21, 1847 in the Town of Winchester. 1847.

Morgan, Charles S. "The Reformers' Rebuttal." In Peterson, ed., *Democracy Liberty, and Property,* 408–9.

Myers, Samuel H. *Address Delivered by W. Samuel H. Myers, PM in the Masons' Hall, in the City of Richmond, on Thursday June 24, 1847, Being St. John's Day, before and at the Request of Lodge No's 10, 14, 19, and 36.* Richmond: John Warrock, 1847. UVA.

Nicholas, Philip. "The Freehold Suffrage Defended." In Peterson, ed., *Democracy, Liberty, Property,* 386–95.

"Non-Freeholders' Memorial." In Peterson, ed., *Democracy, Liberty, and Property,* 377–86.

"Odd-Fellows' Hall in Richmond." *Independent Odd-Fellow* 1 (September 1841): 95–96.

"Odd-fellowship." *Independent Odd-Fellow* 1 (September 1841): 73–74.

Peyton, J. Lewis. *History of Augusta County, Virginia.* Staunton: Samuel M. Yost, 1882.

Powers, Pike. *Address Delivered before the Sons of Temperance, in Staunton, July 4, 1845.* Staunton: Spectator Office, 1845. Duke.

Proceedings of the Grand Annual Communication of the Grand Lodge of Virginia. Richmond, 1838–60. GLVA.

Proceedings of the National Division of the Sons of Temperance: Fourth Annual Session. Philadelphia: William P. Geddes, 1847.

Proceedings of the Right Worthy Grand Lodge of Virginia, IOOF, *Held in the City of Richmond, at Its Annual Communication on the 15th, 16th, and 17th of April 1857.* Richmond: MacFarlane and Fergusson, 1857.

"Public Celebration." *Odd-Fellows' Magazine* 1 (May 1839): 39–41.

"Quid Nunc?" *Independent Odd-Fellow* 3 (May 1843): 31–34.

Raleigh, Daniel T. "Oration: Delivered in Trinity Church, Richmond, Virginia, on the 25th of March, 1841 on the Occasion of Laying the Corner-stone of the Odd-Fellows' Hall." *Independent Odd-Fellow* 1 (June 1841): 5–12. VHS.

Randolph, John. "Randolph on the Federal Issue." In Peterson, ed., *Democracy, Liberty, Property,* 351–60.

Rooker, William Y. *Oration before the Independent Order of Odd Fellows at the Dedication of the Hall of Winchester Lodge No. 25, October 28, 1846.* Winchester: J. P. Bentley's Book and Job Office, 1846. Duke.

Ruffin, Edmund. *The Political Economy of Slavery; or, The Institution Considered in Regard to Its Influence on Public Wealth and the General Welfare.* Washington D.C.: Lemuel Towers, 1853.

Rules of Order, Constitution, and General Laws, of the R. W. Grand Lodge of Virginia, IOOF, *as Amended up to April Communication, 1860, and A Digest of Decisions of the Right Worthy Grand Lodge of Virginia on Questions of Law.* Richmond: MacFarlane and Fergusson, 1860. VHS.

Shaver, F. L. B. *An Address Delivered before Lebanon Lodge, No. 66,* IOOF, *in the Methodist Episcopal Church, June 16, 1848.* Abingdon: Coale and Barr, 1848. UVA.

"A Short Essay on Odd-fellowship." *Independent Odd-Fellow* 3 (May 1843): 34–38.

Slade, Bartholomew. "Introductory Address." *Independent Odd-Fellow* (December 1841): 171–73.

Smith, D. D. "Oration." *Independent Odd-Fellow* 1 (December 1841): 173–84.

"A Statement Shewing the Number of White Males and White Females, over Twenty-one Years of Age, in the Several Counties, Towns and Grand Divisions of the State of Virginia." In *Documents, Containing Statistics of Virginia, Ordered to Be Printed by the State Convention Sitting in the City of Richmond, 1850–1851.* Richmond: William Culley, 1851.

Strange, John B. *Address Delivered at the Dedication of the New Masonic Hall, in Eastville, Northampton County, Va., on the Anniversary of St. John the Evangelist, December 27, al 5848, ad 1848.* Norfolk: T. G. Broughton and Son, 1849. UVA.

Summers, Lewis. Summers on the Gordon Plan." In Peterson, ed., *Democracy Liberty, and Property,* 364–71.

Taliaferro, Edwin. *An Address, Delivered before the Masonic Fraternity of Williamsburg, Virginia, November 15, 1860.* Richmond: MacFarland and Fergusson, 1861. W&M.

Taylor, Robert J. *Temperance Address, before the Lexington Division Sons of Temperance, No. 45, March 27th, 1850.* Lexington: Samuel Gillock, 1850. VHS.

"To All Odd-Fellows and Others throughout the World." *Independent Odd-Fellow* 1 (September 1841): 92.

"To Our Patrons." *Independent Odd-Fellow* 1 (June 1841): 1–3.

Thomson, R. B. *An Address Delivered before Benevolentia Lodge, Heathsville, Northumberland County, Virginia, on the 27th of December, 1842.* Richmond: J. B. Martin, 1843. Duke.

Upshur, Abel Parker. "Domestic Slavery." *Southern Literary Messenger* 5 (October 1839): 677–87.

U.S. Census Office, Seventh Census of the United States, 1850, Virginia, Free Population Schedules, Buckingham, Appomattox, Augusta, Henrico (City of Richmond), Mathews, and Rockingham Counties.

U.S. Census Office, Seventh Census of the United States, 1850, Virginia, Slave Population Schedules, Buckingham, Appomattox, Augusta, Henrico (City of Richmond), Mathews, and Rockingham Counties.

White, William S. *Total Abstinence from Intoxicating Drinks as a Beverage Expedient.* Lexington: Samuel Gillock, 1849.

Williams, P., Lucian Minor, W. T. Willey, J. T. L. Preston, and J. Cross. *Address to the People of Virginia, by the State Temperance Convention, Held at Staunton, August 4, 1852.* Richmond: H. K. Ellyson, 1853. VHS.

Withers, Robert Enoch. *An Address, Delivered at Masonic Hall, in the City of Lynchburg, on the Anniversary of St John the Baptist, June 23th, ad 1857, al 5857.* Lynchburg: Virginian Job Printing Office, 1857.

Secondary Sources

Adams, Sean Patrick. *Old Dominion, Industrial Commonwealth: Coal, Politics, and Economy in Antebellum America.* Baltimore: Johns Hopkins University Press, 2004.

Albanese, Catherine. *Sons of the Fathers: The Civil Religion of the American Revolution.* Philadelphia: Temple University Press, 1976.

Ambler, Charles H. *Sectionalism in Virginia from 1776 to 1861.* Chicago: University of Chicago Press, 1910.

Ambrosius, Lloyd E., ed. *A Crisis of Republicanism: American Politics in the Civil War Era.* Lincoln: University of Nebraska Press, 1990.

Ashworth, John. *Commerce and Compromise, 1820–1850.* Vol. 1 of *Slavery, Capitalism, and Politics in the Antebellum Republic.* New York: Cambridge University Press, 1995.

Ayers, Edward L. *Vengeance and Justice: Crime and Punishment in the Nineteenth-Century South.* New York: Oxford University Press, 1984.

Baker, Jean H. *Affairs of Party: The Political Culture of Northern Democrats in the Mid-Nineteenth Century.* Ithaca: Cornell University Press, 1983.

Barnes, L. Diane. *Artisan Workers in the Upper South: Petersburg, Virginia, 1820–1865.* Baton Rouge: Louisiana State University Press, 2008.

————. "Southern Artisans, Organization, and the Rise of a Market Economy in Antebellum Petersburg." *Virginia Magazine of History and Biography* 107 (Spring 1999): 159–88.

Bean, William Gleason. "The Ruffner Pamphlet of 1847: An Antislavery Aspect of Virginia Sectionalism." *Virginia Magazine of History and Biography* 61 (July 1953): 260–82.

Bellows, Barbara. *Benevolence among Slaveholders: Assisting the Poor in Charleston, 1670–1860.* Baton Rouge: Louisiana State University Press, 1993.

Beito, David T. *From Mutual Aid to the Welfare State: Fraternal Societies and Social Services, 1890–1967.* Chapel Hill: University of North Carolina Press, 2000.

Berlin, Ira. *Slaves without Masters: The Free Negro in the Antebellum South.* Oxford: Oxford University Press, 1981.

Berlin, Ira, and Herbert Gutman. "Natives and Immigrants, Free Men and Slaves: Urban Workingmen in the Antebellum American South." *American Historical Review* 88 (December 1983): 1175–1200.

Bladek, John David. "'Virginia Is Middle Ground': The Know Nothing Party and the Virginia Gubernatorial Election of 1855." *Virginia Magazine of History and Biography* 106 (Winter 1998): 35–70.

Bledstein, Burton J., "Introduction: Storytellers to the Middle Class." In *The Middling Sorts: Explorations in the History of the American Middle Class,* ed. Burton J. Bledstein and Robert D. Johnstone, 1–30. New York: Routledge, 2001.

Blocker, Jack S., Jr. *American Temperance Movements: Cycles of Reform.* Boston: Twayne, 1989.

Blumin, Stuart. *The Emergence of the Middle Class: Social Experience in the American City, 1760–1900.* New York: Cambridge University Press, 1989.

————. *The Urban Threshold: Growth and Change in a Nineteenth-Century American Community.* Chicago: University of Chicago Press, 1976.

Bogger, Tommy L. *Free Blacks in Norfolk, Virginia, 1790–1860.* Charlottesville: University Press of Virginia, 1997.

Boyer, Paul. *Urban Masses and Moral Order in America, 1820–1920.* Cambridge, Mass.: Harvard University Press, 1978.

Breeden, James O. "Body Snatchers and Anatomy Professors: Medical Education in Nineteenth-Century Virginia." *Virginia Magazine of History and Biography* 83 (1975): 321–45.

Brooke, John L. "Ancient Lodges and Self-Created Societies: Voluntary Association and the Public Sphere in the Early Republic." In Hoffman and Albert, eds., *Launching the "Extended Republic,"* 273–316.

Brooks, Charles H. *The Official History and Manual of the Grand United Order of Odd Fellows in America.* Freeport, N.Y.: Books for Libraries Press, 1971.

Brown, Bertram Wyatt. *Southern Honor: Ethics and Behavior in the Old South*. New York: Oxford University Press, 1982.

Brown, Elsa Barkley. "Negotiating and Transforming the Public Sphere: African American Political Life in the Transition from Slavery to Freedom." *Public Culture* 7 (1994): 107–46.

Brown, Elsa Barkley, and Gregg D. Kimball. "Mapping the Terrain of Black Richmond." *Journal of Urban History* 21 (March 1995): 296–346.

Brown, Kathleen M. *Good Wives, Nasty Wenches, and Anxious Patriarchs: Race, Gender and Power in Colonial Virginia*. Chapel Hill: University of North Carolina Press, 1996.

Brown, Tamara L., Gregory S. Parks, and Clarenda M. Phillips, eds. *African American Fraternities and Sororities: The Legacy and the Vision*. Lexington: University Press of Kentucky, 2005.

Brown, William Moseley. *Blandford Lodge, No. 3 AF&AM: A Bicentennial History*. Petersburg: Plummer Printing, 1957.

———. *Freemasonry in Virginia*. Richmond: Masonic Home Press, 1936.

———. *Freemasonry in Staunton, Virginia*. Staunton: McClure, 1949.

———. *Marshall Lodge, No. 39 AF&AM*. Staunton: McClure, 1953.

Bruce, Dickinson D., Jr. *The Rhetoric of Conservatism: The Virginia Convention of 1829–1830 and the Conservative Tradition in the South*. San Marino: Huntington Library, 1982.

Buckley, Thomas E. *The Great Catastrophe of My Life: Divorce in the Old Dominion*. Chapel Hill: University of North Carolina Press, 2002.

Bullock, Steven C. *Revolutionary Brotherhood: Freemasonry and the Transformation of the American Social Order, 1730–1830*. Chapel Hill: University of North Carolina Press, 1996.

Burke, Janet M. "Leaving the Enlightenment: Women Freemasons after the Revolution." *Eighteenth-Century Studies* 33 (2000): 255–65.

Burnstein, Andrew. *America's Jubilee: How a Generation Remembered Fifty Years of Independence*. New York: Knopf, 2001.

Bushman, Richard L. *The Refinement of America: Persons, Houses, Cities*. New York: Vintage, 1993.

Butler, Anne S. "Black Fraternal and Benevolent Societies in Nineteenth-Century America." In *African American Fraternities and Sororities: The Legacy and the Vision*, ed. Tamara L. Brown, Gregory S. Parks, and Clarenda M. Phillips, 67–93. Lexington: University Press of Kentucky, 2005.

Buza, Melinda S. "'Pledges of Our Love': Marriage among the Virginia Gentry, 1800–1825." In *The Edge of the South: Life in Nineteenth-Century Virginia*, ed. Edward L Ayers and John C. Willis, 9–36. Charlottesville: University Press of Virginia, 1991.

Bynum, Victoria. *Unruly Women: The Politics of Social and Sexual Control in the Old South*. Chapel Hill: University of North Carolina Press, 1992.

Byrne, Frank J. *Becoming Bourgeois: Merchant Culture in the South, 1820–1865.* Lexington: University Press of Kentucky, 2006.

Campbell, James M. *Slavery on Trial: Race, Class, and Criminal Justice in Antebellum Richmond.* Gainesville: University Press of Florida, 2007

Carlson, Douglas W. "'Drinks He to His Own Undoing': Temperance Ideology in the Deep South." *Journal of the Early Republic* (Winter 1998): 659–91.

Carmichael, Peter S. *The Last Generation: Young Virginians in Peace, War, and Reunion.* Chapel Hill: University of North Carolina Press, 2005.

Carnes, Mark C. *Secret Ritual and Manhood in Victorian America.* New Haven: Yale University Press, 1989.

Carnes, Mark C., and Clyde Griffen, eds. *Meanings for Manhood: Constructions of Masculinity in Victorian America.* Chicago: University of Chicago Press, 1990

Cecil-Fronsman, Bill. *Common Whites: Class, Culture in North Carolina.* Lexington, University of Kentucky Press, 1992.

Chalmers, David M. *Hooded Americanism: The History of the Ku Klux Klan.* Durham: Duke University Press, 1987.

Cherry, John W. *The Improved Order of Red Men in Virginia, 1839 to 1916.* Norfolk, 1916.

Clawson, Mary Ann. *Constructing Brotherhood: Class, Gender, and Fraternalism.* Princeton: Princeton University Press, 1989.

Click, Patricia C. *The Spirit of the Times: Amusements in Nineteenth-Century Baltimore, Norfolk, and Richmond.* Charlottesville: University Press of Virginia, 1989.

Cohen, Patricia Cline. *The Murder of Helen Jewett.* New York: Vintage, 1999.

Cott, Nancy F. *The Bonds of Womanhood: "Woman's Sphere" in New England, 1780–1835.* New Haven: Yale University Press, 1977.

Crofts, Daniel W. *Reluctant Confederates: Upper South Unionists in the Secession Crisis.* Chapel Hill: University of North Carolina Press, 1989.

———. "Late Antebellum Virginia Reconsidered." *Virginia Magazine of History and Biography* 107 (Summer 1999): 253–86.

Curl, "The Capitol in Washington, D.C., and Its Freemasonic Connections." In Hoffman and Albert, eds., *Launching the "Extended Republic,"* 214–67.

Dabney, Virginius. *Virginia: The New Dominion.* New York: Doubleday, 1971.

Dailey, Jane. *Before Jim Crow: The Politics of Race in Postemancipation Virginia.* Chapel Hill: University of North Carolina Press, 2000.

Dame, George W. *A Historical Sketch of Roman Eagle Lodge, No. 122.* Danville: J. T. Townes, 1895.

Dannenbaum, Jed. *Drink and Disorder: Temperance Reform in Cincinnati from the Washingtonian Revival to the WCTU.* Urbana: University of Illinois Press, 1984.

Deal, John Gordon. "The Forgotten Southerner: Middle-Class Associationalism in Antebellum Norfolk, Virginia." PhD diss., University of Florida, 2003.

Delfino, Susanna, and Michele Gillespie, eds. *Global Perspectives on Industrial*

Transformation in the American South. Columbia: University of Missouri Press, 2005.

Deyle, Steven. *Carry Me Back: The Domestic Slave Trade in American Life.* Oxford: Oxford University Press, 2005.

Dorsey, Bruce. *Reforming Men and Women: Gender in the Antebellum City.* Ithaca: Cornell University Press, 2004.

Downes, Aviston D. "Freemasonry in Barbados Before 1914: The Limits of Brotherhood." *Journal of Caribbean History* 36, no. 2 (2002): 285–309.

Doyle, Don H. "The Social Functions of Voluntary Associations in a Nineteenth-Century American Town." *Social Science History* 1 (Spring 1977): 333–55.

Duke, Jane Taylor. "The Richmond Home for Boys, 1846–1955." Unpublished ms., 1955. VHS.

Dumenil, Lynn. *Freemasonry and American Culture, 1880–1930.* Princeton: Princeton University Press, 1984.

Durrill, Wayne K. "A Tale of Two Courthouses: Civic Space, Political Power, and Capitalist Development in a New South Community, 1843–1940." *Journal of Social History* 35 (Spring 2002): 659–84.

Eaton, Clement. "Southern Senators and the Right of Instruction, 1789–1860." *Journal of Southern History* 18 (August 1952): 303–19.

Eelman, Bruce W. *Entrepreneurs in the Southern Upcountry: Commercial Culture in Spartanburg, South Carolina, 1845–1880.* Athens: University of Georgia Press, 2008.

Egerton, Douglas R. "Markets without a Market Revolution: Southern Planters and Capitalism." *Journal of the Early Republic* 16 (Summer 1996): 207–21.

Emery, George, and J. C. Emery. *A Young Man's Benefit: The Independent Order of Odd Fellows and Sickness Insurance in the United States and Canada, 1860–1929.* Montreal: McGill-Queen's University Press, 1999.

Engerman, Stanley L. "Southern Industrialization: Myths and Realities." In *Global Perspectives on Industrial Transformation in the American South,* ed. Susanna Delfino and Michele Gillespie, 16–23. Columbia: University of Missouri Press, 2005.

Escott, Paul D. "Yeoman Independence and the Market: Social Status and Economic Development in Antebellum North Carolina." *North Carolina Historical Review* 66 (July 1989): 275–300.

Eslinger, Ellen. "Antebellum Liquor Reform in Lexington, Virginia: The Story of a Small Southern Town." *Virginia Magazine of History and Biography* 99 (April 1991): 163–86.

Etheridge, Harrison M. "The Jordan Hatcher Affair of 1852: Cold Justice and Warm Compassion." *Virginia Magazine of History and Biography* 84 (October 1976): 446–63.

Fahey, David M. *Temperance and Racism: John Bull, Johnny Reb, and the Good Templars.* Lexington: University Press of Kentucky, 1996.

———. "Who Joined the Sons of Temperance? Livelihood and the Age in the Black Book and Minutes, Phoenix Division, Dexter, Michigan, 1848–1851." *The Old Northwest* 11(Fall/Winter 1985–86): 221–26.

Farnham, Christie Anne. *The Education of the Southern Belle: Higher Education and Student Socialization in the Antebellum South.* New York: New York University Press, 1994.

Ford, Lacy K., Jr. "Making the 'White Man's Country' White: Race Slavery, and State-Building in the Jacksonian South." *Journal of the Early Republic* (Winter 1999): 713–37.

Frederickson, George M. *The Black Image in the White Mind: The Debate on Afro-American Character and Destiny, 1817–1914.* New York: Harper and Row, 1971.

Freehling, Alison Goodyear. *Drift Toward Dissolution: The Virginia Slavery Debate of 1831–1832.* Baton Rouge: Louisiana State University Press, 1982.

Freehling, William W. *The Road to Disunion: Secessionists at Bay, 1776–1854.* New York: Oxford University Press, 1990.

Friend, Craig Thompson, and Lorri Glover. "Rethinking Southern Masculinity: An Introduction." In *Southern Manhood: Perspectives on Masculinity in the Old South,* ed. Craig Thompson Friend and Lorri Glover, vii–xiv. Athens: University of Georgia Press, 2004.

———, eds. *Southern Manhood: Perspectives on Masculinity in the Old South.* Athens: University of Georgia Press, 2004.

Gaines, Francis Pendleton, Jr. "The Virginia Constitutional Convention of 1850–51: A Study in Sectionalism." PhD diss., University of Virginia, 1950.

Genovese, Eugene. *Roll, Jordan, Roll: The World the Slaves Made.* New York: Vintage, 1974.

Gilkeson, John S., Jr. *Middle-Class Providence, 1820–1940.* Princeton: Princeton University Press, 1986.

Gillespie, Michelle. *Free Labor in an Unfree World: White Artisans in Slaveholding Georgia, 1789–1860.* Athens: University of Georgia Press, 2000.

Glover, Lorri. *Southern Sons: Becoming Men in the New Nation.* Baltimore: Johns Hopkins University Press, 2007.

Goldfield, David R. *Urban Growth in the Age of Sectionalism: Virginia, 1847–1861.* Baton Rouge: Louisiana State University Press, 1977.

Goldfield, David R., and Blaine A. Brownell, eds. *The City in Southern History: The Growth of Urban Civilization in the South.* Port Washington, N.Y.: Kennikat Press, 1977.

Goloboy, Jennifer Lee. "Success to Trade: Charleston's Merchants in the Revolutionary Era." PhD diss., Harvard University, 2003.

Gorn, Elliott J. "'Gouge and Bite, Pull Hair and Scratch': The Social Significance of Fighting in the Southern Backcountry." *American Historical Review* 90 (February 1985): 18–43.

Green, Elna C. *This Business of Relief: Confronting Poverty in a Southern City, 1740–1940*. Athens: University of Georgia Press, 2003.

Greenberg, Amy S. *Cause for Alarm: The Volunteer Fire Department in the Nineteenth-Century City*. Princeton: Princeton University Press, 1998.

———. *Manifest Manhood and the Antebellum American Empire*. New York: Cambridge University Press, 2005.

Greenberg, Brian. "Free Labor Fraternalism: The Independent Order of Odd Fellows in Albany." In *Worker and Community: Response to Industrialization in a Nineteenth-Century American City, Albany, New York, 1850–1884*, 89–101. Albany: State University of New York Press, 1985.

Greenberg, Kenneth S. *Honor and Slavery: Lies, Duels, Noses, Masks, Dressing as a Woman, Gifts, Strangers, Humanitarianism, Death, Slave Rebellions, the Proslavery Argument, Baseball, Hunting, and Gambling in the Old South*. Princeton: Princeton University Press, 1996.

———. *Masters and Statesmen: The Political Culture of American Slavery*. Baltimore: Johns Hopkins University Press, 1985.

Hahn, Steven. *The Roots of Southern Populism: Yeoman Farmers and the Transformation of the Georgia Upcountry, 1850–1890*. New York: Oxford University Press, 1983.

Halttunen, Karen. *Confidence Men and Painted Women: A Study of Middle-Class Culture in America, 1830–1870*. New Haven: Yale University Press, 1982.

Harland-Jacobs, Jessica. *Builders of Empire: Freemasonry and British Imperialism, 1717–1927*. Chapel Hill: University of North Carolina Press, 2007.

Harris, Cheryl. "Whiteness as Property." *Harvard Law Review* 106 (June 1993): 1709–91.

Heitmann, John. *A History and Manual of the Independent Order of Odd Fellows: The History of Odd Fellowship in Virginia*. Accotink: Committee on Publications, 1927.

Heron, James Henry. *Historical Sketch of Fredericksburg Lodge, No. 4: Mother Lodge of George Washington*. Rev. ed. Fredericksburg, 1950.

Hewitt, Nancy A. *Women's Activism and Social Change: Rochester, New York, 1822–1872*. Ithaca: Cornell University Press, 1984.

Higginbotham, Evelyn Brooks. *Righteous Discontent: The Women's Movement in the Black Baptist Church, 1880–1920*. Cambridge, Mass.: Harvard University Press, 1993.

Hill, McCoy. "Sons of Temperance." *Augusta Historical Bulletin* 29 (Fall 1993): 60–63.

Hobsbawm, Eric. "Introduction: Invented Traditions." In *The Invention of Tradition*, ed. Eric Hobsbawm and Terence Ranger, 1–12. London: Cambridge University Press, 1983.

Hoffman, Ronald, and Peter J. Albert, eds. *Launching the "Extended Republic": The Federalist Period*. Charlottesville: University Press of Virginia, 1996.

Hoffman, Stefan-Ludwig. "Civility, Male Friendship, and Masonic Sociability in Nineteenth-Century Germany." *Gender & History* 13 (August 2001): 224–48.

———. *The Politics of Sociability: Freemasonry and German Civil Society, 1840–1918.* Ann Arbor: University of Michigan Press, 2007.

Holton, Woody. *Forced Founders: Indians, Debtors, Slaves, and the Making of the American Revolution in Virginia.* Chapel Hill: University of North Carolina Press, 1999.

Irons, Charles F. *The Origins of Proslavery Christianity: White and Black Evangelicals in Colonial and Antebellum Virginia.* Chapel Hill: University of North Carolina Press, 2008.

Isenberg, Nancy. *Sex and Citizenship in Antebellum America.* Chapel Hill: University of North Carolina Press, 1998.

Jabour, Anya. 'Grown Girls, Highly Cultivated': Female Education in an Antebellum Southern Family." *Journal of Southern History* 64 (1998): 23–64.

———. "Male Friendship and the Early National South: William Wirt and His Friends." *Journal of the Early Republic* 20 (Spring 2000): 83–111.

———. *Scarlett's Sisters: Young Women in the Old South.* Chapel Hill: University of North Carolina Press, 2007.

Jacob, Margaret C. *Living the Enlightenment: Freemasonry and Politics in Eighteenth-Century Europe.* New York: Oxford University Press, 1991.

Johnson, Paul E. "The Market Revolution." In vol. 1 of *Encyclopedia of American Social History,* ed. Mary Kupiec Cayton, Elliott J. Gorn, and Peter Williams, 545–59. New York: Charles Scribner's Sons, 1993.

———. *A Shopkeeper's Millennium: Society and Revivals in Rochester, New York, 1815–1837.* New York: Hill and Wang, 1978.

Johnson, Walter. *Soul by Soul: Life Inside the Antebellum Slave Market.* Cambridge, Mass.: Harvard University Press, 1999.

Kaestle, Carl F. *Pillars of the Republic: Common Schools and American Society, 1780–1860.* New York: Hill and Wang, 1983.

Kammen, Michael. *A Season of Youth: The American Revolution and the Historical Imagination.* New York: Knopf, 1978.

Kann, Mark E. *The Gendering of American Politics: Founding Mothers, Founding Fathers, and Political Patriarchy.* Westport, Conn.: Praeger, 1999.

Karpeil, Frank J. "Mystic Ties of Brotherhood: Freemasonry, Royalty and Ritual in Hawaii, 1843–1910." PhD diss., University of Hawaii, 1998.

Kaufman, Jason. *For the Common Good? American Civic Life and the Golden Age of Fraternity.* New York: Oxford University Press, 2002.

Kelley, Robin D. G. "'We are not what we seem': Rethinking Working-Class Opposition in the Jim Crow South." *Journal of American History* 80 (June 1993): 75–112.

Kennon, Donald, ed. *A Republic for the Ages: The United States Capitol and the*

Political Culture of the Early Republic. Charlottesville: University Press of Virginia, 1999.

Kerber, Linda. "The Republican Mother: Women and the Enlightenment, an American Perspective." In *Toward an Intellectual History of Women*, 42–43. Chapel Hill: University of North Carolina Press, 1997.

———. "Separate Spheres, Female Worlds, Woman's Place: The Rhetoric of Women's History." In *Toward an Intellectual History of Women*, 155–99. Chapel Hill: University of North Carolina Press, 1997.

———. *Women of the Republic: Intellect and Ideology in Revolutionary America*. Chapel Hill: University of North Carolina Press, 1984.

Kimball, Gregg D. *American City, Southern Place: A Cultural History of Antebellum Richmond*. Athens: University of Georgia Press, 2000.

Koch, Adrienne, and William Peden, eds. *The Life and Selected Writings of Thomas Jefferson*. New York: Random House, 1993.

Kruman, Marc W. "The Second American Party System and the Transformation of Revolutionary Republicanism." *Journal of the Early Republic* 12 (Winter 1992): 509–37.

Laderman, Gary. *The Sacred Remains: American Attitudes toward Death, 1799–1883*. New Haven: Yale University Press, 1996.

Laurie, Bruce. "'We are Not Afraid to Work': Master Mechanic and the Market Revolution in the Antebellum North." In *The Middling Sorts: Explorations in the History of the American Middle Class*, ed. Burton J. Bledstein and Robert D. Johnstone, 50–68. New York: Routledge, 2001.

Lebsock, Suzanne. *The Free Women of Petersburg: Status and Culture in a Southern Town, 1784–1860*. New York: Norton, 1984.

Lindsay, George, et al. *The Official History of the Improved Order of Red Men*. Boston: Fraternity Publishing, 1893.

Link, William A. "The Jordan Hatcher Case: Politics and 'A Spirit of Insubordination' in Antebellum Virginia." *Journal of Southern History* 64 (November 1998): 615–48.

———. *The Roots of Secession: Slavery and Politics in Antebellum Virginia*. Chapel Hill: University of North Carolina Press, 2003.

Lipson, Dorothy Ann. *Freemasonry in Federalist Connecticut, 1789–1835*. Princeton: Princeton University Press, 1979.

Lockley, Timothy. *Welfare and Charity in the Antebellum South*. Gainesville: University Press of Florida, 2007.

Maddox, William A. *The Free School Idea in Virginia before the Civil War*. Arno Press, 1969.

Majewski, John. *A House Dividing: Economic Development in Pennsylvania and Virginia Before the Civil War*. New York: Cambridge University Press, 2000.

Marion, Forrest L. 'All That Is Pure in Religion and Valuable in Society':

Presbyterians, the Virginia Society, and the Sabbath, 1830–1836." *Virginia Magazine of History and Biography* 109 (2001): 187–218.

Martin, Jonathan D. *Divided Mastery: Slave Hiring in the American South*. Cambridge: Harvard University Press, 2004.

McCurry, Stephanie. *Masters of Small Worlds: Yeoman Households, Gender Relations, and the Political Culture of the Antebellum South Carolina Low Country*. New York: Oxford University Press, 1995.

McVeigh, Rory. "Structural Incentives for Conservative Mobilization: Power Devaluation and the Rise of the Ku Klux Klan, 1915–1925." *Social Forces* 77 (June 1999): 1461–99.

Merrill, Michael. "Cash Is Good to Eat: Self-Sufficiency and Exchange in the Rural Economy of the United States." *Radical History Review* 15 (Winter 1977): 43–71.

Mintz, Steven. *Moralists and Modernizers: America's Pre–Civil War Reformers*. Baltimore: Johns Hopkins University Press, 1995.

Munn, Sheldon A. *Freemasons at Gettysburg*. Gettysburg: Thomas Publications, 1993.

Murphy, Sharon Ann. "Securing Human Property: Slavery, Life Insurance, and Industrialization in the Upper South." *Journal of the Early Republic* 25 (Winter 2005): 615–52.

Naragon, Michael Douglas. "Ballots, Bullets, and Blood: The Political Transformation of Richmond, Virginia, 1850–1874." PhD diss., University of Pittsburgh, 1996.

Nelson, Dana D. *National Manhood: Capitalist Citizenship and the Imagined Fraternity of White Men*. Durham: Duke University Press, 1998.

Newman, Simon P. *Parades and the Politics of the Street: Festive Culture in the Early American Republic*. Philadelphia: University of Pennsylvania Press, 1997.

Noe, Kenneth W. *Southwest Virginia's Railroad: Modernization and the Sectional Crisis*. Urbana: University of Illinois Press, 1994.

Norton, Mary Beth. "The Evolution of White Women's Experience in America." *American Historical Review* 89 (June 1984): 593–619.

Oakes, James. *The Ruling Race: A History of American Slaveholders*. New York: Vintage, 1982.

"Order of United American Mechanics." In *The Cyclopedia of Fraternities*, ed. Albert C. Stevens. New York: E. B. Treat, 1907.

Palmer, Edward N. "Negro Secret Societies." *Social Forces* 23 (December 1944): 207–12.

Parsons, Elaine Franz. *Manhood Lost: Fallen Drunkards and Redeeming Women in the Nineteenth-Century United States*. Baltimore: Johns Hopkins University Press, 2003.

Pearson, C. C., and J. Edwin Hendricks. *Liquor and Anti-Liquor in Virginia, 1619–1919*. Durham: Duke University Press, 1967.

Peterson, Merrill D. *The Jefferson Image in the American Mind.* New York: Oxford University Press, 1960.

———. "The Virginia Convention of 1829-1830: Introduction." In Peterson, ed., *Democracy, Liberty, and Property*, 271–85.

———, ed. *Democracy, Liberty, Property: State Constitutional Conventions of the 1820s.* New York: Bobbs-Merrill, 1966.

Presidential Elections, 1789–1992. Washington, D.C.: Congressional Quarterly, 1995.

Prince Hall, "History of the Prince Hall Masons in Virginia." <http://www.mwphgl-va.org/id2.html>

Proctor, Nicolas W. *Bathed in Blood: Hunting and Mastery in the Old South.* Charlottesville: University of Virginia Press, 2002.

Pulley, Raymond. "General Cocke and the Temperance Crusade: The Master of Bremo Led the First Campaign against Alcohol in Virginia." *Virginia Cavalcade* 15 (Summer 1956): 22–27.

Pulliam, David L. *The Constitutional Conventions of Virginia from the Foundation of the Commonwealth to the Present Time.* Richmond: John T. West, 1901.

Purcell, Sarah J. *Sealed with Blood: War Sacrifice and Memory in Revolutionary America.* Philadelphia: University of Pennsylvania Press, 2002.

Quist, John W. *Restless Visionaries: The Social Roots of Antebellum Reform in Alabama and Michigan.* Baton Rouge: Louisiana State University Press, 1998.

Rady, Charles P. *History of Richmond Randolph Lodge, No. 19, af and am.* Richmond: J. W. Fergusson and Sons, 1888.

Reynolds, David S. *George Lippard.* Boston: Twayne Publishers, 1982.

Roberts, Allen E. *House Undivided: The Story of Freemasonry and the Civil War.* Richmond: Macoy, 1961.

Roediger, David. *The Wages of Whiteness: Race and the Making of the American Working Class.* Rev. ed. New York: Verso Press, 2007.

Rorabaugh, W. J. "The Sons of Temperance in Antebellum Jasper County." *Georgia Historical Quarterly* 64 (Fall 1980): 263–79.

Ross, Steven J. "The Transformation of Republican Ideology." *Journal of the Early Republic* 10 (Fall 1990): 323–30.

Ruggles, Jeffery. *The Unboxing of Henry Brown.* Richmond: Library of Virginia, 2003.

Rutyna, Richard A., and Peter C. Stewart. *The History of Freemasonry in Virginia.* Lanham, Md.: University Press of America, 1998.

Ryan, Mary P. "The American Parade: Representations of Nineteenth-Century Social Order." In *The New Cultural History*, ed. Lynn Hunt, 131–53. Los Angeles: University of California Press, 1989.

———. *Civic Wars: Democracy and Public Life in the American City during the Nineteenth Century.* Los Angeles: University of California Press, 1997.

———. *Cradle of the Middle Class: The Family in Oneida County, New York.* New York: Cambridge University Press, 1981.

————. "Gender and Public Access: Women's Politics in Nineteenth-Century America." In *Habermas and the Public Sphere*, ed. Craig Calhoun, 259–88. Cambridge, Mass.: MIT Press, 1992.

————. *Women in Public: Between Banners and Ballots, 1825–1880*. Baltimore: Johns Hopkins University Press, 1990.

Schechter, Patricia A. "Free and Slave Labor in the Old South: The Tredegar Ironworkers' Strike of 1847." *Labor History* 35 (Spring 1994): 165–86.

Schlotterbeck, John T. "The 'Social Economy' of an Upper South Community: Orange and Greene Counties, Virginia, 1815–1860." In *Class, Conflict, and Consensus: Antebellum Southern Community Studies*, ed. Orville Vernon Burton and Robert C. McMath Jr., 3–28. Westport, Conn.: Greenwood Press, 1982.

Schweiger, Bath Barton. *The Gospel Working Up: Progress and the Pulpit in Nineteenth-Century Virginia*. New York: Oxford University Press, 2000.

Sellers, Charles. *The Market Revolution: Jacksonian America, 1815–1846*. New York: Oxford University Press, 1991.

Shade, William. *Democratizing the Old Dominion: Virginia and the Second Party System, 1824–1861*. Charlottesville: University Press of Virginia, 1996.

Sheehan-Dean, Aaron. *Why Confederates Fought: Family and Nation in Civil War Virginia*. Chapel Hill: University of North Carolina Press, 2007.

Siegel, Frederick F. *The Roots of Southern Distinctiveness: Tobacco and Society in Danville, Virginia, 1780–1865*. Chapel Hill: University of North Carolina Press, 1987.

Simpson, Craig. "Political Compromise and the Protection of Slavery: Henry Wise and the Virginia Constitutional Convention of 1850–1851." *Virginia Magazine of History and Biography* 83 (October 1975): 388, 395–96.

Skocpol, Theda, and Jennifer Lynn Oser. "Organization despite Adversity: The Origins and Development of African American Fraternal Associations." *Social Science History* 28 (Fall 2004): 367–438.

Smith-Rosenberg, Carroll. "The Female World of Love and Ritual: Relations between Women in Nineteenth-Century America." In *Feminism and History*, ed. Joan Wallach Scott, 366–97. New York: Oxford University Press, 1996.

Stanley, Amy Dru. "Home Life and the Morality of the Market." In Stokes and Conway, eds., *The Market Revolution in America*, 74–96.

Stansell, Christine. *City of Women: Sex and Class in New York, 1787–1860*. New York: Knopf, 1986.

Steger, Werner H. "'United to Support, But Not Combined to Injure': Free Workers and Immigrants in Richmond, Virginia during the Era of Sectionalism, 1847–1865." PhD diss., George Washington University, 1999.

Stewart, James Brewer. "The Emergence of Racial Modernity and the Rise of the White North, 1790–1840." *Journal of the Early Republic* 18 (Spring 1998): 181–217.

Stokes, Melvyn. Introduction. In Stokes and Conway, eds., *The Market Revolution in America*, 1–20.

Stokes, Melvyn, and Stephen Conway, eds. *The Market Revolution in America: Social, Political, and Religious Expressions.* Charlottesville: University Press of Virginia, 1996.

Sutton, Robert P. *Revolution to Secession: Constitution Making in the Old Dominion.* Charlottesville: University Press of Virginia, 1989.

Syrett, Nicholas L. *The Company He Keeps: A History of White College Fraternities.* Chapel Hill: University of North Carolina Press, 2009.

Tabbert, Mark A. *American Freemasons: Three Centuries of Building Communities.* New York: New York University Press, 2005.

Takagi, Midori. *"Rearing Wolves to Our Own Destruction": Slavery in Richmond, Virginia, 1782–1865.* Charlottesville: University Press of Virginia, 1999.

Tarter, Brent. "The New Virginia Bookshelf." *Virginia Magazine of History and Biography* 104 (Winter 1996): 7–102.

Tate, Adam L. "Republicanism and Society: John Randolph of Roanoke, Joseph Glover Baldwin, and the Quest for Social Order." *Virginia Magazine of History and Biography* 111(Fall 2003): 263–98.

Towers, Frank. *The Urban South and the Coming of the Civil War.* Charlottesville: University of Virginia Press, 2004.

Travers, Len. *Celebrating the Fourth: Independence Day and Rites of Nationalism in the Early Republic.* Amherst: University of Massachusetts Press, 1997.

———. "'In the Greatest Solemn Dignity.'" In Hoffman and Albert, eds., *Launching the "Extended Republic,"* 155–176.

Tripp, Steven Elliott. *Yankee Town, Southern City: Race and Class Relations in Civil War Lynchburg.* New York: New York University Press, 1997.

Tyrrell, Ian. "Drink and Temperance in the Antebellum South: An Overview and Interpretation." *Journal of Southern History* 48 (November 1982): 485–510.

———. *Sobering Up: From Temperance to Prohibition in Antebellum America, 1800–1860.* Westport, Conn.: Greenwood Press, 1979.

Van Zelm, Antoinette G. "Virginia Women as Public Citizens: Emancipation Day Celebrations and Lost Cause Commemorations, 1863–1890." In *Negotiating Boundaries of Southern Womanhood: Dealing with the Powers That Be,* ed. Janet L. Coryell et al., 71–88. Columbia: University of Missouri Press, 2000.

Varon, Elizabeth. *We Mean to Be Counted: White Women and Politics in Antebellum Virginia.* Chapel Hill: University of North Carolina Press, 1996.

Vaughn, William Preston. *The Antimasonic Party in the United States, 1826–1843.* Lexington: University Press of Kentucky, 1983.

Voorhis, Harold Van Buren. *The Eastern Star: The Evolution from a Rite to an Order.* Richmond: Macoy, 1976.

Waldstreicher, David. *In the Midst of Perpetual Fetes: The Making of American Nationalism, 1776–1820.* Chapel Hill: University of North Carolina Press, 1997.

Walker, Corey D. B. "'The Freemasonry of the Race': The Cultural Politics of

Ritual, Race, and Place in Post-emancipation Virginia." PhD diss., College of William and Mary, 2001.

Walters, Ronald. *American Reformers, 1815–1860*. New York: Hill and Wang, 1978.

Walthall, David K. *History of Richmond Lodge, No. 10, AF&AM*. Richmond: Ware and Duke, 1909.

Watson, Harry L. "Slavery and the Development in a Dual Economy: The South and the Market Revolution." In Stokes and Conway, eds., *The Market Revolution in America*, 43–73.

Watson, Samuel J. "Flexible Gender Roles during the Market Revolution: Family, Friendship, Marriage, and Masculinity among U.S. Army Officers, 1815–1846." *Journal of Social History* 29 (Fall 1995): 81–107.

Weisberger, R. William, Wallace McLeod, and S. Brent Morris, eds. *Freemasonry on Both Sides of the Atlantic: Essays Concerning the Craft in the British Isles, Europe, the United States, and Mexico*. New York: Columbia University Press, 2002.

Wells, Jonathan Daniel. *The Origins of the Southern Middle Class, 1800–1861*. Chapel Hill: University of North Carolina Press, 2004.

White, Shane. "'It was a Proud Day': African Americans, Festivals, and Parades in the North, 1741–1834." *Journal of American History* 81 (June 1994): 13–50.

Wilentz, Sean. *Chants Democratic: New York City and the Rise of the American Working Class, 1788–1850*. New York: Oxford University Press, 1984.

Williams, Loretta J. *Black Freemasonry and Middle-Class Realities*. Columbia: University of Missouri Press, 1980.

Wood, Gordon S. *The Radicalism of the American Revolution*. New York: Vintage, 1991.

Yacovone, Donald. "Abolitionists and 'The Language of Fraternal Love.'" In *Meanings for Manhood: Constructions of Masculinity in Victorian America*, 85–95. Chicago: University of Chicago Press, 1990.

Zaborney, John J. "Slaves for Rent: Slave Hiring in Virginia." PhD diss., University of Maine, 1997.

Zelinsky, Wilbur. *Nation into State: The Shifting Symbolic Foundations of American Nationalism*. Chapel Hill: University of North Carolina Press, 1988.

INDEX

Abiff, Hiram, 88
abolitionist movement, 33, 129n13
African American fraternal orders:
African Lodge, no. 459, 45; Grand
United Order of Odd Fellows
(GUOOF), 44, 46–47; Peter Ogden, 47;
postbellum Virginia, 44; Prince Hall
Masons, 44–46; Sons of Temperance
and, 47–48
African American Freemasonry. See
Prince Hall Masons
African Americans: access to public
space, 99–101; alcohol, restricted access to, 48–49; exclusion of (see racial
policies); fraternal organizations,
44–46; mutual aid societies, 44. See
also free blacks; slavery
African Lodge, no. 459 (Freemasons),
45
agriculture, 15, 16–17
alcohol use: abstinence from, 67–68; in
antebellum secret fraternal orders,
30; in early Masonic history, 28–29;
in other men's associations, 27; restricting black access to, 48–49; role
of fraternal orders in discouraging,
76; Sons of Temperance and, 32
American Colonization Society, 74
American Revolution, 28, 82–84
American Temperance Union, 32, 33, 74
Anderson, Joseph Reid, 19–20
anniversary celebrations, 110–13
anti-Masonic movement: Antimasonic
Party, 29–30; Morgan Affair, 28, 29,
33–34
Appeal to the Coloured Citizens of the
World (Walker), 45

Appomattox Lodge, no. 16 (Odd
Fellows), 91–92
Appomattox Lodge, no. 107 (Freemasons), 38, 43
Arnold, Benedict, 84–85
artisans and mechanics: class identity,
6–7, 125; membership in fraternal
order, 23, 36–40, 50, 53, 118; slave
hiring, 18–19; urbanization 16–17
Association for the Improvement of
the Condition of the Poor, 74

Barboursville Division (Sons of
Temperance), 48
Barnes, L. Diane, 16
basis issue, 22
Baxter, Sidney S., 46
behavior, proper, 66–67
Bell, John, 121
benefits of membership: becoming
established in a new town, 59; death
benefits, 30–31, 78–81; introduction of
system of, 37; safety in travel, 56–57,
59; sick benefits, 30–31, 78–81; worthy
poor, 75–76, 78–79
benevolent reform, 74–76, 77–78, 97, 105.
See also charity work
black book of expelled members, 56,
138n17
Bledsoe, Alfred, 130n14
body snatchers, 109, 150n49
British jurisdiction, 45, 46–47
British Masons, 45
British Odd Fellows, 46
Broadus, John A., 96–97
brotherhood, 33; benefits of, 73–82; as
evidence of white male unity, 10;

brotherhood (*continued*)
promoted by rituals, 63, 66; Sons of
Temperance and, 33, 36. *See also* civic
brotherhood
Brotherhood of the Union, 24, 30, 84
Bullock, Steven, 60
business and fraternal orders: business
directories, 55; business relationships
among lodge brothers, 51–55; lending
and borrowing, 54–56; travel, 56–57

Caldwell, David, 57, 61
Caldwell Masonic Institute, 92
Capitol Square, 115–18
Carmichael, Peter, 4
Carnes, Marc, 28–29
celebrations: anniversary, 110–13; civic,
101–6; community, 113–19; fraternal,
100–106
cemeteries, privatization of, 149–50n40
Charity Division, no. 6 (Sons of
Temperance), 43, 112
charity work, 104–6, 110. *See also*
benevolent reform
Chesapeake Lodge, no. 89 (Odd Fellows), 37, 40, 43
citizenship, white male, 100, 101
civic brotherhood, 2, 5, 99–119;
anniversary celebrations, 110–13;
community celebrations, 113–19;
fraternal celebrations and public
space, 100–106; funerals, 106–10. *See
also* brotherhood
civic celebrations, 101–6. *See also*
celebrations
civic responsibilities, 89–90
civic virtue, 72–73, 75
class status: as displayed at funerals,
107–8; distinctions, 2–3, 5; and
identity, 6–7, 101; market revolution,
51–52; softened by secret fraternal

orders, 24–25, 35–36, 100, 110, 112–13,
122
Clay, Henry, 113
college fraternities, 26
colleges and academies, 92
community celebrations, 113–19
Compromise of 1850, 22
conduct, code and standards of, 37, 53,
66–69
"conduct unbecoming," 68–69
confidence men, 9, 52–53, 68, 74
Conservative Party, 13
cornerstone laying, 10, 28, 51, 72, 86,
99–101, 104, 112, 115–16
Covington Division (Sons of Temperance), 104, 114
creation mythology, 82–84. *See also*
invented lineage
crime, increase in, 73–74
crop diversification, 16–17

Dame, George W., 92
Daniel, Raleigh T., 51, 79
Danville Female Academy, 92
Daughters of Temperance, 96
death announcements, 109
death benefits, 30–31, 78–79, 80–81. *See
also* funerals
deaths of national figures, 113
Declaration of Independence signers,
144n71
Democratic Party, 21, 27
Dew, Thomas, 130n14
disabilities, membership and, 79–80
disagreements moderated privately
among members, 69–70
"divided mastery," 18–19
divisions, use of word, 134n21
"Domestic Slavery" (Upshur), 14–15
domestic sphere. *See* separate spheres
Dorcas Society, 74

Dove, John, 46; *Masonic Textbook*, 31, 65
Druids, 24, 30, 134n21
dual economy, 3
dues, 34, 69–70, 78

eastern slaveholders, political power of, 20–21
education: colleges and academies, 92, 112; equal education for white children, 91, 94, 145n93; fraternal promotion of, 90–95; gender and, 92–94
equality, white male: founding fathers and, 85, 88, 116–118; in fraternal rhetoric, 30, 35–36, 97; proslavery ideology, 14–15
eulogies, 108–9
Evans, Thomas J., 33
expulsion, 55–56, 68–70

Faulkner, Charles J., 22
fictive kinship, 30, 37, 59–60, 66, 70, 122. *See also* brotherhood
Finley, I. Randolph, 89
Flournoy, Thomas, 23
Floyd, John B., 115, 118
founding fathers, 84–86, 144n69
Fourth of July. *See* Independence Day celebrations
Franklin, Benjamin, 84–85, 144n71
Franklin Society and Library Company, 21
fraternal buildings, 103
fraternal celebrations, public space and, 100–106
fraternal republicanism, 10, 82, 97. *See also* republicanism
Fredericksburg Divisions (Sons of Temperance), 41, 42
Fredericksburg Lodges (Freemasons), 38, 42

Frederickson, George M., 129n11
free blacks: abolition and, 129–30n13; access to alcohol, 39; competition for jobs and, 18–19; exclusion of, 37, 46–50; fraternal organizations, 44–46; funerals, 150n49; lack of respect for in death, 109–10; public space restrictions, 100–101, 115. *See also* African Americans
Freemasons: African Americans, 45; American Revolution, 28; charitable funds and, 30, 78; colleges and academies, 92; in the colonial era and early America, 28–29; cornerstone laying, 115–18; creation mythology, 82–83; education, 91–92, 145n93; European origins, 44; exclusion of women, 88–89; founding fathers and, 84–85, 144n69; governance of, 31, 34; growth of, 33–34; introduction to, 2; lodges, 134n21; *Masonic Textbook*, 65; membership, 31–32, 152n1 (*see also* membership); occupational distribution, 38; racial policies, 46; regalia, 64; as republican form of government, 82; slaveholders in, 42–43; George Washington and, 84–87, 116–18
Friend to Friend Masonic Memorial, 152n8
funerals: commercialization of, 149–50n40; eulogies, 108–9; free blacks, 150n49; functions of, 106–7; ideals of society defined, 108–9; processions, 107–8; resolutions, 109

General Union for Promoting Observance of the Christian Sabbath, 74
Gentlemen's Benevolent Society, 27
Glover, Lorri, 4
good character, 52–53, 74–75

governance of antebellum fraternities, 31, 33, 34
Grand Division of Virginia (Sons of Temperance), 33, 41, 42, 96
Grand Lodge of United States, IOOF, 47
Grand Lodge of Virginia (Freemasons), 28, 31, 35, 46, 63, 91, 116, 121
Grand Lodge of Virginia (Odd Fellows), 40, 42
Grand United Order of Odd Fellows (GUOOF), 44, 46–47
Gratitude Lodge, no. 24 (Odd Fellows), 70
Grattan, Robert, 107
Greenberg, Amy S., 5
Greene, Nathanael, 84
gubernatorial election of 1855 (Virginia), 23

Hall, Prince, 45
herrenvolk ideology, 13, 15, 23, 79, 129n11
hierarchy, internal, 61, 63
Higginbotham Male and Female Academy, 92, 145n93
hiring out, 18–19
history of fraternal orders in early America, 28–34; anti-Masonic movement, 29–30; Freemasons, 28–29, 31, 33–34; growth, 31–32; Odd Fellows, 29; Sons of Temperance, 30, 31–33
Hollywood Cemetery, 149–50n40
Hunter, Edmund Pendleton, 108
Hyneman, Leon: *The Universal Masonic Record and Directory*, 55

Illustrations of Masonry (Morgan), 29
Imboden, John, 112
Improved Order of Red Men, 24, 30, 83–84, 134n21, 143–44n66
Independence Day celebrations, 114–15
Independent Order of Odd Fellows (IOOF): black members in North,

46–47; British Odd Fellows, 46; charitable funds and, 78–79; colleges and academies, 92; cornerstone ceremony, 51; creation mythology, 83; education 91–92, 145n93; emergence of in U.S., 29; lodges, 105–6, 134n21; membership, 31, 152n1 (*see also* membership); mutual benefit system, 30–31; occupational distribution, 37, 39, 40; racial policies, 46–47; slaveholders in, 42–43, 136n54
Independent Order of Rechabites, 30
Independent Order of St. Luke, 44
industrialization, southern, 3–4, 15
initiation rituals, 1–2, 35, 60–61
internal improvements, conflict over, 20
invented lineage: American Revolution, 82–84; civic responsibilities, 89–90; creation mythology, 82–84; founding fathers, 84–86; republicanism, 82–86, 88; women's exclusion, 88–89, 122
investigation, committee of, 34–35

Jackson, Andrew, 113
James and Kanawha Canal, 15, 20–21
joining the lodge, 34–36

Kemper, James Lawson, 60, 81, 88
Kinney, Chesley, 108

labor strikes, 19–20
Ladies Association for Erecting a Statue of Henry Clay, 102, 103
Lebanon Lodge, no. 66 (Odd Fellows), 67–68
Lebsock, Suzanne, 95–96, 97–98, 123
Leigh, Benjamin Watkins, 12–13
Leitch, J. A., 108
Lexington Division, no. 45 (Sons of Temperance), 36, 67
lodge, 59–71; abstinence from alcohol

use, 67–68; brotherhood, 63, 66; disagreements moderated privately among members, 69–70; dues, 69–70; proper behavior, 66–69; as public space, 103–6; as refuge from partisan politics, 30, 60, 94–95; regalia, 61, 63; rituals, 60–61, 63, 66, 68
lodge, use of word, 134n21
Lynchburg Hose Company, 27

Madison Division (Sons of Temperance), 55, 80
Maffitt Lodge (Odd Fellows), 70
male friendships. *See* brotherhood
manhood, 4–5, 89, 123. *See also* masculinity
market capitalism: effect on antebellum South, 3–4; reconciliation with slavery, 18; as threat to republicanism, 72
Marshall, John, 84
Marshall Division, no. 3 (Sons of Temperance), 41, 42, 142n41
Marshall Lodge, no. 44 (Odd Fellows), 37, 40, 43
Martha Washington Female College, 92, 93
martial manhood, 5
Martin, Alexander, 33, 76
masculine civic responsibility, 89–96
masculine independence, 9, 14, 24–25
masculinity, 4–5, 52, 79, 105
Masonic School of Virginia, 92
Masonic Textbook (Dove), 31, 65
Mayo, Joseph, 99, 118
McCabe, James D., 35, 72, 93, 114–15, 146n105
McCabe Lodge, no. 56 (Odd Fellows), 93, 114–15, 146n105
Meade, Richard K., 114
membership: composition of, 2, 6–7, 23–24, 36–44; as marker of good

character, 53; requirements for, 34–35; slave ownership, 39, 44. *See also* racial policies
men's associations (other than fraternal orders), 26–28
middle class: and civic groups, 27; definition of in antebellum South, 6; expansion of, 4, 16; in fraternal orders, 2–3, 37; identity, 6–7; and temperance movement, 32–33, 37; use of term, 125
militia groups, 27
"mixed-basis" representation, 22
Monguy Division, no. 226 (Sons of Temperance), 41, 43
moral character: as component of manhood, 5; importance of in market culture, 51; as means to exclude blacks, 44, 46, 47; membership in fraternal orders, 7, 34–36, 44, 52–53; movement to improve, 75–76; poverty and, 79 (*see also* worthy poor); preservation of, 73; women and, 77
Morgan, Charles, 13, 14, 129n10
Morgan, William, 29; *Illustrations of Masonry*, 29
Morgan affair, 28, 29, 33–34
Mossy Creek Division (Sons of Temperance), 67
Mount Crawford Division (Sons of Temperance), 41, 69, 104, 110, 138n9, 138n17
Mount Vernon, 86
Mount Vernon Ladies Association, 86
muskrat episode, 69–70
mutual benefit system, 30–31, 78–79
Myers, Samuel H., 46, 75
Myrtle Lodge, no. 50 (Odd Fellows), 40, 42
mythology. *See* creation mythology; invented lineage

Nat Turner's rebellion, 14, 121–22. *See also* Turner, Nat
natural rights ideology, 36, 129n13
New York State Women's Temperance Society, 96
Nicholas, Philip, 11

occupational distribution, 126; agricultural v. nonagricultural, 17–18, 23–24, 36–37; Freemasons, 38, 126; Odd Fellows, 40; Sons of Temperance, 41
Odd Fellows. *See* Independent Order of Odd Fellows (IOOF)
Ogden, Peter, 47
Order of the Eastern Star (OES), 96
Order of United American Mechanics, 30, 134n21
orphans/orphanages, 74, 91, 145n94

parades. *See* public celebrations
partisan divisions: as basis for membership in other men's associations, 27; fraternal orders role in assuaging, 73, 85, 94–95, 122; lodge as refuge from, 30, 60, 94–95; and partisan harmony, 10, 98, 100; and partisan strife, 94–95, 97, 120–21
passwords, 2, 52–53, 63
patriotic celebrations, 114–15. *See also* celebrations
patriotism, lodge work as, 81–82
Petersburg Benevolent Mechanic Association, 26
Petersburg Grays, 27
Pfifer, James, 69–70, 140n59
Plecker, Adam, 54, 138n9
Points, Benjamin, 108
Polk, James K., 113
Pollitz, Jacob, 112–13
poor relief, 74–75. *See also* benevolent reform; charity work

poverty, 74–75. *See also* charity work; worthy poor
Powers, Pike, 33, 91
preexisting illnesses, membership and, 80
Prince Hall Masons, 44–45, 46
processions, 107–8, 151n56
professional class, 37
property ownership: fraternal orders and, 104; masculine independence and, 24; mixed basis, 20; and voting, 11–14, 22, 27; and white manhood, 5
proslavery ideology, 12, 14–15, 75, 79, 130n14
public celebrations, 101–6, 110–13, 113–19, 122–23
public processions. *See* celebrations; funerals
public schools. *See* education
public space, 101; anniversary celebrations, 110–13; black access to, 99, 115–16; changes in use of by free blacks and slaves, 100–101; control of, 99–100, 115–16, 118–19; fraternal celebrations, 100–106

racial policies, 44–50; black fraternal organizations, 44–46; Freemasons, 46; Independent Order of Odd Fellows, 46–47; proposal to allow free blacks membership, 46; Sons of Temperance, 47–49
Randolph Lodge, no. 19 (Freemasons), 35, 55
Rebekah degree, 96
refuge, lodge as. *See* lodge
regalia: Freemasons, 64; image of, 62; Improved Order of Red Men, 84; as military costume, 115; public celebrations, 101, 105, 110, 118; purpose of, 2, 53, 61, 63, 101; social harmony, 63, 66

republicanism: antebellum emphasis
on, 101; duty to protect, 122; importance of education, 94; invented
lineage and, 82–86, 88; market
culture as threat to, 72; miniature
republics and, 86, 88; preservation
of, 72–73
republican motherhood, 93–94
respectability, 37
restrained manhood, 5
Richmond, 24, 104–5, 115–18
Richmond city lodges (Freemasons),
38, 42
Richmond Light Infantry Blues, 27
Richmond Male Orphan Society, 27
rituals: as defense against outsiders,
66, 68; distinction from other men's
associations, 26; importance of, 2,
37, 63, 66; initiation, 35; invented
lineage, 82; Morgan affair, 29; Odd
Fellows, 78; in other groups, 26, 27,
84; as protection against swindlers,
52–53; purpose of, 9, 24, 30–31, 52–53,
60–67, 75–76, 122; Sons of Temperance, 32–33, 83; strengthening bonds,
60–61; women and, 96
Robinson, Jacob H., 70
Rockingham Union Lodge, no. 27
(Freemasons), 38, 42, 126
Roller, Peter S., 54, 104, 138n9, 148n23
Roman Eagle Lodge (Freemasons),
92
Rooker, William, 52–53, 66
Ruffner, Henry, 21, 132n42
Ryan, Mary P., 101, 103, 112

safety from strangers, 52–59; in business
relationships, 54–55; reputation damage if expelled from fraternal order,
55–56; travel and reliance on fraternal
brothers, 56–57, 59

Samson Division, no. 4 (Sons of
Temperance), 56
Scott, Robert G., Jr., 35, 46, 85, 116, 118,
144n69
Second Great Awakening, 32
secret fraternal orders: attraction of,
70–71; compared to other men's associations, 26–28; differences between
early groups and antebellum groups,
30; percent of adult white males in,
24; popularity of, 23–25, 29–30, 75–76;
rebirth of after Civil War, 121–22;
resurgence of, 30; role in reunifying
North and South after Civil War,
121–22
separate spheres, 77, 89, 90, 94, 97. *See
also* women
Shade, William, 12
Shaver, F. L. B., 67
Sheffey, Hugh W., 112
sick benefits, 30–31, 78–81
signals, 52–53, 57
Sisters of Temperance, 147n122
skilled labor. *See* artisans and mechanics
slave hiring, 18–19, 100–101, 122
slaveholders in fraternal orders, 39,
42–43, 44, 136n54, 136n55
slavery, 8–9; criticism of, 21; effect on
market development, 4; fraternal orders on, 8; hiring out and, 18–19, 100;
"living out," 19, 100–101; poverty and,
75, 79; problem of, 14; reconciliation
with market culture, 18; temperance
and, 39, 83; trade, 18
Smithfield Lodge, no. 20 (Odd Fellows), 59
social harmony, 63, 66
solidarity, white male, 12, 18, 25
Sons of Temperance: alcohol and, 32;
anniversary celebrations, 110, 112;

Sons of Temperance (*continued*)
colleges and academies, 92; creation
mythology, 83; disagreements moderated privately among members,
69; divisions, 134n21; education
for white children, 91–92, 145n93;
funerals, 106–7; governance of, 33;
initiation rite, 1–2; introduction to, 2;
membership, 31–32, 152n1; men with
disabilities and, 80; occupational
distribution, 39, 41; origins of, 30;
pledge, 34; popularity of, 32–33; promotion of abstinence from alcohol
use, 76; racial policies, 47–49; regalia,
62, 63; slaveholders in, 42–43, 136n55;
temperance movement, 31–33, 36;
white male equality, 36
Special Grand Charity Fund, 91
Spotsylvania County divisions (Sons
of Temperance), 41, 42
state constitutional convention (1829):
Benjamin Watkins Leigh, 12–13;
Charles Morgan, 13, 14, 129n10;
Philip Nicholas, 11; suffrage, 11,
12–14; Abel Parker Upshur, 14–15,
130n14
state constitutional convention (1850):
Charles, J. Faulkner, 22; legislative
representation, 20–22; suffrage, 11–12,
22–23; Henry A. Wise, 21–22, 23.
Staunton Lodge, no. 13 (Freemasons),
38, 43, 108, 115
Staunton Lodge, no. 45 (Odd Fellows),
43
Stevenson, Levi L., 112
Strange, John Bowie, 35, 60, 85
Stringfellow, Thornton, 130n14
suffrage requirements, 11, 12–13,
148–49n24
Sunday schools, 74

Taylor, Zachary, 99, 113, 116, 118

temperance: controlling black behavior
and, 48–49; and middle class, 37;
republicanism, 83; restrained manhood, 5; and slavery, 39; stressed by
fraternal orders, 30. *See also* Sons of
Temperance
temperance movement, 31–33, 49, 112,
114
Thomson, Mason R. B., 84
tobacco, 16–17
transportation networks, expansion of,
15–16
travel, safety in, 56–57, 59
Tredegar Iron Works, 19–20
Trout, Nicholas K., 112
Turner, Nat, 14, 45. *See also* Nat Turner's
rebellion
Tyler, John, 116

Union Grand Lodge (Prince Hall
Freemasons), 46
Union Hotel, 118
United Ancient Order of Druids. *See*
Druids
United Order of American Mechanics,
24, 83–84
United Order of Galilean Fisherman,
44
unity, white male, 14–15
Universal Lodge, no. 1 (Prince Hall
Freemasons), 45, 137n63
*Universal Masonic Record and Directory,
The* (Hyneman), 55
University of Virginia, 109
unworthy poor, 74
Upshur, Abel Parker, 14–15, 130n14;
"Domestic Slavery," 14–15
urbanization, 3–4, 17, 51–52

Valley Lodge, no. 40 (Odd Fellows),
40, 42
Varon, Elizabeth, 94

vice, fraternal orders role in fighting, 76–77
Virginia House of Delegates, 21
volunteer firemen, 27

Walker, David, 45; *Appeal to the Coloured Citizens of the World*, 45
Warren, Joseph, 84
Washington, George: birthday celebration, 115–118; equestrian statue of, 99, 115; as fraternity brother, 28, 84–87; Mount Vernon, 86; Washington National Monument, 86. *See also* founding fathers
Washingtonians, 32, 33
Wells, Jonathan Daniel, 6, 19–20, 125
Wesleyan Female Seminary, 112
Whig Party, 21, 27
Whig womanhood, 102, 103
"white-basis" representation, 22
white male solidarity, 12, 14–15, 18, 25
widows and orphans, support for, 80–81
Wildey, Thomas, 29

Williamsburg Lodge, no. 6 (Freemasons), 34, 38, 43
Wilmot Proviso, 21
Wise, Henry A., 21–22, 23
Withers, Robert Enoch, 53, 67, 88
women: benevolent and moral reform efforts, 73–75, 77, 97; benevolent reform, marginalization in, 77–78, 81, 88–89; changing roles of in antebellum era, 5–6; economic equality for, 147n124; education, changing role in, 92–93; exclusion of, 88–89, 102; fear of "female masculinity," 97; partisan events, 94, 102–3; partisan strife, role in mollification of, 94; public behavior of, 102–3; public sphere, marginalization in, 73, 95–98, 103; as republican mothers, 93–94; separate spheres, 77, 89, 90, 94, 97; support for education of, 92–94. *See also* separate spheres
women's auxiliaries, 96, 147n122
worthy poor, 74, 78